Also Available From the American Academy of Pediatrics

Common Conditions

Allergies and Asthma: What Every Parent Needs to Know

The Big Book of Symptoms: A–Z Guide to Your Child's Health

Mama Doc Medicine: Finding Calm and Confidence in Parenting, Child Health, and Work-Life Balance

My Child Is Sick! Expert Advice for Managing Common Illnesses and Injuries

Sleep: What Every Parent Needs to Know

Waking Up Dry: A Guide to Help Children Overcome Bedwetting

Developmental, Behavioral, and Psychosocial Information

ADHD: What Every Parent Needs to Know

Autism Spectrum Disorders: What Every Parent Needs to Know

CyberSafe: Protecting and Empowering Kids in the Digital World of Texting, Gaming, and Social Media

Mental Health, Naturally: The Family Guide to Holistic Care for a Healthy Mind and Body

Newborns, Infants, and Toddlers

Caring for Your Baby and Young Child: Birth to Age 5*

Dad to Dad: Parenting Like a Pro

Guide to Toilet Training*

Heading Home With Your Newborn: From Birth to Reality

Mommy Calls: Dr. Tanya Answers Parents' Top 101 Questions About Babies and Toddlers

New Mother's Guide to Breastfeeding*

Newborn Intensive Care: What Every Parent Needs to Know

Retro Baby: Cut Back on All the Gear and Boost Your Baby's Development With More Than 100 Time-tested Activities

Your Baby's First Year*

Nutrition and Fitness

Food Fights: Winning the Nutritional Challenges of Parenthood Armed With Insight, Humor, and a Bottle of Ketchup

Nutrition: What Every Parent Needs to Know

A Parent's Guide to Childhood Obesity: A Road Map to Health

Sports Success R_x! Your Child's Prescription for the Best Experience

School-aged Children and Adolescents

Building Resilience in Children and Teens: Giving Kids Roots and Wings

Caring for Your School-Age Child: Ages 5 to 12

Caring for Your Teenager

Less Stress, More Success: A New Approach to Guiding Your Teen Through College Admissions and Beyond

**For additional parenting resources, visit the HealthyChildren bookstore at
shop.aap.org/for-parents/.**

healthy children.org
Powered by pediatricians. Trusted by parents.
from the American Academy of Pediatrics

*This book is also available in Spanish.

2ND EDITION

RAISING
TWINS

Parenting Multiples
From Pregnancy
Through the School Years

SHELLY VAZIRI FLAIS, MD, FAAP

American Academy of Pediatrics
DEDICATED TO THE HEALTH OF ALL CHILDREN™

American Academy of Pediatrics Department of Marketing and Publications

Director, Department of Marketing and Publications
Maureen DeRosa, MPA

Director, Division of Product Development
Mark Grimes

Manager, Consumer Publishing
Kathryn Sparks

Director, Division of Publishing and Production Services
Sandi King, MS

Editorial Specialist
Amanda Cozza

Publishing and Production Services Specialist
Shannan Martin

Manager, Art Direction and Production
Linda Diamond

Digital Content and Production Specialist
Houston Adams

Director, Division of Marketing and Sales
Julia Lee

Manager, Consumer Product Marketing
Mary Jo Reynolds

Published by the American Academy of Pediatrics
141 Northwest Point Blvd, Elk Grove Village, IL 60007-1019
847/434-4000
Fax: 847/434-8000
www.aap.org

Cover design by Daniel Rembert
Book design by Linda Diamond
Illustrations by Tony LeTourneau

First Edition—2009
Library of Congress Control Number: 2014935004
ISBN: 978-1-58110-865-1
eBook: 978-1-58110-869-9
EPUB: 978-1-58110-878-1
Kindle: 978-1-58110-879-8

The recommendations in this publication do not indicate an exclusive course of treatment or serve as a standard of medical care. Variations, taking into account individual circumstances, may be appropriate.

Statements and opinions expressed are those of the author and not necessarily those of the American Academy of Pediatrics.

Products are mentioned for informational purposes only. Inclusion in this publication does not imply endorsement by the American Academy of Pediatrics.

The persons whose photographs are depicted in this publication are professional models. They have no relation to the issues discussed. Any characters they are portraying are fictional.

Every effort is made to keep *Raising Twins: Parenting Multiples From Pregnancy Through the School Years* consistent with the most recent advice and information possible.

CB0079
9-355

1 2 3 4 5 6 7 8 9 10

What People Are Saying

—〰—

Dr Flais has the experience and training as a mother of twins and a pediatrician to get it right. She knows how to double the joy of being a parent.

— Marc Weissbluth, MD, FAAP
   Author of *Healthy Sleep Habits, Happy Twins*

—〰—

Raising Twins: Parenting Multiples From Pregnancy Through the School Years, 2nd Edition, by Shelly Vaziri Flais, MD, FAAP, is a book I wish I had when my multiples were younger. Raising multiples is a challenging task, and as the mother of 20-year-old fraternal girls and a teenage son, I have navigated more emotional waters than I want to remember! Through the support of my multiples club on the local and state levels, I found wise and helpful "anchors" to help me cope with those sometimes turbulent times. Dr Flais' book discusses how family dynamic changes when multiples arrive and offers insights on schedules, equipment, feedings, and other care issues. This must-have book contains indispensable information and guidance that mothers of multiples can reference for years. The perspective Dr Flais provides as a pediatrician and mother of twins is invaluable.

— Denise Anderson
   President, Illinois Organization of Mothers of Twins Clubs, Inc,
   2009–2010

—〰—

This book is chock-full of useful advice and comforting anecdotes for parents of multiples. I wish it had been on the bookshelf when I had mine!

— Gale Gand
   Chef, author, and mother of twins

—〰—

————

Who better to hold your hand and help prepare you for the multiple joys (and challenges) of parenting twins than a pediatrician-mother of twins? By combining a medically sound foundation with a fully updated, reality-based approach, *Raising Twins* continues to provide new and expectant parents of twins a double dose of valuable advice and insight, while adding welcomed new and expanded second-edition insights including parenting premature infants and multiples.

— Laura A. Jana, MD, FAAP
  Pediatrician; coauthor of the award-winning books *Heading Home With Your Newborn: From Birth to Reality* and *Food Fights: Winning the Nutritional Challenges of Parenthood Armed With Insight, Humor, and a Bottle of Ketchup;* and an identical twin!

————

If you've just learned you're expecting twins or if you want strategies and tips from a mom of multiples who has been there, *Raising Twins* is the book you need.

Raising Twins is an invaluable resource for any family with twins. Dr Flais gives detailed, practical strategies for gracefully handling the daily challenges of having multiple children of the same age (schedules, feeding, sleep training, discipline) and does it with the voice of experience. Knowing Dr Flais is not only a pediatrician but also a mother of 4 (including twins) made me sit up and listen to her practical tips. I especially appreciate her thoughts on the importance of nurturing and appreciating each child as an individual. The tone of the book is easy and conversational; you can tell Dr Flais is speaking from experience.

— Lisa Zollner
  Attorney, mother of 3 (including twins)

————

Contents

Chapter 4
Early Infancy and Getting on a Schedule (cont)

Chapter 5
Older Infancy and First Birthday

Chapter 6
The Toddler Years (1- and 2-Year-Olds)

Acknowledgments

I have many people to thank for playing a special role in my life and in the development of both editions of this book. The opportunity to write *Raising Twins* has been a complete joy and honor. It combines the passion I have as a pediatrician to help other parents raise their children happily and healthfully with the practical knowledge I have gained while raising twins in addition to single-born siblings close in age.

I thank my amazing husband Mike, Michael J. Flais, MD, for being a constant source of love and support. I thank you for being the most wonderful husband, partner, and father to our children. Your humor and steadfast calm help us through any challenge in life. I am grateful to be a mother to our children, Matthew, Andrew, Ryan, and Nancy—four remarkable, unique individuals whose presence makes this world a better place. I also thank our extended Vaziri and Flais families for their love and support.

For both the first and second editions, I thank Sarah Lacey Pilarowski, MD, FAAP, IBCLC, assistant clinical professor at the University of Colorado School of Medicine, Department of Pediatrics, and a Denver community pediatrician, for her invaluable peer review of book content, as well as a rewarding long-term friendship. I also thank Kristina Ferro Keating, MD, FAAP, of Lake Forest Pediatric Associates in Lake Forest, Illinois, for her invaluable peer review of book content and years of friendship.

As always, a big thanks to the wonderful people at the American Academy of Pediatrics (AAP) for their guidance and expertise—Mark Grimes, director, division of product development; Kathryn Sparks, manager, consumer publishing; and the entire production team. I also acknowledge Carolyn Kolbaba, former manager of AAP consumer publishing, for her thorough and insightful involvement with the production of our first edition.

A hearty thanks to the numerous wonderful families with multiples who helpfully shared their thoughts, experiences, and notes with me during the process of writing both the first and second editions.

Adler Family

Bell Family

Buteau/Erickson Family

Coleman Family

DeGuzman Family

Derk Family

DeRome Family

Didrickson Family

Dooyema Family

DuMais Family

Fraser Family

Graf Family

Greenawalt Family

Henderson Family

Hepokoski Family

Hynek Family

Irhke Family

Janson Family

Kowynia Family

LaMonte Family

Lange Family

Long Family

Morris Family

Orrico Family

Peters Family

Rappoport Family

Sayles Family

Scheidler Family

Slinde Family

Styzcen Family

Vervack Family

Winkler Family

Zollner Family

And I thank you, our readers. Congratulations on joining our ranks of families with multiples! Our multiples community is incredibly supportive of one other through all the challenges and triumphs of parenting twins, triplets, and more. You will learn much about parenting multiples; please pay it forward, and share this knowledge with others. In *Star Wars: Episode VI: Return of the Jedi,* Yoda asked of Luke Skywalker, a well-known twin, "Pass on what you have learned." Spread the love and pass on the lessons you have learned to other families with multiples.

To all families with multiples, and to my
beloved husband and children.

"Remember you are over the Edge of the Wild now,
and in for all sorts of fun wherever you go."

— Gandalf, *The Hobbit; or,*

There and Back Again,

J. R. R. Tolkien

CHAPTER 1

Introduction:
A New Adventure

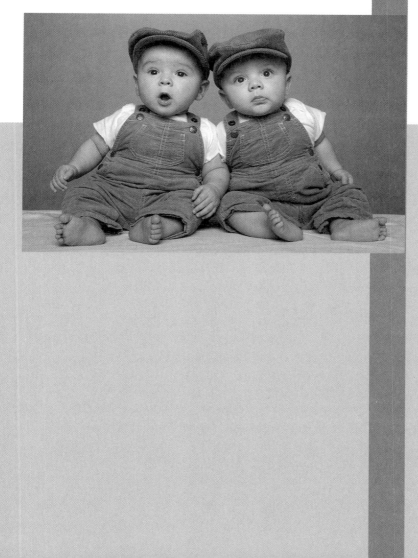

One beautiful August day, the skies were blue and the sun was shining. "Can we take our training wheels off our bikes, please?" My husband and I had heard this request countless times before, and on this clear day, my preschool-aged identical twin boys' summer-long pleas were finally answered. Managing a busy family with 4 young kids, we had been hesitant to remove our safety net of the training wheels. Were the boys ready to make this adjustment? Were we, their parents, ready to let our sons take a leap forward toward greater independence?

Ryan's bike was first. Being fascinated by tools and gears, he watched intently as Dad removed the unwanted support system. Eager to practice, he hopped on his streamlined bike and quickly learned that starting and stopping required some new adjustments. Once he gained momentum, however, there was no stopping him! With Ryan happily practicing his new skills, it was Andrew's turn. Andrew waited patiently and cheered Ryan's success. Within moments, each boy was off and cycling, learning the ropes for the new method of riding their bikes.

As I watched each of my boys race past me on the sidewalk, I felt a strange sensation. It was as if it was just a week earlier that we learned we were pregnant with twins. How was it that we went from seeing 2 heartbeats on an ultrasound to watching these 2 growing, unique kids whiz by on bicycles?

Your New Life With Multiples

If you are expecting or are already parenting twins, triplets, or more, congratulations! If you are nervous about the challenges of raising multiples, remain calm and take a deep breath. With preparation, planning, organization, and the support of those around you, you can do it. You may be unsure of your abilities to parent multiples, a natural feeling because it is a completely new experience and responsibility, but you will surprise yourself with your ability to adapt to your new family dynamic. You'll spend the first year or so synchronizing the babies' schedules to make life easier. As they grow, you will nurture each of them as an individual. In the blink of an eye, your children will ride their bikes in figure-eight patterns around you; in 2 blinks, you'll help them register for drivers' education classes!

As a child learns to ride a bike without training wheels, she has some initial adjustments to make as she figures out a new way of cycling. Similarly, as parents welcome multiples into their family, they adjust and learn a new way of managing family life. You soon get a feel for how to handle your new life and therefore cruise along, free of your training wheels.

How will you handle more than one baby? You can care for twins or more by keeping in mind the basics of good parenting. A good parent provides love, safety, and security. Babies only need a few things— something to eat (breast milk or formula), something to pee and poop into (diaper), a safe place to sleep (crib), and a safe way to ride in the car (car safety seat). If you streamline your newborns' needs, you will be able to provide what is important to your newborns. Being able to tell the difference between basic requirements and the extras helps you stay organized and keep your sanity.

When you have baby twins, triplets, or more, the most important mantra to remember is to *keep the babies on the same schedule.* It is the best way to happily survive their first year of life. When one baby wakes up to eat, it doesn't matter how cute the other one looks sleeping; you have to wake them both up for the feeding. If the babies' feedings are uncoordinated, you could easily spend the entire 24 hours of any given day feeding them, one after the other. If you feed 2 babies on 2 different schedules, you may not be able to sleep much, spend any time with an older child in the family, or recognize that vaguely familiar-looking person over there who reminds you of your spouse.

Parenting Support

Lisa, mom of twin toddlers, shares, "The best advice I got was to get and keep the babies on the same schedule. Managing the 2- to 3-hour bursts of handling the newborns' needs provides you some time to catch your breath when they are both sleeping, and it might possibly be the only shower opportunity one might have!"

The News Flash of a Lifetime

Your reaction to the news that you have more than one baby on the way is most likely a mix of strong emotions. I admit, the first month after discovering I was pregnant with twins, I looked like a deer staring in the headlights. A hundred questions ran through my mind. How could I be having twins?

Is this really happening? How on earth could we handle 2 newborns at once?

You and your spouse may have very different reactions. While I was nervous, my husband was thrilled and breezily optimistic. He told me, "Relax, it will be great! Everything will work out just fine." I appreciated his joy and confidence, but I felt frustrated that he wasn't showing fear of the unknown, while I felt unsure of my ability to handle the situation. I wondered just how steep our learning curve would be to find our groove.

Here we are, years later, and we have not only survived but enjoyed the chaos and excitement of our twins' early years. I was so nervous when pregnant that I had imagined it would be more difficult than it actually was to raise younger twins. In reality, the day-to-day routine of taking care of 2 little babies at the same time is very doable; it is key to take things one step at a time, as well as one day at a time. Once your family starts using some strategies to streamline your babies' care, you'll breathe more easily and enjoy the whole process.

The challenges of raising multiples are what make the parenting successes, and the overall experience, even sweeter. It is fascinating to watch as each child's unique personality evolves and develops over time. The highs and lows of the parenting experience are amplified for parents of multiples. You'll have moments of intense exhaustion but also moments of unsurpassed joy.

Have faith in yourself and your parenting abilities. The human spirit has an amazing ability to rise to a challenge. You can successfully parent multiples, one day at a time. Any challenge in life must be tackled one step at a time, and parenting multiples is no exception. One particularly tough day may feel like it lasts an eternity, but soon a time will come when you look back and wonder how the early weeks and months flew by so quickly.

Parenting Support

There is no one-size-fits-all parenting technique for raising multiples. Accept the advice of others, but do what works for *your* family.

How the Parenting Experience Changes Over the Early Years

The job of parenting multiples requires different skills from you at different stages. The earliest weeks and months with twins require stamina and an ability to streamline your daily tasks to survive with some semblance of sanity remaining. As time wears on, you can ease out of survival mode and adjust to a different mindset. You will be a master of understanding human emotions and interactions as you navigate all the different personalities that live under your roof, and you'll have as good of a grasp of interpersonal relations as an international diplomat.

Pregnancy

During your pregnancy, channel your nervous energy into preparing your nest for your babies. Twins and other multiples tend to deliver earlier than single-born babies, so prepare for this in case it happens (see the "If Your Multiples Are Born Early" chapter on page 211 for more information). Of course, another reason you should prepare early is because your belly will get quite large and uncomfortable as you approach your due date. Start attending your local Parents of Multiples club meetings to meet other parents of multiples and start collecting helpful tips. Pregnancy is also the time to enlist family and friends for help in the early weeks and months of your babies' lives.

Early Infancy

During the newborn period, your family will adjust quickly to a brand-new routine. The daily schedule will be filled with feedings, burpings, diaper changes, and catnaps, cycling through the days and nights. You and your newborns will begin a relationship with each other that will strengthen with your love and consistent responses to their basic needs. If there are older siblings in your family, continue to show love and positive atten-tion to them as well, and help them feel as much a part of the process as possible. You may discover during this period that while your newborns were born at the same time, they may have very different temperaments and personalities.

Later Infancy

During the later infancy months, you'll coax everyone into a more predictable schedule, and kids and parents alike will know what to expect at certain times. Your babies are becoming little people and you begin to see what makes each of them tick.

The Toddler Years

When they are toddlers, life is overall much easier to handle, but you've got some major milestones to negotiate, such as toilet training and transitioning to big-kid beds. Strategies that work for single-born children need to be tweaked a bit when you're toilet training kids of the same age in the same home. All toddlers start to realize at some point that they are independent people, separate from their parents and their siblings. As a parent, help your toddlers make more decisions for themselves within an acceptable framework of behavior.

The Preschool Years

The preschool years with multiples are such a great payoff for your years of effort. Your home evolves into their imagination factory. They sleep all night (for the most part!); they use the toilet to pee and poop (for the most part!); and you're now able to enjoy them even more and nurture each of them as unique individuals. As I have seen, one of the many benefits of having twins is that their "twinship" teaches them about patience and sharing; the multiples experience provides built-in life lessons. Many experts believe that multiples may be more socially savvy than their single-born peers because of the relationships they've grown with since infancy.

The School Years and Beyond

In kindergarten and the school years, your multiples' world is rapidly expanding. As the years progress, keep in mind that parenting means raising future independent adults. Decisions will be made regarding classroom placement, participation in activities, social dynamics, and more. Your children may be quite independent, or you may be dealing with a fair amount of competition between the siblings. We will hear some advice from multiples themselves as well as gain insight into raising multiples.

Enjoying the Parenting Experience

Parenting multiples can be quite hectic, and in the early days and weeks, it can consume your days *and* nights. You don't want to merely *survive* raising them; you want to enjoy the experience, retain your sanity, and maintain a good relationship with your spouse and other children. Each day is only 24 hours long. There are always the mundane things that we must do to keep the home running, and then there are the fun bonding experiences we'd like to enjoy more. Instead of folding laundry all day, it would be nice to have a moment to cuddle with your kids and read them another good book. Not all of us can afford to hire babysitters or outside help on a regular basis, and not all of us have available family nearby who are able to help make our personal or couple time a routine experience.

As a parent of multiples, you'll need strategizing and creative planning to streamline and organize the everyday, necessary tasks as much as you can. That way, you have more time and energy to simply *be* with your kids and *enjoy* them. Another part of the equation of happy parenting is finding time for yourself, for your friends, and to exercise, as well as dedicating time to your relationship with your partner.

Implementing and maintaining a routine household schedule will go a long way toward protecting special time for your multiples, your other children, yourself, and your partner. Your best ally during your twins' early years is their need for *sleep*. Young children need plenty of sleep. If the family works together to maintain a routine bedtime for the kids once they have grown past the newborn stage, you will have a couple of hours every night for personal or free time, or at least the ability to think a complete sentence in your head without interruption! A happy parent is a better parent. It is not selfish to seek out personal or couple time; it is healthy and will have positive effects on everyone in the family.

Families With Multiples:
One Size Does Not Fit All

My firsthand experiences taught me a lot as a parent and as a pediatrician. Our oldest son was only 18 months of age when our identical twin boys were born. My husband and I had to quickly figure out how to care for 3 kids, all younger than 2 years. I remember making a phone call to our crib manufacturer when we had a problem with one of our cribs. The woman helping me simply could not believe we had 3 kids in 3 cribs at the same time. Efficiency became our middle name as we coaxed ourselves and our 3 young sons to operate on a daily schedule so that we could all survive. We were both practicing physicians and had no outside child care assistance. My husband handled our sons solo on the days that I worked in my pediatric practice, and I handled the boys solo on his working days. Our fourth child, a daughter who was born a month before our oldest son turned 4 years of age, rounded out our family.

I continued to practice clinical pediatrics part-time through my twins' toddler years, and then I made the decision to stay home temporarily while my 4 children were young. I returned to clinical practice when all 4 kids were on a more regular school schedule. I can appreciate twin parenting from both perspectives—working outside the home, pumping breast milk and all, and being at home as the children's primary caregiver. My professional knowledge and real-life experience with 4 young kids has helped me to efficiently, healthfully, and lovingly parent my children, and I appreciate the opportunity to share some of my insights with you and your family. While this chapter and a few others in this book cover births of multiples in general, the following chapters from preparing for your babies arrival to the school years will focus on raising twins. However, all principals, strategies, tips, and advice mentioned throughout these sections universally apply to families raising triplets, quadruplets, or more! For an individual chapter on triplets and more, please see page 221, as well as page 229 for some fun multiple facts.

At times, there will be friends, family, and health care professionals giving you advice and encouragement as you embark on *your* journey raising multiples. Listen to what everyone has to say and give ideas a try, but ultimately, only you can figure out what will work for your family and your situation. Not all families with multiples are the same. A family with 2 older kids and twins needs to operate much differently than a family of solely twin children or a family with triplets and one younger sibling. Accept the support and camaraderie of others, but *you* as the parent will find what works for your individual family. Have confidence in your own parenting judgment and abilities and you will not only survive their early years, you will enjoy them.

CHAPTER 2

Preparing for Your Twins' Arrival

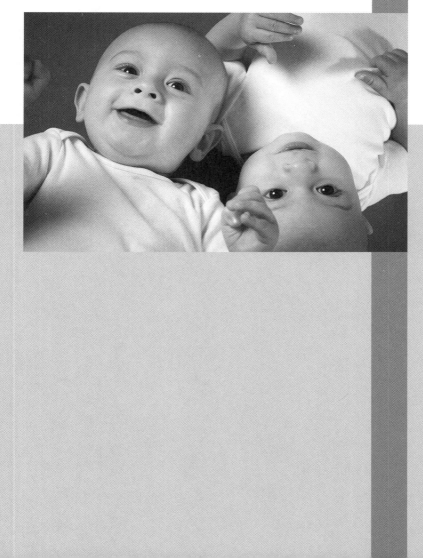

"*L*et's get an ultrasound just to be safe." I hadn't expected to be strolling my first son, still just a baby, toward the ultrasound suite during the first routine prenatal visit for my second pregnancy.

My husband and I always hoped to raise a big family. We were eager to get pregnant again soon after our first child was born. Happily, our home pregnancy test soon turned positive, and at the 6-week mark I brought baby Matthew along to visit the obstetrician for what I thought would be a straightforward initial checkup.

I mentioned to my obstetrician that I experienced some minimal bleeding, yet was otherwise well. Apparently the bleeding was enough to warrant an ultrasound.

Matthew and I entered the small ultrasound room. The tiny room felt toasty warm from the large ultrasound machine and other running equipment. As we began the study, Matthew began to fuss in his stroller, so I hoisted him up onto the examination table with me and held him tight as I tried to lie flat on my back. Matthew was finally content when he saw how fun it was to swat at the examination table's crinkly paper. I securely held onto Matthew so he wouldn't fall, which is no small feat during an uncomfortable vaginal ultrasound.

The ultrasound technician seemed to be taking quite a while with the study. "Hmm…well, that's what I thought. OK, take a look at this," she said as she turned the monitor so I could see it.

When you're looking at a fuzzy, moving, black-and-white image, it is challenging to interpret what you're seeing. But what I saw on that screen was unmistakable—2 tiny spots flickering repeatedly, each to its own rhythm. Two hearts! The world stopped, as I was sure I just stepped into someone else's life. Utter shock and disbelief. I hadn't planned on twins. Believe me, I plan everything—this wasn't part of my plan!

Through my dizzy blur of emotions, clutching onto a wriggling, oblivious Matthew, I kept focusing on those 2 blips on the screen. They were so beautiful, so innocent, sending their rhythmic beats across the ultrasound waves like communicating stars in the Milky Way. I was mesmerized and terrified at the same time, all the while having what felt like an out-of-body experience.

The Emotional Roller Coaster

Congratulations! You are about to enter the world of twins. This world is an incredible and remarkable place in which you will share many beautiful moments in your children's lives. It is also an experience that can be chaotic and challenging, but have confidence in your abilities to navigate the road ahead. Just as generations of parents before you have survived and succeeded, you will as well. Unexpected joys are yours as you watch your twins grow and develop relationships with each other and everyone in your family. Becoming a parent changes your life forever, but becoming a parent to multiples is truly a gift.

You will never forget the moment you learned you were pregnant with twins. Whether you conceived the babies naturally or with the assistance of fertility treatments, the reality that you are already the mother to more than one growing, living being is incredible. You may be very emotional about the news. Pregnancy, with all of its associated hormones, is already an emotional time. The fact that you'll have 2 (or more) bundles of joy, arriving at the same time, can increase the emotions even more so. You may feel elated and joyous one moment, anxious and panicked the next. It doesn't matter if your pregnancy was a surprise or planned for years; your emotional roller coaster is completely normal.

Twin Support

Talk about your emotions during your twin pregnancy. Seek out good listeners to support you during this exciting time.

Preserve your emotional well-being by discussing your feelings with your partner, your family, and your friends—anyone who is a good listener. Your excitement can transform into fear in mere moments, and discussion with loved ones is the best way to sort out your thoughts and begin to devise coping strategies. Make good use of your support network as a sounding board for what you are experiencing.

Your support network includes family and friends. These people know your history, and you may be able to share your deepest fears with them. However, along your new journey you'll be developing new relationships as well. I suggest you reach out to your local Parents of Multiples club, at which you'll meet new families, in addition to registering for a multiples

> ## Twin Support
>
> In the classic novel *The Hobbit; or There and Back Again* by J. R. R. Tolkien, the wizard Gandalf shows up on Bilbo Baggins' doorstep, informing him that he is to partake in a grand adventure involving dwarves, mountains, and a dragon. Bilbo, who loves the comfort of home and all that is familiar, is dumbfounded and incredulous that this is indeed his future. Parents of multiples, regardless of the means of conception, may feel similar emotions to Bilbo's, feeling that they have been nudged to begin an adventure into the unknown with little preamble, warning, or preparation.

prenatal class at the hospital where you plan on delivering your babies. (For more information on finding a Parents of Multiples club near you, see the "Support, Emotional Health, and Time-savers for Families With Multiples" chapter on page 193) You may find that your new friends who are pregnant with or already have twins or other multiples relate to your situation better. It is comforting to talk with someone who is living a similar experience to yours. There are advantages to different kinds of support.

Ideally, the people you include in your support network should be positive and upbeat. Many well-meaning people may put their feet in their mouths when they learn that you are expecting multiples. These people are as surprised and shocked as you, and when they learn the news they may have poorly thought-out remarks or questions. In most cases, these people mean well and are simply blurting out their comments without realizing that they might be insensitive. Inconsiderate remarks may feel hurtful to you, especially in your state of emotional overdrive. Try not to let these comments get under your skin. The best way to respond is to simply say, "We are very surprised and happy." The nature of your children's conception isn't anyone else's business.

> ## Twin Support
>
> You will likely have strangers asking you inappropriate questions about the conception of your twins, how much weight you have gained, and so on. Unfortunately, intrusive questions are not exclusive to those of us with multiples. I once read that Mary Kay Ash, founder of Mary Kay Cosmetics, was asked by a television personality, "How old are you?" She looked her right in the eye and answered, "How much do you weigh?" Whether you respond with humor or sarcasm, don't let these interactions faze you; respond concisely, and move forward.

Another option is to infuse humor. One mother I know had a standard response whenever anyone asked her, "What are you going to *do*?!" She would reply, "I'll just sell one of them on eBay!" The absurdity of this comment alerts the questioner that he or she has asked an unhelpful and silly question. Regardless of how you choose to respond, don't be caught off guard; have your answer planned ahead of time so that you are prepared for this inevitable exchange. Most importantly, after your witty or concise reply, leave it at that. You don't need to get into details with the offender, and it will not help your emotional state to have this kind of conversation. If certain people in your life cannot be upbeat and supportive about your twin pregnancy, you may need to maintain some emotional distance from those people for your sanity. Now is the time to take care of your body, your emotional status, and your babies.

You may feel scared at times, but remind yourself that you are up to the task. Human nature has an amazing ability to adapt. Even though you may not have expected twins, have confidence. It is important, however, to envision your life with your new babies realistically. Don't expect to become the perfect parent of twins. There are no perfect parents, even of single-born children. You are going to do the best you can. Your main job will be to provide love and a nurturing environment for your twins.

Twin Support

Have confidence in your ability to raise twins. The characteristics of good parenting are universal, whether you have 1, 2, or more babies at a time. If you can provide love, food, and safety to your babies, you can successfully parent twins.

Your local Parents of Multiples club meetings are a great source of support. Even if you cannot attend in person on a regular basis, it can be quite informative, as well as soothing, to be surrounded by a room full of parents who are expecting or already have multiples. (Read more about Parents of Multiples clubs in the support chapter on page 193.) This is important because people who haven't lived it just cannot relate to the exceptional experiences you're about to have.

You may feel alone and scared, but if you reach out, you will find other twin families who not only had a similar situation but also *survived* it and are richer people for having had the experience. Thanks to the prevalence of social networking online, for those of us who have difficulties getting to Parents of Multiples club meetings in person, there are plenty of public and private groups online for further support (read more in the support chapter on page 193). This may be a necessity for you if you need to go on bed rest for any amount of time during your pregnancy.

Twin Support

During my twin pregnancy, I was very worried about how young my first son was, as well as the fact that he would only be 18 months of age when the twins would be born. I met a woman right away at a Mother of Twins meeting who was due to have her twins around her daughter's first birthday. I had been thinking I'd be the only mom in the country with 3 kids younger than 2 years, and suddenly here was a room full of people who could relate. Meeting these other parents diminished my feelings of isolation.

Emotionally, allow yourself time to let go of your plans for a straight-forward single-baby pregnancy. We have all daydreamed for years about the perfect, typical singleton baby and about the way that baby would fit into our lives and families. It is quite an adjustment from any preconceived hopes to learn that you will have more than one little baby entering into your life and family at the same time. Allow yourself time to let go of the old fantasy. Twins may not be what you expected or planned, but they have a way of providing you with happiness and love that you never thought possible. You are in for the treat of a lifetime!

Twin Tip

Seek out advice from other families with twins. Speaking with these families can help you remember that you are not alone.

When you feel overwhelmed or even nervous that you are expecting twins, feelings of guilt may not be far behind. You may think, "All of my friends have it so easy, with only one baby at a time. It would be so much easier to give birth to just *one* baby than to have twins. But I shouldn't feel this way, shame on me. How can I feel this way when I am so lucky to be having twins?" You are human and entitled to waver in your happiness. Allow yourself to feel the full range of emotions as need be, and let go of the guilt. If you feel disappointed at times, acknowledge your feelings and then move forward. Use this time to talk with your partner. Also, get cracking on your to-do lists. A good way to relieve some stress is by using your nesting instincts to prepare for your twins' arrival.

Twin Tales

Jon, dad to infant twins and a preschool-aged singleton, shares, "I wish I knew how elastic the human capacity for love and care truly is. My worry that we wouldn't be able to deftly handle all of the intricacies of infant care times 2, *and* still find time to soak up all the love and wonder without going crazy, quickly gave way to a rhythm that—almost as quickly as it fell upon us—became the 'new normal.' We can't even imagine 'only' having one baby."

Taking Care of Your Body and the Pregnancy

The fact that you are carrying more than one baby does place you in a special category in the eyes of obstetricians. A pregnancy with twins is classified as a *high-risk* pregnancy, which can be translated as, "We will need to follow this pregnancy more closely." Also in the high-risk category are mothers with diabetes, those with a history of preterm labor with prior pregnancies, or those who have other major health issues. Most twin pregnancies progress smoothly, and the odds of a healthy pregnancy increase if you take better care of yourself.

According to the National Vital Statistics Reports, about 60% of twins, more than 90% of triplets, and virtually all quadruplets and higher-order multiples are born prematurely. On average, most single-baby pregnancies last for 39 weeks; for twins, 35 weeks; for triplets, 32 weeks; and for quadruplets, 29 weeks. The length of pregnancy decreases with each additional baby. The American College of Obstetricians and Gynecologists has defined *early term* (preterm) babies as those born 37⁶∕₇ weeks of gestation through 38⁶∕₇ weeks of gestation and *full term* as 39⁰∕₇ weeks of gestation through 40⁶∕₇ weeks of gestation; it is important for parents expecting twins or more to be aware of the greater likelihood of premature deliveries. For more information on premature delivery, please refer to the "If Your Multiples Are Born Early" chapter on page 211.

A very important consideration during your pregnancy is proper nutrition. Pregnant mothers should take a prenatal vitamin with folic acid, ideally starting a few months ahead of when they hope to conceive, if possible. Folic acid, an important ingredient in prenatal vitamins, has definitively been proven to reduce the chances of neural tube defects such as spina bifida. If you haven't started taking a prenatal vitamin daily yet, don't fret about the missed time, but do start now. Take your prenatal vitamin with food to reduce nausea, and applaud yourself for taking yet another step to keep your babies as healthy as possible. Moms of twins don't need 2 prenatal vitamins a day; one is enough.

Eating the proper foods and the right amount of calories is critical during a twin pregnancy. Whereas single-baby pregnancies require 300 extra calories a day, most experts agree that twin pregnancies require around 1,000 extra calories a day. Morning sickness—or in most women's cases, all-day sickness—can be eased by eating small, healthy snacks frequently and can help you reach your caloric goals each day. Keeping a little something in your stomach at all times can help take the edge off of the nausea. Low-fat yogurt, fruit, smoothies, crackers, and protein shakes are all good options.

In addition to consuming extra calories, it is important to drink water throughout the day. Keeping well hydrated may drive you crazy in later months when it seems like you're running to the bathroom every 5 minutes; however, your babies' extra blood flow and removal of wastes depend on it. It may help to drink more water earlier in the day and then stop after 8:00 pm so that you can sleep longer stretches at night between bathroom breaks.

Twin Tip

Remind yourself to drink plenty of water, even during a busy day at work. Every morning, pre-fill your daily water needs in individual water bottles or a bigger container. Take sips of water every hour. At the end of the day, empty bottles will tell you that you drank what you needed.

Listening to Your Body's Signs

Proper nutrition and hydration is important for your twin pregnancy, as is listening to your body. Any new pregnancy symptoms you notice *must* be brought to your obstetrician's attention; seemingly minor things could be a sign of something more serious. Because twins have an increased chance of being born early, any symptoms or concerns *must* be addressed for the safety of your babies. Bleeding or vaginal discharge, contractions that are becoming more frequent, pressure in the pelvis or lower back, or even diarrhea can all be signs of preterm labor. And while early bleeding in the first trimester could be the normal phenomenon of the twins implanting in the uterine wall, you should call your obstetrician if you experience bleeding at any point.

📖 Twin Tales

Lisa, mom to toddler twins, shares, "In retrospect, I think that anyone expecting multiples should get a lot more information about what to expect in the event of a C-section. Looking back, I wish I'd been a little more prepared for it."

Twin pregnancies can also increase the chances of preeclampsia, a condition in which the mother has increased blood pressure, protein in the urine (detectable by urinalysis), and more swelling than is normal in pregnancy. If you notice rapid weight gain or headaches, alert your obstetrician so you may be examined as soon as possible. Depending on the severity of the situation, treatment may range from bed rest to hospital-administered medications to immediate delivery of the babies (the only "cure" for preeclampsia). Have you heard of TTTS? It stands for *twin-to-twin transfusion syndrome.* It is a rare occurrence for identical twins (10%–20% of monochorionic twin pregnancies, meaning identical twins who share one placenta). The 2 babies' blood can mix in a connection between placental vessels, resulting in one baby receiving too much blood, while the other baby receives too little. Prenatal ultrasounds can allow obstetricians to study the placenta, blood flow, and growth and development of identical twins.

An optimistic yet attentive attitude during your pregnancy will help your mental state and hence help your babies thrive during pregnancy as long as possible. Take things one day at a time and one week at a time. Eat well and pay attention to what your body and your babies are telling you. Every extra day that your babies spend inside the womb will help them once delivery day arrives. The bigger your belly gets, the bigger your smile should be because you're creating 2 miracles!

Pregnancy Preparations

The more you do now to prepare for twins will help immensely once your babies arrive. If you are on a form of bed rest because of pregnancy complications, you will need to delegate preparation tasks or use the Internet as much as possible. Consider obtaining necessary items, such as cribs, a bit earlier in the pregnancy than you would for a traditional single-baby pregnancy so you're ready in case the babies decide to show up early.

New Information

Similar to offering support, Parents of Multiples club meetings can provide useful information and learning tools. Even 1 or 2 useful tidbits may really help you out. That one tip you learn could potentially save you hours of time and effort down the line. It was at a twin club meeting that I learned about the existence of a twin-feeding pillow, a large foam-filled device specially designed to make it easy to nurse or bottle-feed both babies simultaneously. I had never heard of them before, even though I was a pediatrician! This single tip made our family's lives incredibly easier during those first few months. I cannot imagine surviving those early weeks without my trusty twin-feeding pillow. At Parents of Multiples club meetings you'll hear these nuggets of information and meet other women who are in the same boat, as well as listen to how they survived and prospered.

Shopping for Twins

Twin clubs also host clothing and equipment swaps and sales of gently used items from other members. Real bargains can be found at these sales.

Twin Tales

Lisa, mom to 9-year-old twin boys, advises, "You don't need 2 of everything. Two babies means you get twice the practice diapering, feeding, bathing, and burping. You get good pretty quickly. Oh, and buy the twin nursing pillow—foam, not inflatable."

You must shop carefully when preparing your nest for twins. The baby product industry would have you believe that you need 20 pairs of baby booties, a dust ruffle for the crib, a baby wipe warmer, and a diaper pail for every room in the house. Advertisers even go as far as to publish "handy" checklists with many unnecessary or irrelevant items. Feel free to use these lists as reminders or guides, but don't feel obligated to buy all the items on them.

First-time parents especially need to be aware of the baby product marketing phenomenon. Because they are your first babies, you want to prepare as best you can. That is what being a good parent involves, right? Baby product companies take advantage of new parents' feelings of anticipation, anxiety, and inexperience by subtly hinting that if you are to be a good parent, you'll definitely purchase the crib mobile with the alphabet on it for just $49.99. Expensive things are *not* what make you a good parent. A good parent provides love, safety, and security. All the other bells and whistles are just extras; keep this in mind as you prepare your budget.

Twin Tip

Is your head spinning over too many must-have baby items? Many baby products are unnecessary. As long as you have food, diapers, cribs, and car safety seats, you're set. Anything else is a bonus.

Parents of twins need to make budgeting a priority; you'll note how expensive it is, requiring double of many items. You have to buy or launder twice as many diapers, and you need twice the bottle supplies if you are pumping or not nursing.

You will probably need to streamline other areas that are negotiable. It is important to note, however, that over the long haul, twins are not much more expensive than 2 babies born separately; it's just that you need certain things at the same time.

Now is the time to start asking for help. Make a call or send a mass e-mail out to your extended family and friends, inform them of your soon-to-arrive twins, and ask for baby items to borrow. Borrowing baby items is wonderful because a lot of baby gear has a limited life span and is only usable for a few months. Bouncy seats, carriers, and baby swings are quickly outgrown. For example, a soft-pack front carrier can start to be used when a baby is around 8 pounds (check the specific manufacturer's instructions) and continue to be used until the baby is up to around 20 pounds, which is usually by 9 months of age. Don't be overly particular about hand-me-downs. I remember during my first pregnancy, I wanted to buy everything new and fresh for my son. Months later, after numerous spit-ups and diaper overflows, I realized hey, it really isn't a big deal to borrow a baby swing and save some cash.

Investigate different ways to streamline your budget. When it comes to toys, consider Internet-based companies that rent age-appropriate toys to families. Once a batch of toys is outgrown, it is mailed back and a new, age-appropriate set of toys is mailed out. A toy-rental service is a creative way to save on costs, as well as reduce clutter and minimize waste.

Make sure you carefully examine and clean borrowed equipment to ensure that it is safe and clean. Verify that there are no loose or broken parts. When you borrow items, you also need to make sure they are not on any safety recall listings. Check out the US Consumer Product Safety Commission Web site at www.cpsc.gov to make sure your borrowed items have not been recalled. This is especially important for cribs because your twins will probably spend most of their time there.

Twin Tip

When preparing your nest for twins, stay on a budget by borrowing extra baby equipment. Make sure that borrowed or secondhand baby gear has not been recalled by checking the US Consumer Product Safety Commission Web site (www.cpsc.gov).

If you are pregnant and on bed rest, or even after the delivery of your newborn twins, it is a lifesaver to have an Internet lifeline available to help. Housebound by your pregnancy or newborns, it is gratifying to be able to point and click on your computer and have the things you need delivered to you. A little research will help you figure out who offers free or low-cost shipping. Many parents even find ordering drugstore necessities, diapers, or groceries online for delivery to be helpful for the first few months after the twins arrive. If you are the fortunate recipient of a baby shower, many Web sites can help you set up a shower gift registry online, saving you repeated trips to the store.

Other must-have baby items are usually unnecessary. You'll have to decide for yourself whether certain items are worth buying to have a cute nursery or if you'd rather save the money. A good example is a crib bumper. It may surprise you to learn that a bumper is unnecessary, and in fact, the American Academy of Pediatrics recommends not using one at all. Crib bumpers (or bumper pads) may seem as though they can help protect babies from drafts and bumps, but they should not be used in cribs. There is no evidence that bumper pads can prevent serious injuries, and they pose a risk of suffocation, strangulation, or entrapment. In addition, older babies can use them for climbing out of the crib. Babies usually do not roll over for the first 3 or 4 months, so you don't need to worry about them hitting their heads on the rails. Evaluate so-called necessary baby items to ensure that they are needed or even safe. Parents of multiples need to streamline and prioritize their babies' needs.

Twin Baby Gear: What You Need

I cannot stress this enough: babies require your love and hugs more than stuff or cute outfits. Here is a list of items your babies will need, along with items you may not necessarily need but that will save your sanity. This list is not all-inclusive, but it includes important points for the parents of twin babies to remember in the early months. Items that are useful later in your twins' lives will be discussed in subsequent chapters.

- **Cribs.** Your twins will sleep safely and comfortably in separate cribs. Either buy 2 new cribs or just 1 if an older sibling has outgrown his or her crib that meets current safety standards. (Check www.cpsc.gov for the most up–to-date recall information.) If a trusted friend or family member has an extra crib you can use, great, but do your home-work and make sure the crib is not on a safety recall list or broken. Any crib's slats should be no wider than 2⅜ inches. The top of the crib rail should be at least 26 inches from the top of the mattress. Periodically lower the mattress as your children get taller. Implemented in 2011, federal safety standards prohibit the manufacture or sale of drop-side rail cribs to prevent suffocation or strangulation that leads to infant deaths.

- **Car safety seats.** You definitely need 2 of these. A car safety seat is the one item (or should I say 2 items?) you should not borrow or take as a hand-me-down. If a car safety seat has been involved in even a minor accident, it must be replaced. Car safety seats have a Lower Anchors and Tethers for Children (LATCH) system that makes proper installa-tion much easier for a car that is LATCH-ready. (This system became standard in 2002.) You can install your car safety seats by LATCH or by seat belts; make sure you read your specific car owner's manual carefully for instructions, as well as the instructions that come with the car safety seats. Because twins are small at birth, you'll need an *infant* car safety seat, preferably with head and neck support. Don't worry about convertible car safety seats until later, as your newborns will probably not be the designated minimum weight at birth. (For more information on infant car safety seats, visit HealthyChildren.org.)

- **Breast milk or formula.** Ideally, this will be breast milk in the begin-ning weeks of your babies' lives, but you may want or need to use infant formula to supplement breastfeeding or feed exclusively. We will discuss breast milk and formula-feeding issues at length in later chapters.

- **Bottles, nipple rings, and silicone nipples.** You'll find that a dishwasher will make cleaning these much easier. The sanitizing settings on most modern dishwashers will effectively sterilize your equipment for you. Small plastic dishwashing baskets (available in the baby section of any big-box store) can hold the nipples and nipple rings in place during a dishwashing cycle. Also make sure that you have newborn slow-flow nipples on hand (there are medium- and fast-flow options for when your twins have grown). Newborns typically feed on breast milk 8 to 12 times in 24 hours (on formula, a little less frequently), so you should estimate your needs and know that you may need as many as 16 nipples in 24 hours. You could always have less, but then you'll need to wash the used nipples several times throughout the day. If you'll be using a breast pump, make sure your bottle supplies are compatible with the pump.

- **Breast pump.** A pump is infinitely useful if you plan on nursing your twins. If you find that you need to boost your milk supply, pumping will help stimulate your breasts to produce more milk, and you can store your precious, nutritious milk for a later feeding. A high-quality electric double breast pump will be worth the investment when it saves you time and energy collecting breast milk. Many moms choose to rent a breast pump rather than buy one up front; rentals allow parents a little more flexibility in the budget. Breastfeeding twins will be discussed further in subsequent chapters.

- **Diapers.** Disposable diapers are quite convenient but expensive. Log onto major diaper manufacturers' Web sites to obtain coupons for parents of multiples. You may need to wait until you have birth certificates because some companies want proof that you actually have twins. Many families use cloth diapers and launder them themselves or use a cloth diaper service. The cost and availability of these services vary from region to region, so you will need to do some investigation. Cloth diapers can be more environmentally friendly than filling up landfills with all the disposables, but on the other hand, they require energy and water use for all the washings.

- **Twin-feeding pillow.** I recommend getting a twin-feeding pillow before you are 6 months pregnant so that you are ready in case the twins deliver early. The twin-feeding pillow is a wonderful yet simple invention that makes simultaneous feeding much easier. It is helpful for either breast-feeding or bottle-feeding 2 babies at the same time. I used mine from the time my twins were born to about when they were 7 or 8 months of age. Type "twin feeding pillow" into your Internet search engine to find some great examples. Feeding your babies simultaneously saves time and helps keep the twins on the same daily schedule.

- **Changing table.** Once you have changed a few diapers while slouching over the bed or the floor, you'll realize the health and comfort of your back may depend on a changing table. Even if you have a safety strap on the changing pad, *never* step away from the table, even for a moment. Even a newborn can wiggle her way off the table if you are not there holding a hand on her. Our family mounted a changing pad on a dresser upstairs so we could have one changing area upstairs and one downstairs. A second changing table is not a necessity, but it sure made life easier for those first few months.

- **Clothing.** Do you prefer to let laundry pile up and deal with it once a week? Or do you prefer to launder more manageable piles more frequently? Your answer to these laundry questions will help you decide how much clothing to obtain for your twins. For clothes to wear at home, no one cares if your twins stay in pajamas all day. You may need 2 or 3 outfits a day per twin depending on spit-ups and overflowed diapers. Babies grow fast, so don't buy too many newborn-sized clothes—these may be outgrown quickly. Important clothing and layette items include
  - All-in-one shirts that snap closed at the crotch, as well as separate tops and bottoms
  - Socks (Shoes are not needed until the babies are walking.)
  - "Swaddle sacks" for ease in safely swaddling your babies
  - Footed pajama sets
  - Sack-like pajamas with an open bottom hem to simplify overnight diaper changes
  - Receiving blankets for swaddling
  - Baby washcloths and hooded towels for bath time

- **Infant washtub for bathing.**

- **Twin stroller.** There is a range of prices and styles for twin strollers. A tandem front-back stroller is more convenient for younger babies because you can often snap the infant car safety seats right into it. This type of stroller is also narrower and thus easier to get through doorways for your pediatrician visits (which are more frequent in the first months). Side-by-side strollers are nicer for older babies and toddlers because the twins can interact more in this style. They are wider than the tandem front-back strollers and do not fit through standard doorways, but they usually fit in doorways wide enough for a wheelchair. The more expensive options can be quite lightweight, so if you live in a city and use your stroller every day you may want to make this investment. Be sure to check the stroller's baby weight minimum and maximum rules to be sure your babies will be safe in the stroller.

- **Waterproof mattress pads to protect crib mattresses.** In addition, smaller waterproof pads placed on top of the crib sheet makes cleaning after spit-ups or other spills much easier. You simply take away the soiled pad and replace with a fresh pad, saving the time of remaking the entire crib with new sheets.

- **Front-pack carrier, wrap, or sling.** These carriers have a limited life span but can make your life easier trying to get things done around the house. A second carrier means your partner can carry the other twin and no one gets jealous. Baby slings are another great option. As with all baby equipment, ensure that your sling meets current safety standards and that you are using it properly to avoid suffocation risks.

- **Play yard(s).** These are useful for keeping your babies safe in different areas of your home when you need to answer the phone or run to the bathroom. Some models come with a changing table attachment so that you can have a diaper changing station in your main family area; extra diapers, wipes, and burp cloths can be stored in the lower compartment. When choosing to use this, do not add a supplemental mattress or any other padding to the play yard.

- **Digital camera.** Thankfully, smartphones usually come with a terrific digital camera and video option. With twins you'll take countless pictures, but only a small proportion of all shots taken may be photo-print worthy. The more babies in the picture, the more likely someone will be moving and have a blurry face. You will save money in the long run if you can select which pictures should be printed. Be sure to back up your photos onto an external hard drive. I admit, I fell behind quickly on logging our digital images into printed photo books. However, I am hoping that my stored digital images will find fresh light with future technology.

Twin Tip

Take plenty of pictures of each of your twins *alone,* as well as together. They will thank you later for treating them as individuals. How can you remember who is who in the pictures? Color-coding their clothes will help you identify them years later, if you aren't able to label the photos in a timely fashion. Boys and girls lend themselves to different color codes pretty easily. For girl twins, you can use purple for one and pink for the other. For boy twins, you can use blue for one and red for the other. Alternatively, one twin can wear primarily solid colors, while the other wears prints or stripes.

- **Diaper pail with deodorizer system.** Diaper pails trap odors with varying degrees of success and usually require daily disposal to eliminate odors. Breast milk stools don't have much of a foul odor, so if you are nursing, a diaper pail may be unnecessary. In my experience, when solid foods are started at around 6 months of age, the diapers start to emit a stronger odor that even the best pail can't cover up. Our family found it easiest to store dirty diapers in an ordinary lined trash can kept inside the garage, away from our noses.

- **Rocking chair or glider.** Once your twins are strong enough, they can sit on your lap with support while the 3 of you read a book together. This is especially nice as part of your nighttime routine to help signal to your babies that it will soon be time to sleep. In the early months you will probably need your spouse's help in picking up the twins when you have finished reading, but you'll find yourself becoming more self-sufficient with such tasks as time progresses and your babies' muscle tone strengthens.

- **Bulletin board or comparable organizational system.** It is important to keep track of infant feedings and soiled diapers, and record-keeping can quickly become overwhelming. Have a system for recording your babies' feeds, wet diapers, and poopy diapers in a central location of your home. Such a system is all the more important if your twins were born early, small, or both. If you weren't already an organized person, don't worry; parents of multiples become quite organized very quickly to keep up with everybody's needs. Smartphone apps can also come in handy for recording breastfeeding and soiled diaper data, but you may prefer an old-fashioned board posted in your home as a centralized method of record-keeping so that multiple caregivers can consult and make notes on it.

Twin Preparation Checklist

• Two cribs	• Infant washtub for bathing
• Two car safety seats	• Twin stroller
• Breast milk or formula	• Waterproof mattress pads
• Bottles, nipple rings, and silicone nipples	• Front-pack carrier, wrap, or sling
• Breast pump	• Play yard(s)
• Diapers	• Digital camera
• Twin-feeding pillow	• Diaper pail with deodorizer system
• Changing table	• Rocking chair or glider
• Clothing	• Bulletin board or comparable organizational system

---

Preparing Older Siblings

The arrival of a new baby creates a whole new family environment, requiring adjustment on behalf of all family members. With the arrival of twins, the new family dynamic changes even more dramatically. Older siblings' lives will invariably change with the arrival of 2 or more newborns that rely on the parents to take care of all their needs. The proper way to prepare your older children for the twin birth depends on their ages and developmental levels.

If your child will be younger than 2 years when the twins are born, you will deal with fewer sibling rivalry issues. Toddlers younger than 2 are much more adaptable and seem to take the birth of a new baby more in stride. The greatest challenge is for a child 2 to 3 years of age. As an older child, he has a better understanding of what is going on, yet still craves lots of love and attention from his parents, as any child would.

> ## Twin Support
>
> When preparing older siblings for the birth of twins, *books* are a terrific resource. Age-appropriate books are an excellent way to help a child of any age through a multitude of transitions.

In the first trimester before the pregnancy begins to show, you may want to hold off on explanations to children younger than 3. A good time to periodically talk about the arrival of new babies is after the pregnancy has progressed 12 weeks and you are starting to show. Toddlers especially enjoy picture books of babies, and age-appropriate baby doll sets are a fun way to pretend play before the babies' arrival. Keep in mind that it will be difficult for your child to imagine life with the twins until it actually happens.

Twin Tales

Jon, dad to infant twins plus an older son, says, "I wish I'd been more prepared to introduce my firstborn (singleton) to his siblings. I was a nervous wreck. 'Will we still be best buds? Will I be able to devote to him anything close to the attention he received before the twins arrived?' He was fine, of course, and immediately fell in love with his sisters."

Once the twins arrive and come home, they will mainly require feeding, changing, and snuggling; all this can be accomplished while you engage your older child in conversation and play. Your twins' language development will benefit from observing you and their older siblings chat. Let the twins relax in their bouncy chairs and watch while, for example, you and their big sister work on a craft project together.

It is important to try to avoid major lifestyle changes for older siblings around the time that the twins are born. Becoming a big brother or sister is enough of a lifestyle transition for a young child already. Now is not the time to move your older child to a big-kid bed, for example. If a room trade must be made for space issues, make the trade earlier in the pregnancy so your child does not feel he has been replaced by your twins. If your older child has been potty trained, you might expect some accidents. Regressive behaviors during the adjustment period are normal and common as a child adjusts to life with new siblings in the family. You will have a lot on your plate caring for 2 new babies, and you might find yourself frustrated if your older child is acting out as a call for attention. Be as understanding of your older child as you can be, as challenging as that may be, given all your new responsibilities.

If sibling rivalry issues take hold, make sure to make time for one-on-one attention with your older child. He can go shopping with just Mom, have bath time with just Dad, or have other fun "together" activities that you enjoyed before the twins' birth. Daily special time together, apart from the babies, will go a long way to reassure your older child that he'll always be loved. Even if you don't have babysitting available for the twins so you can take your older child on an outing, you can use the babies' nap times for special one-on-one time with your older child. Newborns sleep most of the 24 hours in a day, so this will allow more time to spend with your other child than you may think. Of course the big challenge, which will be discussed in subsequent chapters, is to help the twins sleep *at the same time* so that everyone can live a healthier, calmer, less chaotic life.

Nearing the Delivery

As you advance through your pregnancy and prepare for your babies' big arrival, your belly will expand as you've never thought possible. Your big belly is illustrative of your growing and thriving twins. As challenging as carrying 2 babies can be, savor each day of your pregnancy. Every day in the womb is so critical for your babies' development. Applaud yourself for eating well and keeping them healthy. Start packing your hospital bag early, get lots of rest, and put your feet up at every opportunity.

Check with your obstetric team regarding your hospital options for delivery, and refer to the multiples born early chapter on page 211. Be mentally prepared for the fact that a twin delivery means a lot of extra people in the room with you. More manpower and nursing is required to ensure the safety of and provide necessary measures for your babies upon delivery. I delivered my twins in a university hospital setting, so between my own obstetric team, the neonatal intensive care unit teams, and various attendings, residents, and interns, it made for quite the crowd. When a friend of mine delivered quadruplets, her hospital used 2 operating rooms so there was enough space for the delivery team, as well as proper support for immediate care of the 4 babies. Realize, however, that no matter how prepared you feel for the delivery, the reality of it will be quite an adventure. Your delivery experience will be uniquely yours and yours alone.

CHAPTER 3

The Early Days and Weeks

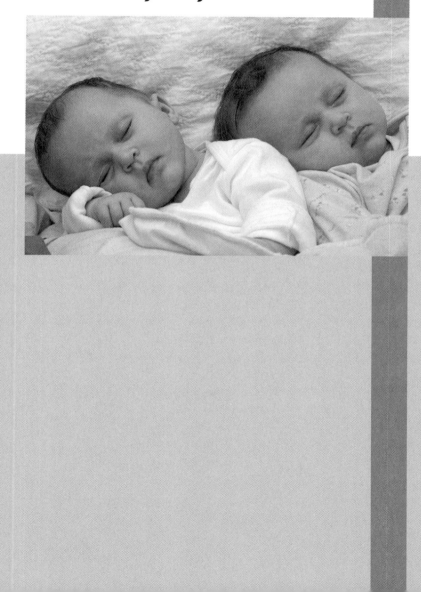

When your delivery day finally arrives, you may feel a mixture of relief and newfound trepidation. The months of wondering what the deliveries would be like and when the deliveries would happen, and perhaps some time on bed rest, are all now at an end. One chapter is closing while a new chapter begins. Hooray! Your twins are here!

In the Hospital

The babies may have been born full-term, or they may have delivered prematurely. In either case, rely on your hospital staff for guidance and advice. Neonatal intensive care unit (NICU) nurses and newborn nursery staff members bring a wealth of experience and knowledge to the table. Avail yourself of the hospital staff's advice at every opportunity. The nurses have seen it all. There is no such thing as a silly question, especially if you are a first-time parent. If possible, arrange for assistance at home ahead of time to care for your older children, which will allow both parents to be present and working together during the hospital stay. Having both partners at the hospital helps Mom recover smoothly from the deliveries. In addition, a teamwork approach starts on day one, which helps align expectations so that caregivers stay on the same page moving forward.

Twin Tales

Mike, dad to school-aged twins (and my husband!), recalls, "Even though we had an older child, and although we felt prepared for the experience, our hospital stay felt surreal—this is really happening!"

Allow the overnight staff to care for your twins so that you can get some nighttime sleep, recover from the births, and prepare for your homecoming. You shouldn't feel that you have to do it all while you are in the hospital. You are still recovering from the births yourself, and if you cannot recover properly, you will not be able to care for anyone else. Think of the emergency procedures on an airplane: first you must put your own oxygen mask on, and then you can help others with their oxygen masks. You cannot effectively care for your babies if you are not operational yourself. There will be plenty of time for you to do it all when you are back home with your babies. Very quickly you will be home, wishing you had someone to ask if your babies' poop looks normal or what good burping positions to try.

Twin Tip

Ask plenty of questions when you are in the hospital after the birth of your twins. With all the excitement, labor, and sleep deprivation, you may forget your important questions as they pop into mind, so keep a pen and notepad or your smartphone by your bedside to jot down thoughts for when your pediatricians and nurses are making rounds and checking in with your family.

While you are in the hospital, the newborn nursery nurses can show you good techniques to swaddle a newborn, a very important lesson for first-time parents. Even seasoned parents can use a refresher course in good swaddling techniques. For more information on swaddling, visit HealthyChildren.org/swaddling. Lactation consultants can help you with the breastfeeding process. Ensure that your pediatrician or registered nurse (RN) orders a lactation consult on your behalf, if the hospital doesn't automatically provide one for you. The consultant can help your babies figure out how to latch on correctly, show you different ways to tandem-feed your twins, and show you how to pump and store your precious breast milk. The NICU nurses also help you learn how to administer medications if your babies will need them.

Twin Support

While breastfeeding is natural, parents have a greater chance of success by educating themselves ahead of time with strong breastfeeding resources. Two excellent references to have on hand are the *New Mother's Guide to Breastfeeding* from the American Academy of Pediatrics and *The Nursing Mother's Companion* by Kathleen Huggins. Also refer to the breastfeeding information found later in this chapter.

All too soon, you will find yourself loading up your babies in their car safety seats, discharge papers in your hand, with the all clear to take your babies home on their maiden voyage outside the womb and the hospital.

Coming Home

Bringing your newborn twins home from the hospital can be a relief. It is good to return to your familiar, comfortable home, bed, and nonhospital food. But then the realization hits—you have 2 little babies to take care of! Where are the helpful nurses and hospital staff with their extra hands?

Take a deep breath and take things one day at a time. The babies will get stronger and bigger every day, and your family will learn a new way of living that includes your new babies. Think of life with your twins as a great sailing adventure on the high seas. Your homecoming is when you start to learn to tie knots and hoist the sails. You're just hitting the waters now, and soon you'll achieve a cruising speed and be sailing on an incredible journey.

A word about your homecoming: if your twins have older siblings, now is a great time to celebrate them and to view the twins' arrival from their viewpoint as well. I recommend discussing the new babies in the most positive terms as possible with your other child. "Here are your new little sisters. How fortunate they are to have you as a big sister!" Lavish as much attention as you can on your older child. The babies have no idea if you're talking to them anyway, but your older child does. You'd be amazed at the great conversations you can have with an older child while you are burping your twins. Extend this philosophy to others; when well-meaning relatives and friends visit to coo over your adorable newborns, remind them ahead of time to please say hello to your older children first and to include them in the conversation as much as possible.

Twin Tip

Your twins' birth means that your older children are now big brothers or big sisters. Some families like to highlight older kids' new title by giving them a big-sibling gift from the new twins to commemorate their new family status.

Keeping Your Twins on the Same Schedule: Starting Now

How will you manage and survive your babies' first weeks of life? Well, the good news is that newborns sleep *a lot*. Eating and sleeping are the 2 main concerns of any newborn. The key to *your* survival is to make sure that your twins start sleeping at similar times. On average, newborns need 16 or 17 hours of sleep in a 24-hour day. The inconvenient aspect of this sleep is that it is evenly divided into daytime and nighttime sleep, with frequent interruptions for feeding. All newborns need to eat at least every 3 hours because their stomachs are so small, yet their caloric needs so great. Breast-fed babies may need to eat every 1 to 2 hours in occasional cluster feeding. Frequent nursing sessions help boost your milk supply and accommodate for your child's growth spurts.

So how do you coordinate the chaos of 2 babies needing to eat and sleep in such frequent spurts? Here is the golden rule for feeding twins: *when one wakes up to eat, both must wake up to eat.* Despite the old saying "never wake a sleeping baby," remember that you will not have enough hours in a day to feed one after the other is fed, day in and day out. Once the babies are awake to eat, feed them at the same time, with burping breaks throughout and a good burping session at the end. If you have a helping hand to feed one twin while you feed the other, great. But if you are breastfeeding, or ever plan on being alone with your twins, you'll need to teach yourself how to feed both babies simultaneously. Both moms *and* dads might as well start learning how to feed the babies simultaneously together early on, while there is still support from the recent deliveries available.

 Twin Tales

Sheri, mom to preschool-aged twins, recalls, "The best advice I received was to feed the babies at the same time. Never would have thought of that on my own."

The best way to feed both twins simultaneously is with a large twin-feeding pillow, which works for breastfeeding and bottle-feeding (Figures 3-1 and 3-2). It is a large U-shaped pillow with a firm foam core that fits around your waist and an opening at the back. Most versions have a safety belt to latch in place so that the pillow remains snug to your body. Each twin gets his or her own side and feeds in the football hold position. You will likely need help positioning the babies on the pillow in the early

Figure 3-1. Double football hold position for breastfeeding.

days, but you will learn how to position them by yourself with time. You will soon be very capable, handling both babies safely simultaneously. If you've had a C-section delivery, you may need to wait a week or so before starting to use a twin-feeding pillow because the pillow's front edge crosses your healing abdomen. In the post-operative period, use bed pillows propped

Figure 3-2. Double football hold position for bottle-feeding.

Figure 3-3. Alternative breastfeeding position with one baby in traditional cradle hold and one baby in football hold.

on both sides to nurse your twins in a double football hold position. An alternative breastfeeding position has one baby in the traditional cradle hold and one baby in the football hold (Figure 3-3). Fathers can jump right in with tandem-feeding the babies, using the specialized pillow, with bottles filled with pumped breast milk or formula.

Positioning standard bed pillows or throw pillows for each feeding is a nuisance in the long run to get the right fit each time for frequent newborn feedings. It is critical that you position yourself and the twins properly for feedings, whether breastfeeding or bottle-feeding, to prevent backaches from poor posture. Hunching over for 20 minutes at a time, 8 to 12 times a day, can take a toll on the body after a few weeks.

 Twin Tales

While we were in the hospital after Andrew and Ryan's birth, I was worried about Ryan. It was always Andrew who awoke for the next feeding, and we found ourselves waking Ryan up with virtually every feeding to stay coordinated with Andrew's schedule. He gained weight just fine in those early weeks, despite always being woken prematurely for feeds. It's more than a decade later and Ryan has proven himself to have a calm, cool, and collected personality, laid-back and relaxed. I am convinced he was illustrating these same characteristics to us as a days-old newborn.

Every baby is different, and each set of twins is different. Twins, especially if born early, have very small stomachs, yet large caloric needs. This is why babies need to feed frequently, both day and night, to properly grow and gain weight in these critical early weeks of life. I will present a suggested newborn schedule here; feel free to tailor this schedule to your own babies' needs. When your twins wake up to eat, look at the clock and make a mental note of the time. Newborns often can only tolerate being awake for an hour or an hour and a half at a stretch, 2 hours tops. The fact that they can only be awake roughly 90 minutes at a time can help you adjust your twins to live on the same schedule. How is the time awake spent? Feeding and burping will take quite some time (especially as Mom and Dad work on positioning the babies correctly). After feeding and burping, the twins should get some time upright to help them digest their milk; this is a nice time to interact, talk, and play with them. Bouncy chairs are helpful to keep one baby upright, safely buckled in, while you cuddle or burp the other twin.

Usually the post-feeding time is an ideal pooping time for babies because of the gastrocolic reflex; food in the stomach stimulates the bowels to move. If you wait a bit after feeding to change diapers, you may save a diaper by anticipating the stool in advance. After all the action of feeding, the burping, and the diaper changing, take another look at the clock. I can assure you it is probably almost time for the twins to go back to sleep. They may not appear particularly fussy, but remember that crying is a late indicator of fatigue. Don't wait for a newborn to cry to put her down to sleep. At that point, she will be overly agitated and stimulated by the crying. You will learn to identify your babies' more subtle clues that they are ready to nap, ahead of the point of no return. Swaddle your twins in swaddling or receiving blankets to mimic the womb environment. At this point, they are fed and burped and have a clean diaper, so they have nothing left on their agenda but to go back to sleep for a couple of hours.

Twin Tip

One of your twins may always be the baby to wake up from his nap hungry for milk. You are not scarring his twin for life by always waking him up to eat with his brother; you are helping him by maintaining his parents' sanity. If you coordinate your twins' schedules, over time each baby's internal clock will align with the other baby's clock, and they will naturally get hungry at similar times.

Then, after a good nap (meaning an hour or more), when one of the twins wakes up, watch the clock. If the other hasn't awoken within 10 minutes, wake him up as well and proceed with the plan again. You can see the emerging pattern. Repeating these cycles of both twins waking up, eating, burping, playing, changing, and going back to sleep is how you can handle 2 newborns at once. Manipulate this suggested schedule to fit your own needs, but make sure that you stick to your version of the schedule. Consistency is the key. Babies can instinctively feel a schedule or routine, and each of you will anticipate the next step if you are consistent.

Twin Tip

When feeding newborn twins during the night, be as boring as possible. Leave the lights low and do not talk or sing to your babies. They will start to learn through these subliminal messages that nighttime is for sleeping.

In these early days, you should not expect your babies to sleep through the night. Your babies will be hungry and eager to feed frequently so that they can keep growing, especially if they were born early or weigh less than 7 pounds. While it is still too soon to expect the miracle of twins sleeping through the night, you should start taking steps from day one to show your babies that daytime is for playing and nighttime is for sleeping. From 8:00 pm or so, through the night until daybreak, keep feedings quiet and efficient. If possible, feed the twins in the room in which they sleep, leaving the lights as low as possible. Only change their diapers if they've had a poop or currently have a diaper rash; modern disposable diapers can hold a lot of urine without leaking or causing too much discomfort. After the feeding and burping, cuddle the twins a bit and coax them back to sleep. The key is to be as unobtrusive as possible. If a diaper does need to be changed, avoid too much eye contact and communication. The middle of the night is not the time to play or coo with your twins. They should be getting plenty of that during the daytime hours. Now is the time to be quiet and efficient. If you are consistent with your nighttime feeds, even newborns can start getting the message that nighttime is for sleeping and daytime is for playing and interacting. I recommend white noise to help infants sleep. A small electric fan in the room can muffle outside noises and signal to the twins that it is sleep time.

Twin Tip

You and your spouse can tag team by alternating overnight feeds so that you each can sleep longer stretches at a time. For example, Dad can handle the midnight feeding (of pumped breast milk or formula) solo, and Mom can handle the 3:00 am feeding solo. This way, each parent can sleep 5 or more hours continuously.

Feeding: Breast Milk or Formula

Every new mother makes a decision whether to breastfeed or formula-feed her babies. The American Academy of Pediatrics encourages breast milk as the optimal nutrition for babies up to 6 months of age, and breastfeeding is strongly encouraged for babies up to 1 year of age (and beyond, if desired). Breastfeeding has many advantages over bottle-feeding. Moms and babies have increased bonding with the physical contact. Breast milk is species-specific for your babies and is easier to digest, does not require mixing or preparation, is already at the right temperature, and contains immunologic factors that have been shown to prevent ear infections, diarrhea, and respiratory illnesses. For the mother, breastfeeding helps the uterus contract to its pre-pregnancy state. Breastfeeding moms also burn more calories, which can help facilitate losing the "baby weight." Potentially delayed ovulation and menstruation are another bonus, but do not rely on breastfeeding as a sole form of birth control.

The decision of what to feed is not so easy, however, if you are expecting twins. You may wonder, "How on earth can I nurse 2 babies? Will I turn into a human feeding machine? Is it even possible to produce enough milk?" Yes, it is very possible to nurse 2 babies. The removal of breast milk from the milk ducts results in more milk produced for the next feeding. The demand for breast milk creates the supply. Double the demand, and you double the supply. So yes, most mothers should be able to produce enough milk for 2 babies. If you are intimidated by the idea of nursing twins, I suggest some hopeful optimism. Start out by learning how to nurse your twins. See how it goes. Take it a day at a time. In the first couple of days or so after delivery, you will produce colostrum ("early milk"). These are challenging days during which to learn to nurse your twins because there is not a lot of volume for your twins to drink. The nursing process becomes simpler once your milk comes in with greater volumes, usually by the fourth or fifth day after delivery. The increased volume of milk helps your twins feel more satisfied after a nursing session.

For healthy twins in the first week of life, if the babies are still hungry after a nursing session and your milk hasn't really come in yet, supplement with a bit of formula. Supplementing with 1 or 2 ounces of formula immediately after your twins have nursed a session at each breast should not inhibit your milk production significantly. Any little bit of colostrum (the early milk) or breast milk the babies ingest is a bonus because it is filled with immunologic factors and other goodies.

Twin Tales

Despite your best efforts, because of factors outside your control you may not be able to breastfeed. Sue, mom to third-grade twins, recalls, "I was hospitalized for a severe case of double mastitis and could not continue breastfeeding as a result. I was very worried about giving up breast milk with preterm babies; it was an unnecessarily difficult period." Be realistic and if breastfeeding is not an option for your family, know you have other options.

Take the experience one week at a time. Ask for help and advice from your pediatrician, and get a referral to a lactation consultant if you need additional resources and support. Try to avoid black-and-white promises to yourself or anyone else that you will exclusively breastfeed your twins for up to 6 months. This is a wonderful goal, and many have done it successfully, but you'll be setting yourself up for extra stress if you decide after 2 months that you need to revisit this decree. The good news is that all infant formula prepared and sold in the United States, whether brand name or store brand, is strictly monitored and contains all the nutritional factors that babies need in the appropriate proportions. You may surprise yourself and make it longer than you expected, simplifying feedings in the long run.

Twin Support

Any amount of breast milk your twins receive is beneficial. Do the best you can and ask for support from your pediatrician and lactation consultant as you need it.

I was able to breastfeed my twins for 3½ months together with some formula supplementation. At that time I made the personal choice, for many reasons, to make the switch to all formula. I will have lifelong wonderful memories of breastfeeding my twin boys on my huge twin-feeding pillow. I also enjoyed the convenience and liberation I felt when we made the switch to formula, so I've seen both sides of the story. Give breastfeeding a try. See what comes of it. If you go back to formula, that's fine too. Again, any amount of breast milk you can give to your babies is beneficial.

Breastfeeding: How Do We Do It?

One of the challenges of breastfeeding any number of babies is wondering how much milk the babies are actually taking in during each nursing session. You will learn each of your baby's feeding patterns. One baby may nurse more quickly than the other, finishing up her meal within 10 minutes, while her twin lingers for more than 15 minutes. Babies who are satisfied at the end of a feeding, burp, have good wet diapers, and are stooling at least once a day are, in general, getting enough to eat. By the end of the first week of life your babies should be having about 4 to 6 wet diapers a day and 3 to 6 stools a day. Many breastfed babies stool with every feed; this is normal and happens because breast milk is so easily digested by your babies. Weight checks at the pediatrician's office are the best way to determine if milk intake is adequate. Especially if your babies were born small, early, or both, you should have extra "weight check" visits to your pediatrician's office after the babies' hospital discharge.

Twin Tip

It is likely that one of your twins will be a more vigorous eater than the other. As long as they are both gaining weight appropriately, try to relax and avoid too many comparisons between them.

Your twins may have 2 different feeding styles, and one twin may be hungrier than the other during a growth spurt. For this reason you may want to remember which baby nursed on which side at each session and then switch sides for the next nursing session. In alternating your twins' nursing sides, you can help even out your milk supply between your left and right breasts so that you don't end up lopsided. In addition, your twins will benefit from lots of experience eating at both sides. Babies can at times develop a preference for just one side, and you can curb that tendency by making sure you switch sides often. You need both sides to produce milk evenly.

I had a hard time remembering who nursed on which side when my twins were newborns, so I taped 2 note cards labeled "Andrew" and "Ryan" onto the edge of my kitchen island. I would switch the position of the cards according to who nursed on which breast to help me remember to alternate. Even with my note card system, I would forget to alternate a few nursing sessions a day, but when you are nursing 8 to 12 times in 24 hours, it's OK; it all evens out. A good friend of mine wore a plastic bracelet on alternating wrists to indicate on which sides the babies should nurse. Smartphones have plenty of apps to help nursing moms keep track of who nurses on which side and when.

Take notes on your twins' feeding, urinating, and stooling patterns by keeping a simple chart. A chart recording feeding information is helpful in the hospital and in the early days at home. In the chart, include the time of day, the time spent at the breast, whether you supplemented with formula afterward, and whether there was a wet or soiled diaper. Such a chart is an easy way to look at the babies' progress over a 24-hour period. You cannot rely on your memory at this sleep-deprived time in your life. Your pediatrician will want to see this chart when you visit the office in the first week after being discharged from the hospital. Feel free to use an app on your smartphone for an electronic method of keeping track.

The most important indicator of adequate breast milk intake is proper weight gain. In the early days, each baby should be gaining at least an ounce a day. This is an important issue that your pediatrician will be following closely with you, especially if your twins were born early or had a low birth weight. Sometimes mothers are concerned that breastfeeding isn't going so well, but the babies' good weight gain bolsters their confidence.

If you are able to pump your breast milk, it is best to store the milk in small increments, no more than 2 or 3 ounces per bottle or freezer bag in the early days. This method prevents waste of any precious breast milk if your baby is not especially hungry. If he needs more milk, you can always thaw another serving. Some moms prefer to freeze their breast milk in specially designed plastic bags; other moms stockpile heat- and freezer-safe bottles that attach directly to the breast pump to simplify collection, storage, and feeding.

If you are exclusively nursing your twins, it is important to focus on feeding at the breast as much as possible for the first 3 weeks of life and to avoid pacifier use to prevent nipple confusion. After 3 weeks, you have a special window of opportunity from 3 to 6 weeks of life during which breastfed babies more easily learn to feed from a bottle without significantly interfering with feedings at the breast. Take advantage of this opportunity to get your twins accustomed to nursing and bottle-feeding formula or pumped breast milk. Bottle-feeding is a great way for fathers to get involved in the babies' care, promote father-baby bonding, and give Mom a break. If you plan on returning to work after a maternity leave, you will need to train the twins to accept milk from a bottle and the breast.

How can you train your twins to feed from bottles? Provide Dad or another loved one with your twins, bottles of expressed milk, and the twin-feeding pillow. (To warm previously frozen or refrigerated pumped breast milk, float the lidded bottles in a larger bowl of warm water 10 minutes in advance. Microwaves create dangerous heat pockets and destroy beneficial proteins in breast milk.) The most important step is that you need to physically leave the room. Babies know when Mom is around and will prefer her familiar breast to any bottle. Be patient with your twins; it may take a few sessions for them to actually drink anything at all from the bottle.

Formula-Feeding: Simplifying the Process

If you are formula-feeding your babies or even just supplementing nursing with formula, it is useful to make batches of formula at a time. Parents of twins simply do not have the time to prepare powdered formula at every feeding. Purchase 1-quart liquid containers and prepare 2 quarts of formula together to save time. Fill each jug with 30 ounces of formula water, and use a funnel to add 15 scoops of powdered formula (double check with the measurements on the side of the can). If you are using concentrated liquid formula, mix equal parts concentrate and water. Gently agitate the jug to blend in the powder; warmer water may help the powder blend in more easily. Store the jugs of prepared formula in the refrigerator, and when it's time for the twins to feed, simply pour out the desired ounces into bottles and warm them up. We found this to be the easiest way to feed 2 hungry babies powdered formula several times a day.

Twin Tip

If you are formula-feeding, don't forget to use newborn slow-flow nipples to help the babies eat and digest more easily without swallowing excess air.

Microwaves are a dangerous way to warm bottles because they can create pockets of heat throughout the liquid, and the milk may be at a scalding temperature, despite feeling relatively cool when held in the hand. The safest way to warm bottles is to float the 2 lidded bottles in a large bowl of warm water in your kitchen sink for about 10 or 15 minutes before the planned feeding time. Anticipate the next feeding ahead of time and get your bottles warming so that they are ready for you when your babies need to feed.

The average number of ounces of formula needed per day depends on the babies' weights and ages. From birth to 2 months of age, each baby can take anywhere from 2 to 5 ounces per feeding. From 2 to 4 months of age, babies usually average 4 to 6 ounces per feed, and from 4 to 6 months of age, 5 to 7 ounces per feed. After 6 months, your babies will also be eating solid foods for additional calories, so you really won't need bottles bigger than 7 ounces total. After 12 months, healthy babies can transition to whole milk.

Twin Tales

Danielle, mom to 8-year-old twin boys, recalls, "For bottle-feeding, the best advice I got was to make a big batch of formula at the same time and put it in bottles all at once. Much easier to grab a premade bottle out of the fridge than to measure everything out individually each time."

If you find a 5- or 6-ounce bottle brand and type that you like, you should stockpile the bottle. Your twins will be formula-feeding every 3 hours on average, which calculates into 16 bottles a day. Decide whether you want to wash bottles frequently or in one big batch once a day. Once your twins are about 1 year of age they will be ready to transition to drinking from a cup.

Burping and Reflux

Whether nursing or bottle-feeding, and whether prone to spit-ups or not, all babies benefit from burping breaks. About halfway through a nursing session, or after 1 or 2 ounces of a formula bottle, give your twins some time to change their position a bit and burp them. Releasing any excess gas that may have gotten caught in the stomach is a good way to help your baby take the rest of the feeding. I have seen many hungry babies inhale a feed quickly, only to spit up a significant portion of the feed because of inhaled air in the stomach. These big spit-ups are not necessarily reflux; often the spit-ups reflect *improper pacing of the feed*, or even overfeeding. Proper pacing of a feed means giving your babies time to rest and time for any air bubbles in the stomach to rise up and be released before the babies chug the rest of the milk.

Twin Tip

Even if your twins are ravenously hungry, don't be tempted to feed them too quickly; you'll end up with a huge spit-up in your lap.

How long do you burp a baby after the feed is complete? Burp your twins until they burp—and then burp them some more! It sounds silly, but

Figure 3-4. Burping both babies simultaneously using the twin-feeding pillow.

so many times after the big audible burp, there is a smaller bubble that also needs to come out. At times you may not even hear a burp. Not hearing one is more common if you are breastfeeding, but regardless, make sure you burp each baby for at least 5 minutes. Consider the burping time to be cuddle time and enjoy it.

You can burp your twins simultaneously. If you are using a large twin-feeding pillow, you can sit up the twins on either side so that you are hugging and burping both babies at the same time (Figure 3-4). Just make sure you've got a good hold on each of the twins, as their muscle tone is quite weak at this age. Alternatively, you can roll the twins onto their bellies and pat their backs. In this position, make sure to raise your knees so that their heads are inclined up and the milk doesn't come rolling out of their mouths.

Twin Tip

Keep your twins upright for about 20 minutes after each feeding to help them digest their milk more comfortably.

Twins are more likely to be born early, and babies born earlier have a greater chance of developing reflux. Reflux is what its name indicates—milk returning from the stomach, up through the esophagus (the tube that connects the mouth and stomach), and frequently out of the mouth. If your baby spits up frequently but has been gaining weight well, you needn't be too concerned. In this scenario, you may want to make sure the baby isn't getting overfed at each feeding and is being properly paced with burpings midway through the feed. If your baby spits up frequently, is fussy, and is not gaining weight as well as your pediatrician may like, reflux may be the culprit. If you are formula-feeding, your doctor may switch your babies' formula or prescribe a medication, depending on the baby and situation.

After each feeding and burping is complete, try not to lay the baby flat immediately afterward. Imagine eating a big holiday meal and then lying flat; you would feel pretty uncomfortable. Place your twins in bouncy chairs with a 45-degree upright angle, or even wear one of the babies in a front-pack carrier. This way your twins can look around and let the milk settle in their stomachs.

Advice for Outings

For the first 3 weeks that your twins are home with you, I recommend that they lie low and stay at home. I advise this even if your twins were born full-term and healthy. All newborns' immune systems are quite immature. There are a lot of cooties out in the world! Little old ladies at the mall will spy your teeny twins and won't be able to restrain themselves from reaching out to make physical contact. You have enough on your plate without your twin newborns catching a virus. Once you are out and about, be straightforward and direct with overly friendly and curious strangers. They can look, but they can't touch. A simple, "Please don't touch my babies; they're getting over a cold," should fend away curiosity.

Twin Tip

Make sure visitors in your home wash their hands with soap and water or use hand sanitizer before holding your new babies.

Once your twins are older than 3 weeks, getting out of the house periodically is a nice way to keep your sanity. Staring at the same walls of one's home attending to the needs of 2 very high-maintenance little creatures without an occasional glimpse of the outside world is unhealthy. A simple neighborhood walk will give everyone some fresh air. Even a car trip to the drive-through post office mailbox can be a hoot if you are desperate to get out of the house. In case inspiration or necessity strikes, be ready for an outing in advance.

A stocked, ready-to-go diaper bag makes it easier to be spontaneous and take the twins out of the house. You'll have a better chance of going out if your diaper bag is ready to go. In your diaper bag, keep a plastic food storage bag with baby bottles filled with formula water, some packets of powdered formula (the kind that are premeasured—no scoop necessary), and disposable nipples. These ingredients will allow you to easily shake up a tasty meal for the twins while on the road. Of course toss in diapers, wipes, and other necessary items.

If space permits, consider storing your twin stroller in the car trunk so that it is ready to go as well. You won't have to lug it to your car each time you need it to run an errand. It's all about simplification. If you have an older toddler, consider placing him in the twin stroller with one twin and carrying the other twin in a soft front-pack carrier. With this technique you won't have to chase after a runaway toddler; everyone is contained and safe. It may be simpler to pop the twins' infant car safety seats into the stroller, if yours permits.

Twin Tip

After an outing, try to restock your bag when you get a chance so that you're ready for the next trip.

In addition to your usual diaper bag, keep a special bag designated to stay in your car in case of emergency. Usually the hospital or your pediatrician's office has plenty of freebie diaper bags that are great for this purpose. In this bag, toss a couple of bottles of formula water, premeasured packets of powdered formula, extra diapers and wipes, changes of clothes, and some receiving blankets. This bag is meant to carry extras of your babies' necessities, just in case. The emergency stash of supplies is good for peace of mind (eg, in case you ever get a flat tire while driving with your twins). It is also convenient if you're making a quick trip to run an errand and don't feel like checking the status of your usual diaper bag. You know that if your trip runs longer than you expect, you've got supplies on hand if needed. Anything that helps you get out of the house more frequently will be good for your and your twins' sanity—a very healthy thing indeed.

Infant Colic Times 2

And speaking of sanity…colicky babies have been known to endanger the very existence of one's sanity. What does the term *colic* mean, exactly? It is an older term that many people still use today to describe a young infant's tendency to be fussy. In the past, most people believed that a lot of baby crying and fussiness was caused by gas pains. The current thinking is that there is a spectrum of "infantile fussiness" (my preferred term) that may or may not be related to any gas pains. All babies are fussy at various times and to various degrees.

One of your twins may cry more than the other, depending on each individual baby's temperament. Try not to compare your babies, and don't feel guilty if you find yourself annoyed with one twin who cries more than the other. Parents of twins often feel guilty about carrying the fussier twin more often. Do your best to fairly distribute cuddles to both your babies, whether fussy or calm. You're looking to be *fair* to your 2 babies; it is impossible to give them perfectly *equal* experiences.

Infant crying tends to peak in intensity around 6 weeks and is typically vastly improved by 3 months of age. Any time that one or both of your twins are fussy or crying, make it your routine to run down a mental list of potential triggers.

- Is the baby hungry?
- Does the baby need more burping?
- Is the baby's diaper dirty or wet?
- Is the baby cold, hot, or in pain?
- Does the baby need to be swaddled (to mimic the close environment of the womb)?
- Is the baby tired? Look at the clock. Has the baby been awake more than an hour and a half?
- Does the baby need to suck? Show your baby his or her hand and thumb, or use a pacifier if you prefer.

If your baby is still crying after addressing all of these issues, she is probably having a colicky moment. You may notice that late afternoon and dinnertime are particularly noisy at your house. Babies fuss more commonly during these times, in theory because the baby is worn out from all the exciting activity and stimulation during the day. Often the crying can occur a total of 3 hours a day several times a week.

Because we cannot have conversations with babies, no one knows exactly why they sometimes cry for no apparent reason. Studies have shown that the crying of colic does not seem to be related to pain. Rather, it seems to be related to a heightened sensitivity to the environment surrounding the baby. Imagine if you had been living in a cuddly, warm womb for months and were now suddenly expected to live out in the open, noisy, chaotic world. Minor sounds are like nails on a chalkboard to you, thus causing you to cry your heart out.

Colic does seem to have one positive benefit: it can assist parent-baby bonding, as holding a crying baby close usually helps her to calm down. Some have theorized that improved bonding is an evolutionary advantage of colic. Human babies, compared with most other animal species' babies, are very dependent on their parents for their care and survival. Over thousands of years, parents' ears and brains have been hardwired to respond to the sound of their babies crying, resulting in the babies surviving and growing. So even though your twins' crying may drive you crazy at times, the crying does serve a purpose. It ensures that you and your twin babies will get lots of hugs every day.

We do know that all babies of all cultures and ethnicities are affected by colic to varying degrees. We also know that the severity of colic has no correlation to future behavior and development. If one or both of your twins has colic, he still has just as good a chance as any other "calm" baby to develop into a normal grade-schooler, teenager, and adult. Don't worry that your screaming 5-week-old will stay that way forever. He will grow out of it with no harmful effects.

Twin Tip

One twin is usually more "high maintenance" than the other. Don't worry that you are neglecting the calmer twin. Relax—you may hold one twin more than the other some days, but over the months and years it will all even out. In the long run, each of your twins will need more of you at different times.

Because the crying can be related to the stimuli around your babies, the more effective soothing techniques simulate the comforting womb environment. Swaddle your twins well to mimic the tight uterine space. Walk with the babies in front-pack carriers to mimic the swaying in the womb. Rock your twins. A humming fan or even static on an AM radio can create helpful white noise. Your womb had a constant hum of activity; imagine your babies in your uterus, with your aorta rhythmically swooshing near their heads. Although it seems counterintuitive, absolute silence can be new and upsetting to a newborn's ears.

Twin Tales

Lisa, mom to 9-year-old twin boys, shares, "In the first 3 to 4 months, do what it takes to get by. If baby needs a binky to sleep, let him have the binky. What they need today is not what they will need tomorrow."

If you are at your limit listening to the cries of your twins, you need to take a break. Enlist your spouse, a relative, or a friend to watch the twins while you take a walk or a shower. Even an hour's break will help you survive this challenging period. Absolutely never shake a baby in frustration; this could cause irreversible harm to your baby. It is OK to put a crying baby down in a safe spot such as a crib, close the door, and give yourself a break if you are at your wit's end. Remember, your babies will outgrow the crying.

Should We Use Pacifiers?

Whether or not to use pacifiers is something that every set of parents must decide for themselves. Many parents happily and successfully use pacifiers and would use them again. Recent studies have shown that a pacifier can lessen the risk of sudden infant death syndrome. However, pacifiers need to be kept clean and available for newborns to satisfy their need for nonnutritive sucking.

The upshot of a pacifier-free life is that your twins will find a way to soothe themselves. There are 2 of them and 1 of you, and you don't need to hear them crying for you when they can't find their dropped pacifier during a night awakening. Without pacifiers, your twins will find their thumbs and comfort themselves back to sleep while you're catching up on much-needed sleep. Anything that helps your twins become more independent and self-reliant will help you as a parent. However, if your twins are quite fussy and nothing else seems to help, certainly go ahead and use pacifiers. Some families feel it is easier to wean babies off of pacifiers than a thumb, another factor to be considered in your decision.

Seeking Support

Ask, ask, and ask for help. Try to accept everyone's offers for help. Now is not the time to be proud and try to handle everything on your own. Delegate specific tasks, such as picking up a gallon of milk at the store. Well-intentioned friends and family cannot imagine what you're going through unless they have twins themselves, and they may not be able to guess what it is that you need. If a friend or loved one happens to offer, "If you need help, let me know," *do* take them up on it and be specific in what you ask of them. Picking up diapers at the store, dropping off a casserole dinner, or playing with the babies for 20 minutes so that you can take a shower are all good, specific things that won't be difficult for your friend to do and would make such a positive difference for you.

Twin Support

Don't underestimate the kindness of strangers. Look beyond family and friends to neighbors and your place of worship for support. Many congregations regularly organize meal delivery volunteers to help member families with newborns at home.

Depending on your level of comfort and closeness, you can also ask for assistance with overnight awakenings and feedings. Just one night of 6 hours of uninterrupted sleep will help you function much better. My dearest childhood friend visited us from out of state and offered to get up with the babies overnight so that I could sleep. I hadn't even taken her up on the suggestion, but already I felt such a wave of relief knowing that her help was available. When struggling through difficult times, it is important psychologically to know that you have help, should you need it. If finances allow, many families have found a "night nurse" a way to catch some much needed rest for overnight twin duty. For more, please consult the support chapter on page 193.

It is a good idea to make sure that there is a second trusted adult in your nearby geographic area who is available to help in case one twin gets sick and needs medical attention. If your partner goes out of town on business, this person can be on call to stay home with your other twin and children should you need urgent medical care for one twin. Hopefully you will never need to use this backup, but you don't want to be caught unprepared should something happen.

Going to the Pediatrician

Plan in advance to have an extra pair of hands with you when you bring your twins to the pediatrician for both well-child checkups and sick visits, whether it is your spouse, a family member, or a friend. You will invariably have questions about each of your twins. Have your helper hold one baby while you speak with your doctor about the baby currently being examined. You don't want to be distracted by managing both babies at once; no one can ask important questions this way.

Make sure your pediatrician treats your twins as individuals and gives you an opportunity to discuss one child at length before switching gears to the other. You may have some global questions that involve both twins, but you will need time to discuss each twin independently and to have your questions about that specific twin addressed.

Twin Tip

Write your questions down on note cards or a smartphone in advance so that you don't forget them when going to the pediatrician.

Getting Into a Routine

After your twins' first 2 or 3 months, you'll start to see things settle into more of a routine and less of a chaotic mess. By now, however, you have 8 weeks or so of poor sleep piling up and the exhaustion may be starting to take its toll. Your twins are going to reward you around this time with glimmers of their first social smiles. Suddenly, all the sleep deprivation and chaos is worth it to see these little babies smiling at you. Enjoy it and pat yourself on the back—you've earned these smiles! Now things are really going to get more fun and interesting with each passing month. The twins are becoming more aware of the world around them and are ready to interact more with you and each other. Now that you have learned the fundamentals of caring for your twins, you're ready to relax a bit and enjoy the beautiful moments of your journey with twins.

CHAPTER 4

Early Infancy and Getting on a Schedule

Congratulations! You have survived the first couple of months with your twins, which is no small feat! Remind yourself frequently that the toughest days are likely behind you. With every passing week, you and your babies are getting to know each other more and more. Your babies are gaining weight each day and becoming stronger. You are learning the best ways to soothe them. They are learning to trust in you and your loving care. Your twins are comforted by the sight and smell of you, and they have grown to be aware of and anticipate your consistent love and responses on a very primary and basic level.

Your household routine is growing more regular and consistent. A consistent home routine will simplify your life and your care of the babies. On a regular schedule, your twins will know what to expect, and they will be calmer in general. A regular schedule will benefit you as a parent as well. You will know what your twins will need at what times—whether it be a bottle of milk, more burping, or a nap.

What do young infants do all day? Sleep and eat! Your babies' basic needs of milk and sleep are more easily handled with a consistent schedule. When parents of twins synchronize these 2 basic needs, there is more free time each day to enjoy the babies. You will run yourself ragged if your babies nap on different schedules and are fed separately. You will have more energy and be a much better, more effective parent with synchronized daily schedules.

Sleep: Infant Twins (and Parents) Need It

Around the 2-month mark, your twins may be sleeping for longer stretches at a time, but as parents, your energy levels are probably dipping. At this point during the early infancy months, parents of twins can feel as if they are running in the second half of a marathon. The end of the pregnancy was tiring enough, between a huge belly and the inability to get comfortable or a good night's rest. Now you have weeks upon weeks of sleep-deprived nights piling up. During all the feedings and diaper changes, it is also challenging to find time for a break to rejuvenate and reenergize as a parent.

Twin Tip

Be proactive; teach your babies good sleep habits now. The benefits of good sleep are well worth the effort.

All of the sleep deprivation and stress can start to have a cumulative effect. Sleep deprivation affects all areas of a family's life. If Mom and Dad don't get enough sleep, tensions run higher, coping with routine household and relationship issues becomes more difficult, and everyone is cranky. Don't worry—there is a light at the end of the tunnel! Parents of twins can be proactive by helping their children soothe themselves to sleep. A well-rested baby is a happier baby, and a well-rested parent is a more effective parent.

I'll never forget when my eldest, single-born son was 2 months of age and the sleepless nights were starting to take their toll on my husband and me—and we had only *one* baby waking up. A friend reassured us, "Oh, don't worry, my daughter started to sleep through the night when she was 9 months old." She thought she was putting our minds at ease, but the only thing I could think was, "There is *no way* I can keep living like this for 7 more months!" Thankfully, a healthy, otherwise typical baby can sleep through the night sooner than 9 months of age.

How much sleep do babies need in early infancy? On average, 2- to 3-month-olds need 15 hours of sleep in a 24-hour period. About 9 or 10 of the 15 hours of sleep should be nighttime sleep, and the remaining 5 or so hours should be divided into 3 daytime naps. Babies can start transitioning to a 2-nap-a-day schedule around the time they are 6 months of age.

 Twin Tales

Sue, mom of school-aged twins, recalls helpful, practical advice given to her: "I read a sleep book that recommended putting my twins on a sleeping and feeding schedule."

Parents need to make sure that they are not encouraging or prolonging sleep problems by dealing with overnight awakenings incorrectly. Do you enter your babies' room at 2:00 am, turn on some bright lights, and start smiling and cooing to your twins? If you do, you've got some changes to make.

The good news is that most babies can learn to sleep through the night, meaning more than 6 to 8 hours in a stretch, by the time they are 3 months of age and weigh more than 12 pounds. When a baby reaches 12 pounds, his stomach capacity is large enough that overnight feedings are no longer required. All of the baby's daily calories and nutrition can and should be taken during the daytime hours. With less frequent feedings at night, the baby can sleep for longer stretches. If you are breastfeeding, your body will adjust to the changing overnight feeding schedule.

Twin Tip

If your twins were born early or small, they will need overnight feedings a bit longer than a full-term baby would. Once your babies are more than 12 pounds, though, you can confidently proceed with sleep training.

Sharing Space: 2 Cribs or 2 Bedrooms?

Having 2 cribs for your twins ensures that they have the space that they need to comfort themselves to sleep. A borrowed crib that meets national safety standards fits the budget perfectly. You will be especially pleased when time flies and it is time to transition to a big-kid bed. You'll be so glad that you saved the money.

Will it be more difficult to sleep train your twins if they share a bedroom? I don't think so. Your babies become accustomed to their bedroom environment, and they accept the presence of their twin as part of the environment of the room. Most parents of twins have their twin babies share a bedroom because of space restraints in the home. Don't worry about the shared room interfering with the babies' learning process to sleep on their own. You do not need to buy a bigger home with more bedrooms to get your twins to sleep through the night.

It always amazed me how twins have a way of blocking out their twin's noises. Many a time I walked into their bedroom while one boy was screaming his head off and the other was sleeping as peacefully as could be. It boggled my mind! Somehow twins can shut out such overnight noises from their twin, and this skill will extend into the preschool years.

The Science Behind Good Sleep Habits

During overnight sleep, all humans transition through various sleep stages. During these normal transitional episodes, sleep may be interrupted. Even as adults, we may not always be aware of it, but we have various points throughout the night where we are more awake than others. When we briefly awaken between sleep stages, and we are in our familiar bed at our home, we can just get ourselves back to sleep quite easily. However, if we are in an unfamiliar place, it can take longer to fall back asleep.

Twin Tip

During the process of sleep training your babies, it will be important to recognize which of your twins' overnight awakenings are from *hunger* and which are a normal *awakening period* between sleep stages in which they are trying to fall asleep once again. Are your twins crying at 2:00 am? Do they weigh more than 12 pounds? If yes, don't assume the babies are hungry and automatically feed them. Give them a chance to settle themselves back to sleep.

One analogy to this phenomenon is traveling away from home. If you are sleeping in a hotel room and you wake up at 2:00 am with an unfamiliar pillow under your head, you may not be able to fall asleep again as quickly as usual because conditions are slightly different from those at your home. Similarly, your twins' ability to fall asleep can be affected by a change in routine. If a parent is always present when the baby falls asleep, that baby won't be able to fall asleep without the parent. Therefore, your babies should learn from an early age how to fall asleep *without a parent present*.

The time that your babies are falling asleep is the moment during which they need to be in a familiar setting, in conditions in which they have fallen asleep before. It is hardwired into our brains to actively help a wailing baby. If a parent is always immediately rushing in to comfort the baby, that baby will require the parent's presence to fall asleep once again. If your twins are always rocked to sleep, they won't be able to fall asleep without the familiar rocking routine. If your twins always fall asleep when nursing or taking a bottle, they won't be able to put themselves to sleep without drinking milk. Give your babies lots of practice falling asleep on their own at 7:00 or 8:00 pm, and they will be able to get themselves back to sleep on their own if they wake up between sleep cycles at 2:00 am.

A special note: if your twins were born small or prematurely, they may still require overnight feedings at 2 and 3 months of age. But even if your twins still require the overnight feeds, use the following strategies to help them fall back asleep by themselves. As your babies gain more weight, they will be better sleepers.

Strategies for Good Sleep Habits

There are 2 key strategies that will help your twins learn to sleep through the night.

- The first strategy is a good daily schedule and routine. Daytime should be filled with lots of play, interaction, and consistency.
- The second and perhaps more important strategy is that your twins have plenty of practice putting themselves to sleep on their own. Over time, your twins will learn that daytime is for eating, playing, and interacting, and nighttime is for sleeping. When your babies are placed in their cribs *awake* at bedtime, they learn how to fall asleep on their own. Then if they wake up again at 2:00 am, they know what to do—go right back to sleep, without requiring the assistance of Mom or Dad.

Twin Tip

I put a 25-watt light bulb in our twins' bedroom lamp so that diaper changes would not be lit too brightly.

During the overnight hours, keep the bedroom lights as low as possible, even if your twins wake up for a feeding. Try to handle the awakening by night-light only, and only turn on a soft light if you need help changing a poopy diaper. If your babies passed stools, quietly change their diapers, but otherwise, let the diaper be, assuming they are not currently dealing with a diaper rash or skin irritation (for more information on diaper rash, refer to the Diaper Rash section later in this chapter on page 73). A diaper change with all the undressing and air exposure wakes babies from their sleepy state, making it more difficult to settle back to sleep. Modern disposable diapers are strong enough to hold several hours of overnight urine comfortably. Keep your facial expressions as close to a poker face as you can; now is not the time for eye contact, cooing to your twins, or rousing renditions of "The Itsy-Bitsy Spider." Your twins should be getting plenty of fun and games in the daytime.

Keep sending the message that daytime is for playing and nighttime is for sleeping. In the night, when your babies realize they won't be getting much more out of you than a feeding and a burping, they have no choice but to fall asleep. If your twins weigh more than 12 pounds each, they should not get any overnight milk from you.

If just one of your babies is still underweight, however, go ahead and quietly and efficiently feed her as unobtrusively as you can, and then leave the room again. If you are concerned that her twin will get jealous, you can quickly feed your underweight baby in a second, darkened, quiet room before returning her to her bedroom.

Twin Support

Good sleep habits are important for any young child and are especially critical for families with twins or more. Avail yourself of additional sleep resources if need be. *Healthy Sleep Habits, Happy Twins* by Marc Weissbluth, MD, FAAP, has advice specific for the needs of families with multiples. And *Sleep: What Every Parent Needs to Know* by Rachel Y. Moon, MD, FAAP, from the American Academy of Pediatrics, as well as *Solve Your Child's Sleep Problems* by Richard Ferber, MD, FAAP, are filled with excellent sleep advice as well. Children who are good sleepers are happy, healthy children!

It is really challenging to sleep train just 1 baby, let alone 2. But do not procrastinate; the longer sleep training is delayed, the more difficult the overall process will be. As your infants grow, they will begin to develop *object permanence,* meaning that they will know you exist even when you leave the room and are not in their direct sight. If your twins are 9 months of age and aware that you are outside their closed door, sleep training will be that much more difficult. Sleep training is also more challenging if your twins are already sitting up or pulling to a stand. It is preferable to sleep train at an earlier age when your babies are more adaptable.

Twin Tip

Good sleep habits can be temporarily interrupted by illness or travel. You will need to tend to your babies in the overnight hours if they are feverish or coughing. When everyone is healthy once again, you may need to retrain your babies to sleep through the night. If they had previously been sleeping through the night before the illness or travel, they will remember quickly.

The Power of the Bedtime Ritual

Your twins' early infancy months are a good time to initiate a consistent evening ritual. The beauty of the ritual is that if you do it every evening, it will cue your twins that it will soon be time for sleep. If you are consistent with a bedtime routine, you will be richly rewarded in the following several years with children who easily go to bed at a healthy hour.

Of course, there will be occasions that you cannot stick to the usual nighttime routine. Sometimes you will have a date night with your spouse, and your babysitting relatives may do things a bit differently. There will be times when you'll all be out late for some fun event, and that's OK. But for the most part, do your best to keep your evening rituals as consistent as possible.

Twin Tip

A calm, relaxing bedtime routine sets the tone for a good overnight sleep.

Our family has enjoyed the benefits of a bedtime routine for years. Thanks to our evening ritual, for the most part our kids have turned in for the night quite easily with minimal conflict or fuss. An added bonus is that you and your partner will have grown-up evenings to catch up with each other and to do whatever else you need to do.

Our bedtime routine starts with a good toothbrushing session or, in the pre-toothed set, using a clean, wet washcloth to rub the gums. Next comes a quick splash in the bathtub, and I do mean quick. Yes, we give nightly baths, but if it is not summertime and your kid is not particularly stinky or dirty, a quick wash of the face, hands, feet, and lastly the private parts will suffice. Three-month-olds are not crawling around the house picking up dust balls. Thus, you know you can give a quick and effective bath, all the while letting your babies explore the water, learn to splash, and have some fun!

At bath time in the first 6 months of life, babies cannot sit up unsupported yet. We would use an infant bathtub and bathe the boys one at a time in succession. Save some time, water, and energy by using the same bathwater for both twins, assuming that everyone is generally healthy. After the first twin is plucked out of the tub and handed off to your partner, grab a new washcloth and get the second twin in the tub. Having supplies, soap, and towels prepped ahead of time simplifies the logistics of bath time and reduces the chances of a slip or an unintentional injury. Never leave a baby unattended in or near a bathtub. Let the phone ring; the caller can leave a message.

 Twin Tales

Brian, an adult identical twin, recalls, "My mother told us that when she gave us our first bath, afterwards she panicked because she had no way of telling us apart when we were that young. So she made her 'best guess,' and after that she always painted nail polish on one of my brother's toes when we were infants, to help tell us apart. We then developed our individual personalities that very much distinguished us from each other!"

After the baths comes pajama time, and then our favorite, story time. One parent can read to one twin while the other parent reads to the second twin. Alternatively, one parent can read to both twins at the same time. How can you read to 2 kids at once when your young babies don't have the muscle tone to really sit by themselves yet? Get creative. One way is to sit them up in a comfy reading chair together and sit on the floor in front of them. Face them so they don't fall, and hold the book up in front of them as you read. If your partner or another adult can help you, have your helper place one child on each of your thighs in your lap, and you can snuggle and support them as you read. As you read books with your babies, they may not understand the words or images that they see in the books yet, but hearing the rhythm and sound of your voice is soothing. Over time, your twins will start to realize that the images in the books represent real-life things. It is never too early to start reading to your babies!

After reading time is finished, some extra cuddling and a little lullaby song with the lights turned off helps transition your babies to sleep. Then the fan (or your white noise alternative) is turned on, the twins are laid in their cribs while still awake, and the door is closed. They may be awake for the next 30 minutes, but these 30 minutes are when they'll figure out how to put themselves to sleep.

If your babies cry after you leave the room and cannot settle themselves down, you can periodically check to reassure them and make sure they are safe. But afterwards, lay them down awake in their cribs and leave the room. If they can convince you to rock them to sleep one more time, they'll always try to get you to do so. Babies should be left alone in their cribs for increasing stretches of time, with parents periodically checking on and reassuring them, until they learn to finally fall asleep on their own.

Twin Tip

What if one parent works late some nights or all nights? You don't want your babies to miss seeing the working parent. You'll have to devise a system that works for your family. Perhaps you can compromise a couple of nights a week, giving your twins an extra-late nap before dinnertime so that they can spend some quality time with the late-working parent when he or she gets home.

Some of your friends or relatives may question your adherence to a consistent bedtime ritual. Starting good sleep habits now will extend into the next several years. Maybe your friend has only one kid and has no problem taking care of a cranky toddler at 9:30 at night who's asking for more water, but with twins you don't have time for that sort of thing. When you have multiples in your family, you've got to do what it takes to help them go to sleep easily. Your children will be happy and healthy because they are *well* rested.

Twin Tip

The quality and quantity of your twins' sleep is of vital importance to your family. With good sleep habits, your twins will be happier and healthier. Good sleep boosts each baby's immune system to fend off illness more effectively. And if your babies sleep well, you will have extra time in your day to take care of yourself, necessary household tasks, and more. If you haven't quite reached this point yet, hang in there—your current efforts and strategies will ultimately pay off!

Daytime Naps

During the daytime, remember to keep your twins' schedules coordinated with synchronized sleeping, eating, burping, playing, diaper changes, and then more sleep. As mentioned in the previous chapter, babies can only tolerate being awake during the day for a couple of hours. So watch the clock from the time your twins wake up from their nap. Of course, if both twins are not waking up at the same time, you'll need to wake up your second baby so that you can keep the 2 babies on the same schedule.

When your babies have fed, burped, played, and had tummy time, you will probably start to notice some signs of fatigue. Your babies' signs of fatigue will show you when you should scoop them up and initiate the pre-nap routine. This sends the message that sleep is coming. For your routine, you can read the babies a story, give them fresh diapers, dress them in sleepers if you use them, and lay them down in their cribs in a darkened room. At this point, they are fatigued, fed, clean, and content. What else is there to do but close one's eyes and sleep? This is the time when the twins will get practice falling asleep on their own, with their twin doing the same in the other crib across the room.

Twin Tip

Remember that crying is a late sign of fatigue. Look for earlier clues that your twins are sleepy, such as thumb-sucking or rubbing their eyes or ears.

Feeding Your Infant Twins

If you are still able to nurse your twins at this point, good for you! You may be supplementing with formula, which is perfectly fine. Any amount of breast milk your twins can get from you will be beneficial. For our family, daytime nursing with a supplemental evening bottle of formula helped my twins sleep better through the night. The formula "tanked them up," so to speak, and they didn't get as hungry overnight. We referred to their evening formula bottles as their "milkshakes" that tucked them in for the night!

Twin Tip

If your twins are feeding well and not having trouble with spit-ups or reflux, you may consider advancing the nipple speed that you use with your bottles. Many nipple manufacturers make a slow-flow nipple with a small hole for newborns, followed by a medium-flow nipple, and finally a fast-flow nipple with the largest opening.

If your twins are handling feeds well, experiment with a larger nipple opening. If you can safely use a faster nipple speed without causing excessive gas or spit-ups, you can shorten the duration of a milk feeding by 5 minutes. If you can save 5 minutes in each of the 5 feedings a day, you will have 25 extra minutes in your busy day. Simple time-saving tricks can help your life with twins get easier each month!

The American Academy of Pediatrics recommends parents to exclusively breastfeed for a minimum of 4 months, but preferably 6 months. The amount of milk your babies will drink at each feeding will increase as they grow. Their daily intake of milk should be about 30 ounces by 4 months of age, divided over about 5 feedings a day. Again, mixing the batches of formula ahead of time in quart-sized jugs will continue to simplify the process of readying 2 bottles of milk for each feeding.

When your babies are developmentally ready, you can start to feed your babies solid foods, as early as 4 months of age, such as infant cereals as well as pureed and strained vegetables and fruits. Do not be tempted to add infant cereal to the milk bottles to help them sleep through the night; it doesn't work and may lead to excessive weight gain. The way to help your twins sleep all night is by encouraging good sleep habits as previously discussed.

You will need 2 high chairs to feed your twins solid foods. High chairs have a wide range of prices. The safety seats that strap into existing kitchen chairs—the ones with an infant seat belt and eating tray—work well and are also budget friendly. In keeping with a consistent schedule for your twins, feed them solid foods at the same time and place. Place their high chairs close together, in front of you, at a 90-degree angle to one another so that they can see each other as well as you (Figure 4-1). Mealtimes can be a fun bonding time for all of you. Make sure to introduce only one new food at a

time, waiting 3 days or so before introducing another new food to ensure that neither baby has a reaction to the food. Store-bought baby food is just fine; the pureed pears are particularly delicious. If you have lots of energy, you can also prepare food in advance by pureeing, straining,

Figure 4-1. High chairs at a 90-degree angle to one another so the caregiver can feed both babies while creating a nice 3-person social experience at the same time.

and freezing the food in ice cube trays, later popping the cubes of food out and repackaging them in resealable storage bags for safe storage. Do what works for your family.

Twin Tales

Does your neighbor make only homemade baby food for her infant? Do not feel guilty if, because of realistic time constraints in raising twins, your babies are eating store-bought baby food. Sue, mom to school-aged twins, states, "Work within your own boundaries of what is comfortable—and don't feel guilty about it! For me, this meant being realistic about breastfeeding, keeping extensive spreadsheets on the twins' sleep/feeding cycles, and ordering takeout for many meals."

Teaching 2 babies to eat solid foods can get quite messy. In the early days, feeding solid foods once a day is a nice way to slowly introduce the concept. As your twins' skills in eating pureed foods from an offered spoon improve, you can increase the solid feeds over the next several weeks to twice a day and then to 3 times a day.

Twin Tip

Do not be surprised when you discover your infant twins have different taste preferences. They are 2 unique individuals! If one baby is resisting a certain food, do not write off that particular food forever. Keep offering it, and over time your baby will accept it and broaden his palate's horizon. Babies often need to be exposed to food several times before accepting it. Ensure that you as a parent model healthy eating habits as well, even at these early ages.

Get your camera ready! Two babies learning how to eat solid foods is a real photo opportunity. You're taking countless digital pictures of your twins. But who is who in each picture? Other parents of older twins would tell me, "Label your pictures quickly because down the line, you'll forget who is who!" But somehow in my sleep-deprived life with twin babies I couldn't get my act together to label the pictures. What I did do, though, was dress my identical twins in theme colors. Andrew mostly wore blue, and Ryan usually wore red. My pictures never did end up getting labels, but we always know that the little guy in blue is Andrew, and the cutie in red is Ryan. An added benefit: grandparents and friends picked up on our boys' color themes and when they visited us, they immediately knew who each boy was without an explanation.

Twins Getting Stronger

At 2 and 3 months of age, your twins are starting to develop their muscle tone. Their upper trunks and neck muscles are strengthening, and when placed on the floor prone they are able to start lifting their heads on their own. It is our job as parents to become at-home physical therapists and to make sure we give our twins plenty of practice strengthening their muscles.

Tummy time will help your babies gain strength as well as protect their heads from developing plagiocephaly, or in a way that flattens a part of the skull, which can partly result from frequently lying on one's back. The Safe to Sleep campaign, formerly known as the Back to Sleep campaign and introduced in 1992, has been invaluable in educating families about proper sleep positioning to minimize the risk of sudden infant death syndrome, but babies also need plenty of practice holding their bodies in other positions when they are awake and supervised by an adult caregiver.

Twin Tip

Twins outnumber their mom or dad; they can't be held simultaneously all day. As a result, parents of twins love the convenience of bouncy chairs, swings, and the like to entertain and contain our babies. Make sure to *avoid overuse* of such devices. Playtime on the open floor is vitally important and will help your twins develop their muscles and strength.

In the early stages, tummy time can be frustrating for babies and parents alike. Your babies may just cry and fuss immediately, unable to budge their heavy heads up. Tummy time works best if you can give your babies something interesting to look at while on their bellies. It is an advantage to have 2 babies because your twins can face each other with baby toys between them. A mirror to look into is another popular option, but one's own twin can be just as interesting! For comfort's sake, you can position a regular throw or Boppy pillow under the upper chest (Figure 4-2). It gives your twins a slightly higher and more interesting vantage point and if their head droops suddenly, the fall is cushioned.

Figure 4-2. Tummy time fun!

Always supervise tummy time directly. Even if tummy time lasts only 2 minutes and you have to end it because of tears, every minute counts. Try to incorporate tummy time into your daily routine of playing and eating. After a feeding and burping is a good time for tummy time. You can perform tummy time on Mom's or Dad's chest as well, as you lean back while sitting on the couch after burping your baby. Your goal is to give your twins tummy time several times throughout each day.

When you have twins, a parent can come to love bouncy chairs. It is quite a luxury to have the option of keeping your babies safe and comfortable while you tend to things around the house. A word of caution, however: parents of multiples need to make sure that they do not overuse such containment receptacles. It will be difficult for your babies to practice using their muscles if they are strapped and confined in bouncy seats too often. You can briefly use the luxury of your bouncy chairs after a feeding, for example, as the 45-degree incline can help your babies digest their milk, but after you have rinsed out the bottles and put away the jug of formula, pick your babies up and give them time on the open floor.

After the first month of life, your babies learn to visually track and follow you and other objects. They will hear you coming from the next room and turn their heads to your voice. These new skills will help them form relationships and interact with the world around them.

Babies usually start to roll over around 4 months of age. That being said, rolling for the first time could easily happen earlier, surprising both you and your baby. Because you never know when your twin babies will start to roll over, *never ever* leave them unattended in high places such as a bed, couch, or changing table. Consider changing your twins' wet diapers right there on the carpet floor where you are all playing already. If there is no poop in the diaper, save yourself the trip to the changing table where your attention becomes divided between the baby on the table and the baby on the floor. Accidents are more likely to happen when a parent is distracted. You will get very speedy and efficient with diaper changes, trust me!

Twin Tip

Ah, such is the life of a parent of twins—your attention is divided between your babies! Never leave either of your babies in a high position from which they can roll off. You will be busy tending to her twin and won't be able to intervene in time.

Once the twins are 4 months of age, everything seems to get a little bit easier. The babies get better at amusing themselves and each other for increasing amounts of time. Most babies also begin sleeping through the night by 3 months of age and 12 pounds in weight. Solid feedings may have begun and give more structure to the day's activities. At 4 to 6 months, you have time to step back, look at how far you and your twins have come, and enjoy the relative ease of these days compared with those chaotic early weeks.

Diaper Rash

Diaper rash is common among babies after introducing solid foods into their diet. As a parent of twins, you do not have time for diaper rash! Learn how to banish it quickly so that you can all move on with your lives. Be aware of the relationship between solid foods and diaper rash; some preventive care can help keep diaper rash at bay. The warm, moist environment within a diaper triggers diaper rash; unfortunately, modern diapers are excellent at retaining moisture. When changing diapers, do not rush to put the new diaper on. Give your babies' bottoms some air time, or diaper-free time, just for a couple of minutes to truly dry out the skin usually closed up in a diaper.

If you have a case or two of diaper rash in your house, start using a zinc oxide–containing cream with each diaper change. Make sure you are *generous* with the cream. Use the cream like frosting on a cake—you need a bit more than you think. The zinc oxide cream is a barrier cream. There are many zinc oxide–containing creams on the market, all of which work pretty well. My personal favorite brand adds cornstarch to the zinc oxide mix, which together seems to zap the rash quickly. I would also suggest avoiding the use of commercial baby wipes to clean soiled skin when your baby has an active diaper rash.

Another strategy to eliminate diaper rash is to increase your babies' air time between diaper changes. One trick I used when my twins were babies was to have a few pairs of casual, comfy, all-cotton pants on hand as extras, specifically to put on my boys when they were getting air time. The sweatpants helped catch some spills if the boys happened to pee. Warning! Exposure to the air tends to stimulate urination.

Twin Tip

Even wipes labeled "for sensitive skin" contain irritating chemicals. Consider temporarily replacing wipes with 100% cotton balls dipped in a bowl of warm water to clean the skin during diaper rash.

Another trick I used when my boys had diaper rash was to combine air time with tummy time using waterproof pads. A strategically placed waterproof pad makes it possible to combine tummy-air time and catch any unintentional urination that could occur without a diaper. Parents of twins learn to be quite efficient, and you, too, will learn how to multitask this way. Healing up a diaper rash and encouraging upper body strength at the same time is just one example of how you can streamline your life with twins.

Certainly, if a diaper rash is not clearing up as quickly as you'd like or if it looks particularly worrisome, have your pediatrician check it out. Some diaper rashes can progress to a yeast infection of the skin, which requires a prescription medication for treatment.

Twinproofing

Now that the babies are starting to move more and roll over, it is a good time to start intensively childproofing your home. Parents of twins should be extra vigilant and perform "twinproofing" of their home because twins have a way of giving each other ideas. Twins also help each other get into restricted areas that one baby alone could not have ventured into by herself. Some ideas to help you get started with twinproofing your home include

- Safety gates for the top and bottom of staircases
- Doorknob covers
- Electric outlet covers
- Window blind cords secured out of reach

- All nursery furniture far from windows to prevent falls and from getting caught in hanging window blind cords or draperies (It is best to use cordless window products, if possible.)
- Hot water heater set so that water coming out of the faucet is no more than 120°F (48.9 °C) to reduce risk of scald burns
- Dressers and bookshelves secured to the wall with anti-tip devices

Always remember that even the best childproofing gadgets are no substitute for direct supervision of your twins. Do not be fooled into a false sense of security just because you have childproofed your home with all the right equipment; dangerous things can still happen. And certain household features are difficult to twinproof, requiring parents to be watchful and vigilant. For example, a simple bedroom door can cause problems. For a time, my twin boys enjoyed a gleeful but dangerous game in which they would each push on opposite sides of the same door. A foam guard didn't work at these locations, so we had to watch the boys vigilantly and guide them appropriately.

Returning to Work

The decisions of if and when to return to work after having a child are tricky enough but even more complicated for parents of multiples. The cost of child care for 2 kids can be significant, and many families who require 2 working parents need to explore all options and get creative with scheduling.

Options for child care include an outside facility, a home-based day care, a sitter or nanny, or an au pair. Parents may consider working opposite hours or schedules from each other to minimize the amount of time each week that help is needed. Ensure that the outside facility or home-based day care maintains the proper state licensure. If you have 3 or more children, it may be most cost-effective to investigate the nanny or au pair options because your entire family will be covered, as opposed to paying additional rates for each added child. A sitter or nanny comes to your home during the required hours, but an au pair usually lives with the host family, which can be useful if one or both parents need to travel for work. Visit sites, check references, interview with prepared questions, and follow your intuition when making your selection.

Once you've determined your child care and when you'll be returning to work, make sure to make a dry run of the new routine at least a week ahead of time and make necessary adjustments. When back in a working routine, ask your caregivers to take notes on your babies' daily schedules so you have a sense of practical matters such as their feeding and diaper change patterns, as well as the fun stuff such as stroller rides and book preferences. Use special rituals to share special parent-child time when working parents return home from work. The nighttime bath or bedtime story is a perfect way for parents and babies to reconnect and bond after being apart during the daytime.

Toys and Books

Often, the best toys for babies are the toys that do the least. If the toy does less, your child does more. You do not need to spend a lot of money on toys even though you have 2 babies who are the same age. Babies love to explore simple things such as empty, clean yogurt containers and butter tubs. Place a block inside any empty container and shake it up—watch your babies' reactions! Simple containers teach your babies about spatial relationships and help them develop their fine motor skills as they reach for a rattle placed inside a bucket.

Twin Tip

You do not need to purchase 2 of each toy. Infant twins' developmental stage helps them share toys quite nicely because they won't get jealous of each other's toys.

It is never too early to read to your babies. Have plenty of board books on hand, and leave the books around the home in each room so that you can pick one up and start reading at any given moment. Your twins can also find the books on their own and eventually turn pages and leaf through the pictures by themselves. Get into the routine of visiting your local library frequently. You'll be pleasantly surprised by the board book selection for your infant twins. And best of all, the books are free! When you are feeling brave, you can bring your babies to an infant story time as well.

Outings With Your Twins

Continue to make sure you get out of the house periodically to stay sane. Yes, there is still an outside world out there! Keep your diaper bag stocked so running off on a spontaneous errand is easier. You may love your twin stroller, but consider occasionally taking the twins out with a single stroller if you have one, with a front or backpack carrier. This way you can be a little more spry on your feet by not lugging around a huge double stroller.

 Twin Tales

Danielle, mom to school-aged twins, recommends, "Invest in a good double stroller. Don't be afraid to leave the house. Keep a bag of extras—diapers, pacifiers, wipes, etcetera—that you can throw in your trunk or stroller. Get out and get fresh air."

The single stroller/carrier combo comes in handy if you're not in the mood for everyone staring at you and your family. It can't be helped: when people see twins they get so excited and will ask you lots of questions. Some days the attention is fun, but other days you just want to go about your business quickly. Personally, I have been told by countless strangers, "You sure have your hands full!" My standard response if I don't feel like talking? "We are very blessed," and I just keep moving along.

Continue Seeking Support

Do not be shy; ask family and friends for help. You are working very hard to care for your young twins, and you need breaks to stay fresh and healthy. If you do not have immediate family nearby available to help, you will need to think creatively for support. Investigate options through friends and neighbors in your community. Perhaps a family friend's preteen is interested in becoming a babysitter. She can get some hands-on training by being a "mother's helper" to your family. While you address other household chores, she can read to your babies. An extra pair of hands can really help you during the infant stages, so do not be afraid to reach out for help.

Make sure you take time to connect with your spouse. A strong team works more effectively together. Communication is key, and relationships can be difficult when you're sleep deprived. Don't expect your spouse to read your mind; ask for specific help when you need it. Stewing over an ignored household chore is not allowed; simply talk about it in the open and ask for help in getting the chore completed.

Twin Tales

Jon, dad to infant twins, states, "There is marital strain in any new baby circumstance, and we certainly had our bumps upon the birth of our now 4-year-old son. But with so little downtime while tending to twins, the chances for lost patience, curt responses, and general grumpiness is a big and very real—and natural—risk factor for even the greater mom-and-dad partners. I wish we'd acknowledged this prior to actually ending up in the thick of things, and perhaps even had developed some strategies or 'safe words' which could more easily and quickly nip such nonproductive behavior toward one another in the bud."

Bonding With Each Twin

Keeping your twins on the same schedule when they are young infants has many wonderful benefits; however, always keep in the forefront of your mind that your twins are 2 unique individuals. Even at this early age, look for opportunities to connect with each of your twins as individuals. You can take one of your babies out alone for some special individual time while the other twin enjoys special one-on-one time with your spouse or another trusted adult caregiver. Special one-on-one time, even starting in infancy, can help you and each of your twins bond and get to know one another better.

Twin Tip

Even the language that you choose to refer to your twins can affect your (and others') impressions of them as individuals. Try not to refer to your children as "the twins"; rather, name them individually in conversation. Encourage family and friends to refer to your kids by name as well. If others ask you, "How are the twins?" you can respond, "Josh and Billy are great!"

When your twins are babies, you are synchronizing your twins' schedules for survival and sanity, but always remember to regard your twins as the 2 special people they are. As your babies approach 6 months of age, you can start to ease out of survival mode somewhat and begin new family rituals of connecting with each of your twins on a one-on-one basis.

CHAPTER 5

Older Infancy and First Birthday

Your miraculous twins' minds and bodies are growing at amazing rates from 6 months of age to their first birthday. New skills are learned at an incredible rate! Older babies seem to learn new things exponentially rather than merely sequentially. Whether your twins are identical or fraternal, they continue to evolve into 2 unique, individual people. Their distinct personalities are more evident each day.

For the first time in their young lives, your babies can truly illustrate their likes and dislikes to you. Sometimes, these illustrations might be quite crude, such as a swipe at a spoon full of food when they would rather not have another bite. Your babies will make you laugh each day and will keep you guessing as well; one twin will gobble down dinner with an extra helping, while the other eats a mere couple of bites and ends the meal.

Your twins' smiles, coos, and early gestures form patterns of communication. This early communication creates true relationships for them with you, your family, and each other. As you nurture your babies' growth, you will see that as unique individuals, each child will develop at his own rate.

Twin Tales

Jon, dad to twins, states, "In our case, the girls are fraternal, so already there was an expectation of differences, but I wish I'd given more thought to these amazing individuals being thought of, and cared for, as the individuals they are versus the 'couplet' they were in utero, despite the understanding they will forever share this special bond. These days, we rarely, if ever, refer to the girls as 'the twins.' They are sisters, and yes they are twins, but they are individuals first, each with her own traits and quirks."

Sleep Patterns

From 6 months of age to the first birthday, babies should be sleeping about 14 hours total in a 24-hour period to stay healthy and happy. About 11 of these hours should be spent in overnight sleep, and about 3 of these hours are divided up among daytime naps. The daytime sleep is usually divided into 2 naps, morning and afternoon. If you have older children, you may need to be flexible with the twins' nap schedule because of the older kids' carpooling and school activities, but do your best to be as respectful to your babies' sleep requirements as you can. If your twins get their necessary sleep, your family and daily routine will be much more harmonious.

Just as in early infancy, your babies' usual sleep routines may be temporarily disrupted in times of illness or travel. Once the twins are over their illness or you are back home from a trip, get everyone back on board with your usual sleep routine. Sometimes babies can get accustomed to parents tending to them in the middle of the night if they have been congested, coughing, or feverish. When they are healthy once again, help your twin babies get themselves back to sleep. If you need a refresher on good sleep hygiene habits for your multiples, please refer to the previous chapter on early infancy, specifically the Keeping Your Twins on the Same Schedule: Starting Now section on page 37.

Twin Tales

As a guest speaker at a Parents of Multiples club event, I was asked how a parent could help her 11-month-old twins sleep through the night. A few weeks earlier, the mother was concerned her daughter was getting sick and offered a bottle at 2:00 am. Unfortunately, the mother fell into a pattern with this new overnight feeding, and the bottle was disrupting the daughter and her room-sharing twin brother's sleep. A healthy, normally developing 11-month-old does not require overnight feedings, and the new habit had created a learned hunger at a very inconvenient time. Imagine if we, as adults, woke up at 2:00 am to eat a bowl of cereal. After a few nights of this, we'd feel hungry at that time, even though adults do not physiologically need a bowl of cereal at 2:00 am.

Should a mother slowly reduce the ounces offered each night over a week or simply go cold turkey and abruptly stop the bottle? With many parenting questions, there is no one correct answer. Sometimes the slower, more gradual approach can be a kinder, gentler way to go; however, it can prolong the transition over a longer stretch of time. Another analogy is removing a sticky bandage. Should you rip the Band-Aid off quickly (it hurts, but it's over faster) or slowly remove it, prolonging the pain?

In the case of this healthy, normally developing 11-month-old, it is appropriate to eliminate overnight bottles. The cold-turkey approach may result in a lot of tears for the first couple of nights (from both child and parent!). But with consistency, the issue may be resolved more quickly. The strategies to encourage good sleep habits are helpful if implemented anytime during infancy, not just the early months. The difference at this stage, however, is that older babies now understand object permanence, and they know that their parents exist even when they are not in the room with them. Your babies may holler for you to pick them up in the middle of the night, or they might even resist bedtime, but make sure you keep your bedtime and nighttime rituals consistent. Evening baths, pajamas, story time, and perhaps 1 or 2 songs, followed by sweet goodnight kisses, are all that your twins need to be tucked in for the night.

Twin Tip

Your older twin babies are babbling and communicating more. You may notice at bedtime, after you say goodnight and close the door, them "talking" to each other. These exchanges between your twins are adorable and are just one example of the special joys that parents of twins are privileged to experience. Listen at the door if you like, but don't feel the need to reenter the room and shush your babies. They are experimenting with their early language skills. They may chitchat together for a good 30 minutes or so, but as long as they fall asleep eventually, you don't need to interrupt them. For more on early language skills, please refer to the "Toddler Years (1- and 2-Year-Olds)" chapter on page 105.

Mealtime: A Whole New World

Your twin babies' nutrition from 6 months of age up to their first birthday should consist of continued breast milk or infant formula, as well as an increasing variety and amount of solid foods. In addition, table foods should slowly be introduced. It is hard to believe, but by the time your twins turn 1 year of age, they should be eating mostly table foods. If growth and development have been normal, your twins should continue drinking breast milk or infant formula up to the first birthday. Breast milk and infant formula have all the specialized nutrients in just the right proportions, which is especially important if your babies were born small or prematurely. After the first birthday, your twins should be able to switch to vitamin D whole cow's milk.

You will notice that your twins' feeding patterns may begin to change over this period of late infancy. They may noticeably nurse less or drink less formula in a 24-hour period. This is normal and happens for 3 reasons.

- Your babies are eating more solid foods and are more interested in table foods. They are beginning to form taste preferences and may prefer the excitement of a new table food to the routine milk they always drink. Your twins are also mastering the art of self-feeding. Assuming they have been growing properly, the focus should be placed on their increasing independence, not their total caloric intake.

- Your twins are more active and interested in the world around them. They are working on developing their fine motor skills, perfecting their pincer-like grasp, and examining microscopic pieces of fuzz. They would rather crawl around and pull themselves up on the coffee table to see the toy sitting on top. Exploration can be a lot more fun than eating or drinking!

- All babies start to slow their rate of growth as they approach their first birthday. Because the child is not growing quite so quickly, she simply won't have the desire to eat as much as she did a couple of months earlier.

We as parents tend to worry about our kids' eating habits and wonder why a child who ate a certain amount in the past is now eating less. At this age, you need to know that drinking less milk is to be expected.

Twin Tip

Parents of twins must always remind themselves not to compare the 2 children. Do not be surprised or overly concerned if one twin drinks more or less milk than the other. Remember that you have 2 different babies who happen to be the same age, but everyone is an individual. If you have persistent worries, check with your pediatrician.

Monitor each of your babies' total intake of formula in a 24-hour period. After the first birthday, when the switch is made to whole cow's milk, you will be looking for a target maximum of 16 to 18 ounces of milk a day (definitely not more than 24 ounces in a day, which increases the risk of anemia caused by iron deficiency). Plan ahead and make sure that you taper your babies' liquid diets if it is approaching those numbers before their first birthday.

How will you transition your babies' milk after their first birthday? Some parents switch to cow's milk cold turkey after their babies' first birthday. However, some babies do not transition to a new-tasting milk so easily. For our family, I used a system of mixing formula with whole milk, over time increasing the proportion of whole milk to formula. I found that my kids were more willing to accept the new taste if it was introduced more gradually. Over a couple of weeks' time, change the composition of your 6-ounce bottles (eg, from 5 ounces of formula plus 1 ounce milk to 4 ounces of formula plus 2 ounces milk, and so on) until the proportion of the bottle becomes 100% whole milk. This method works with a minimum of resistance from your twins because the taste change has been made over time.

Solid and Table Foods

From 6 months and older, your twins should be eating new foods each week. Introduce a single new food every 3 to 5 days to ensure that there is no food allergy or intolerance. Traditionally, pediatricians recommended a specific order for new foods to be introduced—starting with infant cereals mixed with breast milk or formula, moving on to pureed and strained vegetables, and following with pureed and strained fruits, then meats, and lastly table foods. More recently, however, experts agree that a specific order of introduction is not required. No set order of food type is good news for busy parents of twins—one less "rule" that you need to stress out about! Relax, do not worry about introducing foods in a particular order, and just ensure that you are serving your twins a good variety of food groups and flavors. You are enhancing your babies' palates, as well as providing good nutrition. As always, model good eating habits yourself, even when your children are small; as parents, we are our kids' greatest role models.

While the order of foods may be unimportant to your twins, a good source of iron is. Infant cereals are a great source of iron. At 6 months of age, your twins need a new, additional source of iron to accommodate their growth and red blood cell production, which is especially important for breastfed babies. Mix infant cereals such as rice and oatmeal with pumped breast milk or infant formula instead of plain water to boost the caloric and nutritional value. In addition, your twins are accustomed to the flavor of the milk or formula and will happily recognize the familiar flavor in the new taste of cereal.

Twin Tip

If the weather is nice, feed your babies outside as much as you can. Two babies eating solid foods can get quite messy, and life is easier if you don't have to mop up the floor perfectly after each meal. For indoor meals, some parents like to put a shower curtain or other similar tarp on the floor underneath the 2 high chairs to streamline post-meal cleanup.

In addition to a good source of iron, your babies need fluoride supplementation starting at 6 months of age. If your home water supply is treated municipal water, your fluoride needs are most likely met. If you use well water, you should ask your pediatrician if your twins need a fluoride-multivitamin supplement. More fluoride is not necessarily better; however, babies can develop fluorosis, a condition harmful to teeth and bones, if they receive too much fluoride. Speak with your pediatrician to make sure you have the right balance of fluoride.

Your twins should be ready to try table (finger) foods around 9 months of age. To start eating table foods, they should be able to sit up fully and have a good pincerlike grasp. O-shaped breakfast cereal is a good first finger food because it quickly melts in the mouth, minimizing the risk of choking. To prevent choking, always cut up table foods into lengthwise, manageable sizes for your twins, and make sure foods are cooked well and on the mushy side. You may personally prefer your vegetables with a nice crunch, or your pasta al dente, but for now, serve your babies mushy vegetables, pasta, and other table foods.

Do not be surprised if your twins have different taste preferences. Your babies are unique individuals, after all. Offer an interesting variety of tastes, textures, and flavors at mealtimes. If one or both of your twins reject a food the first time it is offered, do not write off that food just yet. They may not be crazy about green beans the first couple of times they taste it, but keep trying on different occasions. Experts agree that it can take a dozen tries of a new food before a child decides that he likes it. And even from the time that your twins are babies, avoid power struggles at mealtimes.

Twin Tip

Your twin babies love to mimic you. One day soon, they will try to feed each other!

When your babies are seated in their high chairs eating, never leave the room, even for a moment. You never know when one twin may choke on a bit of food. Sometimes, having 2 babies in the house, we can have a false sense of security, as if there is safety in numbers. Always make sure that an adult directly supervises your twins' mealtimes.

Sippy Cup Training: Bye-bye, Bottles!

Your babies will be ready to learn how to drink from a sippy cup around their first birthday. Why do pediatricians encourage families to move forward from the bottle at this age? As babies grow older and become more attached to certain people and certain objects, they tend to form stronger bonds with these objects. Unfortunately, a young child may rely on the bottle for comfort in addition to nutrition, and pediatricians have seen that prolonged exposure to the bottle can cause problems such as excessive weight gain and dental cavities. If a child is sucking on a bottle habitually, the milk or juice inside can cause decay of new teeth, which is known as *early childhood caries.*

As they approach their first birthday, your children need to learn a more mature way of drinking milk. Milk should be enjoyed at standard mealtimes and snack times while sitting upright at a high chair or table. A child should drink and eat at the high chair or table until he feels full, and then he can leave the table to go do other things. A child cannot learn effectively or master new skills if he always has one hand holding a bottle.

A transition to a sippy cup is easier if done sooner rather than later, and as a parent of multiples, you can make your life easier by making the transition sooner. The later you make the transition from a bottle to a cup, the more difficult it will be because 1-year-olds develop their sense of authority more strongly each month. Changing bottles to sippy cups around the time of your twins' first birthday should help make the process more relaxed for all of you.

When you initiate your twins' sippy cup training sessions, you need to start small and work your way up. Initially, select a bottle-feeding session that is not a major feeding—maybe a mid-afternoon feeding. You do not want your twins to be so hungry that they get frustrated at the cup-learning process. Many sippy cup brands have a separate valve insert that is placed inside the lid to prevent spills. Make training easier for your kids and don't use the valve insert at first. These valves prevent milk from flowing freely from the spout and require that the child use more sucking action to pull the milk out. Not using the valve can be a bit messier, but you want to help your twins understand that this new object's purpose is to give them milk and relieve their thirst, even before they can master the proper sucking action.

Twin Tip

As a parent of twins, you are always on a quest for efficiency. The transition to sippy cups may initially seem like a lot of hassle or effort, and you may be tempted to keep handing your twins bottles to drink, especially if they have figured out how to hold the bottles themselves. Remember that the sooner they learn how to drink from sippy cups, the further they are down the road to independence. When your twins are more independent, you can use your time to play and interact with them rather than to continue routine tasks of feeding and cleaning. Which option is more fun?

What about logistics? Seat your twins in their high chairs in front of you and alternate helping each child attempt to drink from the cup and playing with each child. The training sessions should be a pleasant and fun experience because you always want your children to have positive associations with mealtimes. If you find that the twins are getting frustrated or swiping at the cup, or that you yourself are getting annoyed, end the session. You can try again tomorrow. Or if one twin would rather crawl around while the other is interested and actually taking some sips of milk, go ahead and use this opportunity with the interested twin. One-on-one time with each child is always a good thing!

There are a few methods for ultimately making the switch from nursing or bottle-feeding to cup drinking, and every family must choose the method that will work for them, logistically and emotionally. As with most parenting issues, no one solution can fit everybody well.

Some advise a cold turkey approach, claiming that if the breast or a bottle continues to be offered at any time of day in any way, it will cause the child to yearn and hold out for it, preventing the child from getting used to the new method of drinking. I feel that this cold turkey method is a bit harsh

Twin Tip

Your twins have many transitions to make during their early years. Whether it is learning to drink from a sippy cup, toilet training, or moving to a big-kid bed, you as a parent need to be aware of your emotions. Transitioning 2 or more kids through the same thing at the same time is tough! If you find yourself getting frustrated or annoyed, you need to take a step back and regroup. Even young babies can pick up on parental anxiety, and the transition will be that much tougher to make. Do your best to calm down, take a break, and try again another day.

on parents and children. In the case of nursing, it will also cause the mother a great deal of physical pain because she will likely experience some breast engorgement and leaking if nursing is terminated abruptly from 4 sessions a day to none.

A kinder and gentler approach to wean your babies is to gradually switch the style of drinking one session at a time until all the feeding sessions have been replaced with a cup. As mentioned earlier, start with a feeding that usually is lighter so that hunger doesn't upset your babies into being unwilling to try something new. Try this new drinking method at the same session each day for a week or so, and then select a different time of day to switch drinking styles. You can lengthen or shorten the time between additional sessions as you need to make it work for your family. If relatives are visiting for a weekend or some other event is going on, it is fine to wait an additional week here or there as needed to let everyone adjust to the new system. You won't want to switch a morning bottle-feeding to a cup feeding at a time when a lot of other things are happening (eg, at Thanksgiving). If you make things a bit easier on yourself, you will be a happier parent and able to help your babies get through the transition. Over time, the switch will eventually be made for all the feeding sessions of the day.

If you are still nursing, you will notice that once you drop 1 or 2 sessions, your milk supply may take a precipitous dip. You may find that you will need to offer sippy cups more quickly than you had planned. Try not to fret about the total volume of milk that the twins drink. Remember that their growth rates are slowing down, and if they are truly hungry, they'll figure out a way to drink! Your twins are also eating solid foods, so they won't starve. Many nursing moms hold onto one last nursing session, usually at bedtime, for emotional bonding and comfort—a great ritual if you wish to continue it.

Oral Health

Your twins' first teeth may come in, on average, around the time they are 6 months of age. Every child is different, so do not be concerned if your babies get their first teeth a little sooner or later. Ask your pediatrician about any concerns you might have. You can start using an infant toothbrush with toothpaste twice a day when the first tooth has come in. The American Dental Association and the American Academy of Pediatrics recommend that children 2 years and younger use a small smear of fluoride toothpaste, the size of a grain of rice. Even better than a toothbrush at this young age is gently rubbing the teeth and gums with an infant washcloth and water. Get in the habit of cleaning your twins' gums and first teeth with a clean washcloth after a meal. Your babies are probably quite messy with sticky cereal and pureed fruits all over their faces after a meal, and you are wiping them down anyway. Use a fresh washcloth and clean the gums and teeth. We dedicated an entire kitchen drawer to fresh, clean infant washcloths to simplify post-meal cleanups.

Twin Tip

As a parent of twin babies, you perform many of the same child care tasks each day. Step back and evaluate where you store necessary baby supplies. Could you reorganize frequently used items to make them more accessible and streamline caring for your twins?

Play and Development

When your twins start to sit independently, usually around the 6-month mark, they will be able to view the world from an entirely new vantage point. I can promise you that your twins will achieve this milestone on different days; do not fret or compare them. My son Andrew sat up alone a full month or so before his twin brother Ryan. I admit, I was a nervous wreck wondering when little Ryan would sit up by himself! Now looking back, I laugh when I remember how worried I was about Ryan's motor development. Today he is quite a speedy runner, as well as a swimmer.

Twin Tip

When your twins are both sitting up independently, you can do cool new things that will make your life easier. For example, you can fill your big bathtub and bathe them at the same time. But never get a false sense of security. Continue to always attend to your children when they are in or near the bathtub and stay within arm's reach. Soon you will also be able to introduce activity centers (seats surrounded by 360 degrees of toys). Bathing both babies simultaneously or having a new fun place for your babies to spend time while you put together dinner are the sort of things that will streamline your life and make the daily routine easier.

A cause of concern for many parents of singletons and multiples is wondering when their children will take their first steps. Much importance has been placed on the walking motor milestone throughout generations.

You'll often hear grandparents chuckle, "Oh, he didn't walk until 15 months," or others proudly brag, "My daughter walked at 10 months," as if walking makes her a genius. The timing of when a child first walks has no relation to intelligence or future motor dexterity. Walking can start anywhere from 9 to 18 months of age and still be considered within typical range. Each child develops at his own rate, period.

Many parents' anxieties over this issue are fueled at family get-togethers where they hear about similarly aged cousins' physical feats or at playdates with friends because the urge to compare one's child with others is common. What is more, parents of twins have 2 cute little specimens under their noses, and it is human nature to compare them to each other. Try not to do it. Even if your twins are identical, they both need their own time to get where they need to go. The twin who walks first is not better or smarter. The one who walks later will not need special assistance throughout her life.

On average, twins may start walking a bit later than their similarly aged single-born peers. I believe this is for 2 reasons. First, many twins are born early, or preterm, putting their development on a slightly different schedule. Second, when you have 2 babies to keep an eye on, it is simply more difficult to give them individual training sessions. Parents of just one baby have the luxury of being able to hold both of their child's hands and coach him to walk all day long, encouraging a new desire to walk with support. Parents of multiples are not able to focus such constant attention on one child.

Twin Support

When it comes to milestones, you may frequently find yourself comparing the twins with each other. And the comparisons won't end any time soon. Who will count to 100 first? Who will learn to read first? Assuming your twins are generally healthy, they will probably alternate who masters a new skill first. Trust me when I tell you that in the long run, you will be amazed at the fact that each child will take the lead in different areas and alternate being the leader; *it will all balance out.* Enjoy your child's achievement for what it is, without fretting over why her twin hasn't done it yet.

Look at it this way: parents of more than one kid, born at different ages, don't even have such time to devote to one single baby. My fourth child is a singleton. Did I ever have time to hold her hands for more than 5 minutes to help her learn to walk around the house? Definitely not! And she figured it out anyway. Don't worry, it will happen. But do ask your pediatrician about any special concerns you may have about your twins' motor development.

ExerSaucers are toys that our family enjoyed when our twin boys were older infants. These stationary toy centers have a baby seat in the center and are surrounded by colorful toys, music boxes, and activities. These can be pricey and may be too expensive to buy 2. We used our old one from our oldest son and borrowed one from my sister-in-law's family. Your twins can bounce safely in these toy centers, whacking the buttons on the music boxes and having fun together, and you'll know where they are—no wondering if they've crawled into the bathroom and stuck their hand in the toilet. But make sure your twins don't spend more than 15 minutes at a stretch in these toy centers. Your twins do need to move about the house developing their muscles and coordination. But for hectic times such as fixing the family dinner, it was a real helper for me to have my twin boys happily and safely playing for 15 minutes. We have hilarious home videos of our twins bouncing in tandem while giggling madly.

Do not confuse these stationary play centers with old-fashioned walkers that can wheel about the house. Walkers are extremely dangerous, and many children have broken bones or experienced serious head injuries from falling down stairs in walkers. The American Academy of Pediatrics recommends banning the sale of infant walkers. Do not buy one, and do not let any family members hand one down to you. Contrary to the old thinking, walkers do not assist a child in walking earlier. In fact, the walker uses different muscle groups than those used in natural walking and will delay independent walking.

Language and Communication

When it comes to twins' language development, parents may hear concerning generalizations that twins sometimes have language delays compared with their singleton peers, boys more so than girls. Take these generalizations for what they are and focus on your unique children and their abilities.

How can you encourage your twins' early language skills? Narrate experiences to your twins, providing a running dialogue of the day's events, no matter how mundane they may be. "Now we're changing your diaper." "That little dog is barking."

Well before your children utter their first words, they have a growing *receptive* vocabulary of words, meaning they understand what you are saying even if they are not yet talking themselves. You may be mentioning a particular toy to your spouse, and your child may surprise you by crawling over to that toy. You will notice that your twins are starting to imitate words and babble with conversational inflections, as if they are truly saying something. Encourage these early discussions, as they will evolve over time to become the real deal.

Some twins may have an early language delay because of a lack of manpower. Twins simply outnumber a parent 2 to 1, making it logistically difficult to get as much meaningful one-on-one time for talking as a single-born baby would get. The chaos in the daily household routine can make encouraging language development a real challenge. Most days, you're not so concerned with the kids' language skills as you are with trying to make it to bedtime with the house intact.

Twin Tip

How do you handle teaching your babies to talk while life is so crazy? Narrate the events of your daily lives. Your house is hectic—*talk* about it with your twins! "Boy, this room is messy." "Can you believe I haven't showered in 2 days?"

Get as much one-on-one time as possible with each of your twins. Unless you have 4 hands, you can change only one twin's diaper at a time. Diaper changes can be a special opportunity to look into her eyes and talk to her while you change her. Her twin will get his chance when he gets his diaper changed. It's all about capturing those teachable moments.

Studies have shown that some twins may have an early language delay, but most of these kids catch up by 4 or 5 years of age. If you have particular concerns about your twins' language development, talk with your pediatrician to determine if further evaluation or therapy will be needed.

Safety Issues

As your twins become more mobile each day, it becomes more critical to make sure they are constantly supervised. Always monitor your home to make sure the childproofing is as good as it can be, and make adjustments as needed (for further information on "twinproofing," refer to the "Early Infancy and Getting on a Schedule" chapter on page 57). There will always be areas that require protection or modification that you didn't think of, but one of your twins will helpfully demonstrate those to you! It may be a bummer to put away your wine rack for now, but good childproofing will make your life easier in the long run. A well-childproofed home allows your twins more freedom to explore and allows you to avoid redirecting them all day long.

Twin Tip

Remember that the best childproofing in the world does not replace direct supervision. Paper clips or other small choking hazards can unintentionally fall on the ground, ready for inspection by your 10-month-olds. Your twins are little scientist-explorers, making discoveries and charting new territories, but they have little to no sense of what is safe and what is not.

Don't forget the difference between childproofing and twinproofing. Every month your twins are getting smarter, and they will learn as much from their twin's experiences as from their own. They will each try out more things around the house than a singleton because they like to try what their twin just did. Also keep in mind that a pressure-mounted gate which keeps a singleton baby out of a formal room full of breakable knickknacks may not continue to hold against the combined weight of 2 little ones leaning and pushing on it.

Twin Tip

Creatively assess your home to see if you can create a safe designated play area for your growing twins. Safety gates come in a wide assortment and allow parents to contain kids in a particular zone. We did not have a formal living room set up in our home while our kids were young, so it was logical for us to use the space instead as a play area. Parents of singletons can get away with using a portable playpen as a temporary safe zone, but alas, parents of twins need more real estate than a small rectangle!

Now that your twins are becoming increasingly mobile as they crawl with greater speed and are learning to walk, it is nice to maintain some sort of safe zone in which to plop your twins when you cannot keep an eagle eye on them. If you have to run to the bathroom or retrieve something from the hot oven, one of your twins will find a loose button on the carpet at that exact moment and pop it into his mouth for further exploration. To prevent such an ill-timed disaster, keep a large gated play yard set up in some corner of your home.

Several options of gated play yards are commercially available; another option is to gate off a closely inspected and thus safe corner of a room. Your twins may not spend a lot of time playing in the safe zone, but it is good to have the space prepared and ready when you do need it. Keep special baby-safe toys inside, and even rotate toys into the space as needed to keep your twins interested. Inspect the space multiple times a day for surprise choking hazards that may have appeared, such as from a broken toy or an older sibling who brought his Legos nearby.

Discipline: Working Toward Acceptable Behaviors

At this age, your twins do not need discipline in the traditional sense, but you do need to start teaching your twins what is and is not appropriate. It is more difficult to undo bad habits if they have been tolerated even a small number of times in the past. I have used the concept of house rules for our family. Everyone in the house must follow the house rules to stay safe. Instead of saying no repeatedly (which is a great way to teach the word quickly, by the way; you will be hearing it said back to you often if you're not judicious with the use of the word), I try to phrase my instructions beyond a simple "No!" Instead, try, "We don't touch the oven door—it's hot." "Don't pull my hair—it hurts Mommy's head." Another strategy is to tell the child what they *should* do instead of what they *should not* do. Instead of "Stop running!" try "Sit here on my lap."

Twin Tip

Babies' early infractions are usually just the result of early explorers acting on their natural and healthy curiosity, but parents of twins need to draw the line of what is and is not OK. The oven door window is shiny, reflective, and very interesting to an 11-month-old, but even if it is currently off, you don't want your twins thinking it is OK to lean on it and look at it up close. One of these days it *will* be hot, and you may not be right there to intervene.

When your twins engage in inappropriate behavior, intervene *immediately* so that your children connect the action with the consequence. Remove your child from the situation, and redirect your child to a new activity or location. Redirection works well because kids at this age still have a short attention span.

Do not unwittingly encourage behavior that you do not want repeated endlessly in the future. Sometimes parents are caught off guard by a pull to the hair or a bite to the shoulder by a child and in the confusion of the moment, may have even laughed. If you laugh and say how cute it is when your twins pull on your vertical blinds when they are 10 months of age, be prepared for 2 toddlers at 22 months of age to be yanking on them regularly, unless some sort of house rule has been established early on. Be careful to avoid this if you can; your child will think what she has done is funny or somehow good. The child will replicate the action to see if she can get you to laugh again. Biting is not a great habit to encourage. Avert your face if you cannot suppress a laugh, and try to be as consistent in your responses as you can. At times, the word *no* is appropriate, if used selectively and sporadically. In the case of biting, remove the child from your shoulder and firmly say, "No. We do not bite."

Twin Tip

It is easier to encourage good behavior now than to have to undo bad behavior down the line.

Consistency is especially important when you have 2 kids the same age learning the house rules. Two little ones running about can quickly escalate to mayhem without parents actively supervising, intervening, and redirecting. Lessons learned at a young age will carry into the next few years and make your life easier over the long haul.

Twin Tip

Consistency in your response is key. It sounds simple, but it really is not. It is much harder to be consistent when you are fatigued and overworked, running after your twins all day. There will be times when you are tired and do not feel like being on the ball, but these are the days that you have still got to be on your A game and continue to enforce consistent rules.

Your Emotions: How to Stay Sane

The constant supervision of more than one crawling, mobile baby can take a toll on parents. When your babies start crawling and walking, you will need the constant surveillance and vigilance of an air traffic controller—and note that air traffic controller is regarded as one of the most stressful occupations. As with any job or task, to stay fresh, it is important to take breaks. Our theme of *asking for help* comes into play again. Do not consider it a sign of being anything less than a great parent; consider it extremely wise to be able to identify those particularly stressful times when the whole family would benefit from one or both parents getting a break.

Ask your partner for help. Spouses can and should be able to handle the house and all the kids for any stretch of time. Your children's father, for example, is not a babysitter; he is a parent. Do you have relatives or trusted good friends who live nearby? Is there a friendly neighborhood tween looking for "mother's helper" experience before full-fledged babysitting? Investigate all your options for assistance.

What constitutes a break? That is up to you. You could spend an hour with a good book, take a neighborhood run, go to the coffee shop for a couple of hours, spend an evening out with friends, or take an overnight trip—it is up to you.

Twin Tip

Take little and big breaks as needed. If Mommy's not happy, *nobody's* happy!

Asking for help and taking parenting breaks is healthy for you to step back and take a look at how your family is affecting your emotions. Personally, I have experienced a special kind of guilt starting from the time that my twins were born. When I am able to spend some time one-on-one with one boy snuggling, reading a book together, or making pancakes together, there are times I cannot truly enjoy the moment because I already feel guilty that I am not spending this special time with the other guy as well. Sometimes I'll find myself interrupting the special moment to invite the other twin to join us, or I hurry through the moment so I can grab the twin and replicate the moment for him. Of course, interruptions and rushing do not result in meaningful, spontaneous bonding and teaching moments. They just result in one or both twins running off elsewhere while I am left sitting there with the book asking, "Doesn't anyone want to read with Mom?" What have I learned from this? If you've got one of your twins on your lap ready for a story, go ahead and start reading. Over time, there will be plenty of opportunities for the other twin to get his own lap time as well.

Twin Tip

Focus on the *collection of experiences* each twin has over time. The balance will not be perfectly equal, but it should be fair. And each of your twins deserves as much alone time with you as possible. Get over the guilt and enjoy the special time. One-on-one time provides major teachable moments and encourages relationships within your family.

Especially if you are a stay-at-home parent, I'm sure that you have never felt as housebound as you have this year. If you were on bed rest during your pregnancy, it can add to your feelings of being disconnected from the outside world. On a certain level, it may seem easier never to leave the house again! Why would you leave? The milk is in the fridge, the stack of diapers is at the ever-ready changing table, and extra clothes are in the drawers. Packing up your twins for any sort of outing can seem like a lot of hassle. But even if it is just a few times a month, make the effort to take your babies out of the house. It may be as mundane as walking around the mall for 20 minutes, but these experiences will be healthy for you and your twins.

If you are feeling really adventurous, enlist your spouse or another adult to help the family go to a local pool. It may be daunting to plan, prepare, and execute the outing—frankly, it will feel like you are planning a small military operation—but it will be mentally energizing for all involved.

Twin Tales

When our twins were babies, it was always surprising to my husband and me how calm and focused our boys were after even a simple trip to a sandwich shop. Just like for adults, taking twin 11-month-olds out of their usual environment and routine can help them refresh and refocus. They can come back to their familiar play areas and toys with a new perspective and a new appreciation.

Special Time With Each Twin

A child who receives plenty of positive one-on-one time will be less likely to act out in other areas to receive negative attention. Attention, whether positive or negative, is what your twins crave from you. These one-on-one moments of positive interaction are also needed so you can start to recognize the individual and unique traits that each twin has. Even identical twins can have very different ways of looking at the world.

How can a busy family squeeze in one-on-one time with each child? Get creative and look for new ways each week. Every family needs to grocery shop periodically. You can rotate turns each week for special one-on-one shopping trips with a parent. One child gets a fun outing, seeing all the excitement at the store and learning colors and numbers as you select 4 green apples to put in a bag, while the other child gets playtime with the caregiver at home. You won't need to feel guilty about it because the next weekend, it will be the other twin's turn to go. If a relative lives nearby, perhaps he or she can stay home with one twin while you take the other for a walk to talk about things you see in the neighborhood, squeezing in a bit of healthy exercise as well.

The First Birthday

Congratulations! You have survived the first year with your twins! Relish the fact that you've all made it this far. Take a look at your home videos and laugh at how large your pregnant belly was. Smile at your 2 beautiful children who just happened to be born on the same day, and look how far you have all come.

Twin Tales

Danielle, mom to school-aged twins, states, "Even though they share a birthday, we always had separate cakes and sang separately. As my twins get older, they still enjoy getting to pick out their own cake."

If you are going to have a party, make it a small party in the middle of the day. You won't be overwhelmed, the twins won't be overwhelmed, and you can all enjoy the day. Do your children a favor and make sure you bake or purchase 2 birthday cakes, one for each of them. Take photos of each twin alone with her cake, as well as together with both cakes. In our family, we even alternate who gets sung to first each year.

Twin Tip

When the twins are grown, they will appreciate that you treated them as individuals and not as a unit by singing "Happy Birthday" for each of them specifically. Singing twice also sends a message to your family and friends at the party who may have a tendency to refer to your individual children as "the twins."

Year One: An Extraordinary Time That Flies By!

It is a cliché because it is true—these early days of your babies' lives go by very fast! I believe that the time flies even faster than it does with a single-born baby because you are so busy. Of course, you will have days when you think your twins will never sit unsupported, never hold onto a sippy cup and drink by themselves, or never talk. But then you will turn around one day and everything has suddenly changed. They are now running after each other pretending to be puppies, barking loudly, and laughing hysterically.

Keep 2 simple baby books to jot down funny notes and stories. I was too busy to keep perfect baby books, but I did have a system to make frequent updates to each twin's separate book. If one of my twins did something cute, I would jot it down on a note pad. I would pile up my notes and every couple of months, I would rewrite them all at once in the baby books.

Twin Tip

If everything is going wrong, the house is a mess, and your babies are wearing pajamas all day every day, just laugh and enjoy it! Think of all the great stories you will have for family lore. Your children will never remember how clean your house was growing up; they will remember how much fun they had with you.

Invariably, when you take your twins out into the world, people will be interested in your crazy little family. The best encounters for me are from parents who have had twins themselves who are now grown. I remember when an older gentleman spied my husband and me eating lunch in a casual restaurant with our 2-year-old son and 12-month-old twins. He approached us when he and his wife were leaving and told us that they had twins with a closely spaced older brother and they were all grown up now. He paused, gave a sly grin, and said, "It's a lot of fun, isn't it?"

It helps to know that other people have not only survived your situation but also enjoyed it and lived to tell about it. It is easy to feel isolated, especially if you are staying home with your children. The feelings of isolation are normal and will soon be replaced by the hustle and bustle of your twins' toddler and preschool years to come.

CHAPTER 6

The Toddler Years (1- and 2-Year-Olds)

With each passing month and each passing year, life with your twins gets easier and easier. The daytime routine has an increasingly consistent rhythm and flow. Using a fairly dependable schedule, children and parents alike can predict what will happen next. Everyone will get along more harmoniously with a good home schedule because everyone is on the same page. At nighttime, your toddler twins are old enough to sleep through the night consistently and regularly. The more sleep everyone gets at night, Mom and Dad included, the healthier and happier everyone will be.

That being said, life with twins does not become easier in a straightforward manner. On the whole, the day-to-day routine gets easier, but the transitions of the toddler years provide some bumps in the road—discipline and toilet training, for example. Is it easier to care for 15-month-old twins than 3-month-olds? Yes, but 15-month-olds have their own set of matters with which to contend.

Children 1 and 2 years of age have an increasing sense of self; each child is realizing that she is a person separate from her parents and her twin. As your children have a growing sense that they are independent individuals, they will seek to separate themselves from their parents and twin. This independence may sometimes exhibit itself in unpleasant ways.

Twin Tales

Michelle, mom to third-grade twin boys, shares, "What helped most during my sons' toddler years was keeping them on a schedule but also being flexible for changes. The routine, for the most part, stayed the same at bedtime: dinner, bath, and bed. During the day, I had a house to run. I had errands, cleaning, homework with the older kids, activities, etcetera. Then there was the pressure from others to be perfect. Times, schedule, and events would change and I would get so, so frazzled, but then I realized, oh well. I am doing the very best I can, and I started going with the flow. I would be open with people and tell them, 'It is hard for me to get there at this time so I might be late.' Although my intentions were there, I recognized I might not be able to commit. I had that flexibility for my own sanity. I felt as long as I was doing my best, then I needed to not worry about the other stuff."

The toddler years can be exciting and scary for your children. Your role as a parent is to continue to provide the same loving, secure environment as you did in their infancy, while showing them what is appropriate behavior. Your patience, coupled with gentle encouragement, will help guide your toddler twins to mature and grow into well-behaved preschoolers. There will be some challenges during the toddler years, but try not to get too frustrated on the difficult days. Enjoy your children and watch with amazement at how quickly they learn.

Sleep Issues

A child who sleeps well is healthier, gets along with others more easily, and is ready to play and learn. Your twins' nap time is sacred. A regular, consistent sleep schedule keeps your children happy and healthy and can save your sanity. No matter how crazy your days are, there is a predictable chunk of time each day that you know you can work on your to-do list, put away laundry, or take a nap yourself!

Twin Tip

Keep in mind that every family schedule has different needs. When your twins are toddlers, you may need to shift from 2 naps a day to 1 major early afternoon nap a day because of a resistance to the morning nap or to accommodate an older child's needs. Look at your family's schedule to determine the best way to provide your twins with 14 hours of sleep each 24-hour day. Parents who work outside the home may choose to give their kids an early afternoon nap until they are 5 years of age, so the family can have some quality time in the evenings without the kids being overtired.

As your twins grow into toddlers with new interests and abilities, life gets more exciting and the idea of sleep becomes less appealing. Your formerly agreeable "nappers" may suddenly resist the idea of midday slumber. Do not mistake this disinterest as a sign that they don't need naps anymore. On average, 1- and 2-year-olds still require 14 hours of sleep every day in the form of 11 to 12 hours of overnight sleep, as well as 1 or 2 naps a day totaling 2 to 3 hours in length. Every child is different, but some kids may give up naps around 2½ or 3 years of age.

 Twin Tales

Lisa, mom to 9–year-old twin boys, relates, "Be consistent with your twins' sleep. Without good sleep, you have no chance of having a good day. Be consistent with naps, bedtimes, and the routines preceding those."

If your twins are resisting nap time or bedtime, remember that overtired kids may have more difficulty falling asleep than well-rested kids. If your toddler twins are more resistant at nap time, you may want to consider starting nap time earlier to see if they'll go down more easily. Give yourself room to experiment to find out the best solution for your family. If your twins are particularly cranky one week, poor sleep may be the culprit. Try a few days with earlier nap times and bedtimes and see what happens. If the kids are pretty happy with the new schedule, you can be more confident that they're getting enough rest.

If your toddler twins are sleeping well in their cribs, and are not yet climbing out, leave them in their cribs! Some parents celebrate the second birthday with big-kid beds, but I speak from experience when I tell you that big-kid beds will introduce a whole new set of sleep issues. I recommend letting your kids enjoy their cribs as long as possible (as long as they are remaining safely in their cribs), but do be prepared for the big-kid bed transition. You never know when the day that they learn to climb out of their cribs will arrive. When one twin learns how to hop out of the crib, her twin will learn alongside by watching her. If you don't have big-kid beds ready yet and your twins start climbing out of their cribs, a safe, temporary transition is to simply remove the cribs from the room and place the crib mattresses directly on the floor. This will reduce the risk of injuries from falls.

It is in everyone's best interests—the twins, Mom and Dad, and siblings—that a reliable sleep schedule continue as the twins grow older. The benefits extend beyond the twins and parents. For our family, when our twins were 1-year-olds, their nap time was ideal for one-on-one time with our oldest son, who was 3 years of age at the time.

Nap time is also a nice chunk of time to play those board games that toddlers tend to destroy or, at a minimum, mess up the cards and move the players' pieces. Your twins' nap time can be the time to bring out the toys with small parts (to a designated area) that are too difficult to have around when the toddlers of the house are awake. Everyone will become quite adept at cleaning up the choking hazards before the twins wake up from their naps.

Twin Tip

Toddler twins have a way of occupying their parents' complete attention while they are awake; their nap time is a perfect time to give their sibling(s) some much-needed attention.

Transitioning to Big-Kid Beds

Transitioning our twin boys from cribs into big-kid beds was a very challenging time for our family. Even when my twin boys were still infants, I looked ahead and had a great deal of respect for, and fear of, this momentous milestone, having lived through our oldest son's transition. I recalled many a night of our little guy at our bedside at 3:00 am simply because he had the freedom to do so. I was dreading the twins' realization of "I'm free! *We're free!* No crib rails! All-night party!" Or, on the flip side, the twins could be afraid of their new environment; switching to an open bed with no secure, tall rails to keep oneself safe can be scary for a 2-year-old. So whether your twins are elated or terrified that it's 2:00 am and they've found themselves awake in a new bed, chances are they'll do one of these things: have a 2:00 am party in their shared bedroom, examining every nook and cranny of the room, as if they've never laid eyes on their own room before; run to Mom and Dad's bedside repeatedly, crying that they are scared; or a mixture of these. Such shenanigans do not lead to a good night's sleep.

In an ideal world, we would all have homes large enough to give each twin his own bedroom. However, most of us need our twins to share a bedroom for simple reasons of space. And with a shared bedroom comes all the fun of "monkey see, monkey do."

Some families successfully try gimmicks to keep their twins sleeping peacefully all night long in their new big-kid beds. A family we know with triplets (including 2 boys who shared a bedroom) recommended that we get car beds—plastic molded twin-size beds in the shape of a car—for our twin boys. Apparently, their boys were so in love with their car beds that it never occurred to them to climb out of bed in the middle of the night. These car beds sounded so magical that we budgeted the steep price of 2 car beds, thinking that money toward a good night's sleep would be money well spent. To make a long story short, these car beds did not prove to be so magical for my family. We experienced nighttime parties (with draperies being pulled to the floor and night lights being pulled from outlets, the prongs being used to "draw" on the walls), as well as the more straightforward tearful trips to Mom and Dad's bed. This illustrates the point that what works for one family may not work for another family. Because our car beds turned out not to work, we needed to implement some solid strategies to make the transition to big-kid beds smoother for everyone.

How do you make the transition to big-kid beds as smoothly as possible? Be realistic, and remember that no matter how prepared you are and how well you obey the rules of how to keep your kids in their own beds all night, your children are human and there will be some tough nights. Remember that the rough patches are just temporary road bumps, and if you follow the basic sleep rules consistently, your twins will once again be sleeping peacefully each night. Illness, travel, and schedule changes can all affect nighttime sleep; keep this in mind when having a particularly tiresome sleep week (pun intended). This too shall pass and your kids will be on to the next milestone. And in a way, the process of training your toddler twins to stay in their big-kid beds all night is similar to training babies to sleep through the night.

Strategies to Survive

There are some very useful sleep strategies to use during the big-kid bed transition. First of all, when your twins are around 2 years of age and are *not* quite climbing out of their cribs yet, I recommend placing a pressure-mounted gate in their bedroom doorway frame. Placing a gate at the doorway ahead of time will give your children time to get used to the gate's presence while they are still comfortable in their familiar cribs. The gate will become part of the bedroom landscape and will play an important role when the big-kid beds are in place, keeping your twins *in* their bedroom, where they should be sleeping, and preventing them from running around the house, unencumbered, wreaking havoc with no limits. The gate is especially a good idea if you are a heavy sleeper; you might not even hear your twins escape into the kitchen at 4:00 am for a free-for-all.

Twin Tip

A nice idea that may work if your twins share a large bedroom is to put the big-kid beds in the room while the cribs are still there. Have both cribs and both beds in the room at the same time for a couple of days, allowing some time to talk about the change, and you can give each child a choice as to where they want to sleep at night, in the crib or the new bed. Some kids are excited and adventurous and can't wait to try out the new bed. Other kids are a bit more hesitant and want to sleep in their familiar crib a bit longer. Both options are fine. The beauty of this method is that you are giving your twins the power to choose between 2 acceptable choices, and your children will feel empowered and more in control of the situation. At our house, our twin sons shared a small bedroom that did not have the space to use this trick. So instead, we talked about the transition frequently and let the twins check out their older brother's bed. It got to a point where the twins were very ready and excited to use their new beds and felt in control of the situation.

The next step is the selection of the new big-kid bed. Try to involve your twins in the process as much as possible. Discuss the transition often with your children. If there are older kids in the family, point out how the twins can be like their big brother or sister now. Let them explore the older sibling's bed. Look for children's books at your local library about getting a big-kid bed. These steps will help your twins emotionally prepare for the change.

If your big-kid beds don't have built-in sides, you'll need to make sure your kids don't roll out of bed while sleeping. I recommend pushing each bed into a corner of the bedroom and placing a single safety gate on the exposed side. Two gates are much more affordable than 4 safety gates to protect 4 open sides.

Another strategy for a smooth transition to big-kid beds is to keep every other aspect of the nighttime routine the same. Bath time, pajamas, story, bed—whatever your rituals are, keep doing them. Consistent evening rituals will reassure your twins that their entire worlds are not changing, just the bed on which they sleep.

When you tuck your twins into bed, remind them that nighttime is for sleeping. "When it's dark outside, we all sleep. When it's daytime and sunny, that's when we play." Be firm and leave the room. If the twins are not falling asleep or at least being quiet, wait for 10 or 15 minutes, and if necessary, check in on them to get them back in their beds. Don't give in to requests for you to lie with them unless you're prepared to spend the next 5 years sleeping on their bedroom floor. Use the same methods that you used when the twins were 3 months of age: check in on them, be nonchalant and businesslike, tell them to sleep in their beds, and leave the room.

If they have a hard time settling down at night, you may need to start success sticker charts for sleep, one for each twin, to monitor their progress and teach them what to strive for. A night where each child falls asleep quietly earns one sticker on that calendar date. After 5 stickers, for example, the child earns a small prize (your local dollar store is a perfect place to choose such a prize). Start with a low number of stickers to earn a prize so each child has a taste of success, and then raise the bar, increasing the number of stickers to earn a prize as your twins learn acceptable sleep behavior.

If your twins start waking each other and you up in the middle of the night, be businesslike and march them back to their beds as many times as necessary.

Twin Tip

You may be surprised to have just one child waking up a lot, while her sister sleeps peacefully through all the noise. If this happens, be grateful that only one child is awakening, and encourage her to lie quietly in her bed and fall asleep so as not to disturb her sister.

Nighttime awakenings may need to be incorporated into the success sticker charts; each twin earns a sticker for a full night's sleep. I've noticed that when I use success sticker charts with my twin boys, competition sets in and the boys are very eager to do well and earn more stickers. A little friendly competition can be a good thing if it will help everyone sleep through the night again.

Twin Tip

You'll need to evaluate each twin's overall sleep pattern if rough nighttime patterns emerge. Make sure that afternoon naps do not extend past 4:00 pm so as not to interfere with nighttime sleep.

The Need for Naps, or at Least Quiet Time

Later on in the toddler years, when your twins are about to turn 3 years of age and have big-kid beds, it will be a challenge for them to settle down for an early afternoon nap. But if your toddlers are approaching their third birthday and resisting afternoon naps, don't just eliminate naps cold turkey. Transition the early afternoon nap into an hour of enforced quiet time to replace the nap time. Quiet time is an hour where everyone rests quietly, the television is off, and maybe one twin decides to look through a book while the other examines her right foot for a while. Quiet time can happen in the twins' bedroom, Mom and Dad's bedroom, the family room, or whatever location works for you. You can even switch locations as need be. The important thing is for your twins to simply relax and rest before continuing on with the rest of the day.

Twin Tip

A break from a hectic schedule to rest is always a healthy idea, whether you are a child or an adult. If there's a younger baby in your home, coordinate quiet time with the baby's nap time. If there are older kids in the house, have your quiet time the hour before they return home from school or encourage them to have their own quiet time to read or play with toys. An hour of peace and quiet is a precious thing that can assist family harmony.

Each child is an individual, and one twin may still be napping well while the other is clearly finished with daytime naps. In this situation, get creative. Let the napping twin sleep alone in her room so she is not disturbed, and take her twin into your bedroom for an hour of quiet time.

Nutrition and Mealtimes

Feeding toddler twins can be a true adventure! You have 2 unique individuals on your hands. These individuals have different appetites at separate times. Each twin may have various skills when learning how to self-feed, and they may have different taste preferences as well. How do you handle accommodating your unique kids' nutritional needs?

After the first birthday, most healthy children can switch from breast milk or formula to vitamin D whole cow's milk. Your twins should drink whole milk from 12 months until they turn 2 years of age. Whole milk has a higher fat content than 2% or skim, which is important for your twins' still-developing brain and spinal cord. After the second birthday, your twins can drink 2%, 1%, or skim milk.

Whole milk, and all regular cow's milk, is a poor source of iron. Many kids have been known to fill up on milk and have a smaller appetite for nutrient-dense table foods, so keep track of how much milk your toddler twins are drinking each day. Your target amount of milk for each child is 16 to 20 ounces a day (not more than 24 ounces in a day, which would increase the risk of anemia caused by iron deficiency).

Feeding toddler twins is tough enough, so avoid power struggles. If one child is indicating that he is finished with his meal, end his meal. He may say no, shove the spoon away, or throw his sippy cup—these are all signs that you should end his meal. Do not be tempted to keep feeding with tactics such as airplane spoons looking for a runway or a dancing spouse behind your head. Don't worry if his twin is still eating. Trust each of your twins' satiety center, which tells them their tummy is full.

Twin Tip

Just because one of your kids happens to be hungry that day, do not feel the need to force-feed the twin who has a normal appetite. All too often we parents don't feel that we're doing a good job if our kids aren't eating 3 perfect square meals each day, but when you have toddlers, you need to relax. In the long run, you want to avoid recurring battles at mealtimes. Don't stress too much over one individual meal at a time; a meal may not have enough vegetables, for example, but the goal is healthy eating over 2 or 3 days taken as a whole.

Appropriate portion sizes at mealtime can be surprising to parents. A proper meal is a lot smaller than one may think, especially compared with the overly abundant serving sizes at restaurants today. A serving of fruit or vegetables is 1 tablespoon per year of the child's age. A serving of protein (eg, chicken, meats) is about the same size as your child's fist.

Twin Tip

Avoid choking hazards (eg, hot dogs, raw baby carrots, nuts, and whole grapes). Make sure you slice food items lengthwise and into small pieces so they do not block your child's airway if accidentally inhaled.

You may notice that your twins have a smaller appetite as toddlers. Remember that all children at this age start to slow down their rate of growth. The growth rate in the first year of life is astounding, and if the child kept that up for a few more years, he would soon be 9 feet tall! Because the child is not growing quite so quickly, he simply won't have the desire to eat as much as he did a few months earlier.

Enjoy mealtime as a family, even when your twins are toddlers. To simplify life, families sometimes feed young twins dinner earlier in the evening, and the grown-ups eat later. And let's face it, some days can be crazy and you have to do what it takes to survive the week. However, a family meal at least twice a week will show your twins how to enjoy mealtimes and how to socially interact during the experience. Your toddler twins learn a lot by mimicking. It may seem like more work initially, but you'll see that the twins will begin to learn table manners by sitting with their families at mealtimes. Your twins will love spending the special time with you; they find you more fascinating than you would ever imagine.

Serve finger foods to your toddlers, and introduce spoons and forks. Giving your twins more opportunities to self-feed is very challenging in the short run (and gets quite messy), but you'll make your family's life easier in the long run by starting utensil training early. Self-feeding is difficult for some parents to teach their kids, especially if you're a neat person. On a rushed morning, it may seem easier to simply spoon-feed the cereal to your twins. You know that they're getting the nutrition they need, and it's faster, right? But on a less-harried morning, do give your kids a chance to try to scoop that cereal into their own mouths. With practice, they'll soon get there. Imagine how much simpler life will be when they can feed themselves an entire meal. I felt as though my twin boys would never master getting the spoonful of food into their mouths. Not only did they figure it out, but I found them feeding each other on a few occasions!

Twin Tip

Each child's satiety center tells her when her tummy is full of food. Our kids are more aware of how full their stomachs are than we are, and when we allow our kids to *self*-feed, they will truly eat what they need. If they're not eating much, don't sweat it. They'll make up for it at the next meal. If you have persistent worries, check with your pediatrician. A good growth pattern of height, weight, and head circumference can be reassuring.

Are you still concerned that your kids aren't eating well enough? Then ask yourself these questions. Are the twins growing appropriately, as measured at their well-child checkups?

Are they having regular, soft bowel movements, ideally once a day but at least once every 2 to 3 days? Do the kids urinate regularly?

If your twins are peeing well, pooping well, and growing well, trust that they are eating well too. Relax at mealtimes, help your twins learn to feed themselves, and continue to offer a variety of healthy choices for meals and snacks.

Are you concerned that your toddler twins are picky eaters and not eating a proper *variety* of foods? Continue to offer a variety of tastes and textures each day. Model an adventurous palate by eating a healthy variety yourself. Never declare your own finicky food preferences to your kids; if you refuse to eat certain foods, of course your kids will follow suit. You can discuss the issue with your pediatrician. A daily age-appropriate multivitamin may help parents feel better about their twins' nutritional status and relax at mealtimes.

Twin Tip

The home of a family with twins runs more smoothly when everyone has regular bowel habits. It is pretty common for toddlers to experience occasional constipation. Switching to cow's milk and having varied eating patterns (eating like a horse one day, eating like a bird the next) can have its effects on a toddler's bowel movements. Make sure your twins are not drinking too much cow's milk, which could make the constipation worse—no more than 20 ounces a day.

Offer plenty of fresh fruits and vegetables at every opportunity. If you have picky toddlers, keep experimenting until you find a fiber-rich food they love that keeps their bowels moving and their mouths happy. You can try oatmeal or steamed baby carrots, softened and sliced lengthwise, for example. Many kids adore mangoes, a very fiber-rich and nutritious fruit. Fresh apples or pears are great, and for convenience keep canned fruits on hand such as pears, apricots, or peaches. The canned fruits tend to be nice and mushy and easy for a toddler's mouth to handle. When you find a high-fiber food that your twins love, make a mental note of it and use it as your magic bullet when you notice that constipation is starting to set in.

Simplify Mealtime

Parents of toddler twins can simplify life by getting rid of their bib collection. I found that after the first birthday, messy meals never quite landed perfectly on a bib, rendering the bib somewhat useless. A spaghetti dinner with tomato sauce ends up on sleeves, in hair, and on pants. When your twins are learning how to self-feed, you can be sure food won't land on just the bib. Relax during mealtimes and don't fret if the kids are getting messy. Keep an extra stash of clothes near the kitchen for a quick change, if yogurt happens to find its way all over your kids' sleeves or dumped in their laps. When an enormous stash of bibs is given away, there is a drawer now free and available to store something new.

Another mealtime change that makes life easier for parents of twins is changing infant high chairs to booster seats. Most kids around 2 years of age are ready to sit still for a meal and are balanced enough to not fall out of their chair. Every child is an individual, however, and if one or both of your twins tend to run away from the dinner table immediately, or doesn't have the best sense of balance, then hold onto those high chairs a bit longer. Our family used wonderful toddler feeding seats that are placed on regular dining chairs. They are slip-proof, made of a comfortable foam material, do not have complicated straps, are pretty straightforward for a child to climb into and out of, and are easy to wipe clean (or stick in the sink for a deeper cleaning). An added bonus to switching to boosters: they are more streamlined and will reduce the visual clutter in your dining area.

Twin Tip

When you're feeding toddler twins day in, day out, remember to relax and keep your poker face on. If your kids see that they can get a rise out of you, whether it's a positive or negative reaction, they'll try again to get that reaction.

Twins: A Shared Bond, Yet Each Is a Distinctive Individual

Talk to any grown twin and ask about their experiences growing up and you will most commonly hear that efforts made to raise each child as an individual were appreciated. Even when multiples are at the young age of toddlerhood, parents are wise to be aware of avoiding the tendency to parent their multiples as a group.

Twin Tip

Do you have twin boys or twin girls? Help extended family and friends identify who is who. Dress your twins in distinctive clothing and teach them how to introduce themselves. "Hi, I'm Ryan." Your toddler twins, still quite young, probably don't realize that others can confuse them with one another. Helping each of your twins tell others who they are will minimize others' tendency to regard your twins as a unit and encourage the understanding that they are 2 separate individuals.

Yes, in the early months of raising more than one child at the same age, it certainly simplifies the daily routine to coordinate feeding and sleeping as much as possible. As your children grow into toddlers, however, each child is developing his or her unique personality and identity. Smaller steps and habits adopted now grow with the children, and early efforts to treat each child as an individual now will reap rewards over the years to come.

Twin Tales

Dani grew up as an identical twin and is now mom to twin girls in preschool. When asked what she appreciated about how her parents raised her, she responded, "Raising us to live our own separate, adult lives. I was asked at a twins club meeting (as a parent), 'Didn't you have great self-confidence since you were always with your sister?' My answer to that is if you're always with someone else, what happens when you're not with them anymore? Parents need to realize that just as they are raising their kids to be self-sufficient without parents, they also need to be self-sufficient without their twin."

The Importance of Positive One-on-one Time

A child's toddler years are particularly interesting because it is the period that she is evolving into an actual person. Sure, different infants have different temperaments and personalities, but after the first birthday your twins are truly becoming little people. They're not just feeding and burping machines anymore! Spending quality one-on-one time with each twin every day is important during this critical stage.

How is it possible to have daily quality time with each child if you have perhaps other children in your family? It is ideal for you to spend quality time with each of your children each day, whether they are a twin or singleton. There are different strategies for squeezing in quality special time depending on the situation.

If it is the weekend and your partner is home, take one of your twins with you to the grocery store or on errands. Her twin can have special time with her other parent at home. Grocery shopping is something that must be accomplished each week. Multitask and combine the necessary errand with special time with your child. While you're at the store together, point out the colors of the apples you are choosing. Count out loud as you put each apple in a bag. Buying apples may seem mundane to you, but to a 21-month-old who usually has to share her mom with her twin, who rarely gets mom all to herself, buying apples can be a real blast!

On days when Mom and Dad are home, you don't even need to leave the house to get individual special time with your kids. One parent can take one twin out to the yard while the other parent reads with the twin's sibling. One twin can play upstairs with Mom while the other twin colors downstairs with Dad. Make it a natural part of your household routine to occasionally separate the twins. Remind yourself to not simply think of your twins as a unit that cannot be split up.

Twin Tip

If you have to buy stamps at the post office, visit the bank, or even fill up at the gas station, bring just one of your twins with you. Ignore your cell phone and simply *be* with your child. Your child will find the trip fascinating; at this age, children do not need a theme park or a toy store to get excited.

If you are a single parent or your partner works extended hours, be sure to ask grandparents, family, and friends for assistance. See if Grandma can stay with one twin for an hour while you take his twin out. Think creatively and you'll find ways to squeeze in more quality time. Whether your twins are split up between Mom and Dad or Mom and Aunt Jen, each child will get a chunk of time to feel special and have an adult all to herself. Everyone wins!

Twin Tip

When we create special one-on-one time with each of our twins, these are the moments that we hoped to experience when we decided to become parents in the first place. These moments are what parenthood is all about! You're not just feeding and changing diapers, you're *communicating* with your child in a meaningful way. With a busy house full of kids, sometimes we lose sight of that, and we need to remember to figure out what makes each kid tick. When you afford yourself the luxury of being in the company of just one of your kids alone, you have the pleasure of getting to know just who this little person is.

Some stressful days, to be honest, all I wanted to do was escape *alone* to the grocery store, just to think clearly and get a break from the house routine and demands. And definitely, if you feel the need to run an errand *by yourself* for the sake of preserving your sanity, you should. But it may surprise you to see how easy it is to take just *one* child with you to a store! Living with twins each day, you take for granted how hard you're working raising 2 or more kids. If you take just one child on an outing, you'll think to yourself, "Wow, only one kid to take care of!" The special time not only benefits your child, it benefits you as a parent as well. You'll have special moments with your twin that will show you who your child is becoming.

How can you squeeze in one-on-one time during a busy day when you don't have the help of a second adult to care for the other twin? Look for opportunities throughout the day, and take advantage of them. Is one of your 24-month-old twins occupying himself by looking through a picture book? Drop what you're doing and quietly join the other twin and work on a puzzle together for a few moments. Let the laundry sit there—it will still be there later! Any chunk of time spent together meaningfully is beneficial. If the twin interrupts 3 minutes into the puzzle project, it's no big deal. In terms of balance between the twins' special time, you can steal a moment of quality time with the other twin later on.

Obviously you'll want a balance; make sure you're spreading the special time as evenly as possible between your twins. But remember that your twins will never have *exactly* the same amount of one-on-one time with you. It's impossible, and that's OK! You're aiming to be *fair*, but you can never make their experiences perfectly equal. If you notice that one twin has been acting out more frequently, try increasing your positive one-on-one time with him. You'll see an improvement in his behavior as a result.

 Twin Tales

Sue, mom to third-grade twins, advises, "Enjoy every snuggle—it goes quickly!"

Kind but Effective Discipline

Good discipline starts with good communication. When you want to communicate well with someone, whether it is your child, your spouse, a coworker, or a boss, you should look the person in the eyes to convey that you are listening. Eye contact and engagement go a long way to ensure that the person you are speaking with feels validated in what he or she is trying to say. Above all, each of your twins wants you to be engaged with her.

Twin Tip

If you are squeezing in at least 15 minutes of one-on-one time a day with each child, you are doing well. Many refer to this special time as *time-in* (to differentiate it from a time-out). Providing each twin with plenty of time-in will earn you better behavior from your children in the long run. Kids who feel respected, loved, and listened to will not be so desperate for attention that they misbehave. Sprinkle lots of positivity on each of your twins each day, specific to who each child is as an individual, and your twins will feel more emotionally secure and behave better.

Parents of twins have the challenge of 2 young kids at the same age, often pulling a parent in multiple different directions. Additional distractions such as smartphones, television, and tablets do not help matters. Even though it can be hectic with twins and siblings in your home, give your best effort each day to minimize distractions, put away the phone, turn off the TV, and truly listen to each child during pleasant interactions. Each of your twins will have a deeper connection to you, and when the time comes that the child does something she should not, your response as a parent illustrates a clear difference between appropriate and inappropriate behavior. Good communication is the backbone of effective discipline.

Twin Tip

When we discuss proper methods to discipline toddler twins, we need to define what discipline really means. Discipline does not mean the same thing as punishment. When I refer to proper discipline, I am referring to an overall household framework where good behavior is rewarded and unacceptable behavior has appropriate consequences. Discipline takes into consideration lots of positive quality time with your child and then dictates that poor behavior eliminates any kind of attention.

Acceptable Choices and Listening

Give your children plenty of opportunities each day to make acceptable choices. "Would you like the orange cup or the blue cup?" "Would you like the butterfly shirt or the one with the hearts on it?" Help your twins feel empowered in daily interactions by letting them select between 2 acceptable alternatives.

Above all, your toddlers want to be heard. They want to know that you love them and respect them as individuals. When your 20-month-old twins start shrieking for their sippy cups, you should calmly ask them, "What do you need? Do you want your cup? Can you ask nicely please?" You may not feel patient enough every day to have this conversation, but if you remain calm your children will follow suit.

Twin Tip

If you feel your blood pressure rising with your toddler twins' demands, use some tricks to keep your cool. Imagine that you have an audience in the room with you, watching you interact with your twins, and you'll find yourself saying the right things even though you didn't think you could. Or, you can pretend that your twins are from another country and you're slowly introducing them to your language. These ideas may sound a bit silly, but it is key that you keep your cool and remain calm when disciplining your twins, even if you need to use a gimmick to do so.

Make the effort to coach your toddler twins to use their words and language instead of more barbaric behaviors. Even at this early age, if you give your child milk each time he cries for it, you are essentially teaching him to yell every time he wants milk. Start coaching him now to calm down and express himself politely. These behaviors are not magically learned at 4 years of age; it takes gentle encouragement at earlier stages from parents and caregivers.

Encourage good behavior when your twins are toddlers rather than waiting and having more poor behavior to fix later. In the case of toddler twins, you are coaching 2 kids how to be civilized at the same time—a lot of work, but you will reap the rewards in the long run. If you are reaching your limit (and who isn't reaching their limit when dealing with 2 sweet but at times emotional toddlers?), take a moment, catch your breath, and react as consistently as you can. You won't be the perfect parent every day, but if you can do the right thing 80% of the time you're doing pretty well.

Twin Tip

Parents of twins, listen up! Communication and relationships are a 2-way street. Just as you expect your kids to listen to and respect your house rules, you need to give your kids the courtesy of listening to and respecting them as well. To develop trust, avoid making empty promises. As an example, if you promise your child a trip to the playground after visiting the library, make sure you follow through on your promise. If you are consistent and your kids trust you, and they know you will do what you said you would do, your children will be calmer and more patient on the whole.

If for some reason you are unable to follow through, address what your child says to you and acknowledge his feelings. "You're upset, aren't you? Do you wish we were going to the playground? I'm sorry we don't have time for that today; we need to go home and have lunch now." If one child is getting hysterical about something, his twin may pick up on the madness and escalate the situation. When both twins start to lose their cool, calmly call a meeting to order. Get down to your twins' eye level. Talk in a low, calm voice. Use every fiber in your being to not lose *your* cool! "We do not yell in our house. Please use your words. Dad said that it is bath time, and that means we are going to take our baths now." And most importantly, follow through.

Temper Tantrums

If one or both of your twins truly start to melt down into a temper tantrum, you need to ignore the hysterics. Just make sure that your child is safe and won't hurt himself or anyone else during the tantrum, and let him scream. You don't want to reward a tantrum with bribes, pleading, or any kind of attention—unless you would like to have more tantrums in your house on a daily basis, that is.

Consistency Is Key

Be consistent with your house rules every day, even on days when you're exhausted. I think that this is the most challenging aspect of good discipline. Sure, we all know to be consistent and have the same expectations of our kids' behavior each day, but in the real world, when the twins were up all night with colds and you are about to pass out from fatigue, guess what? You've still got to be on your A game when it comes to parenting. Whether you're having a great day or a bad day, you still need to be consistent with your house rules so that your toddler twins learn that the rules exist no matter what day of the week it is.

I like using the term *house rule* with my kids because it removes the individuals from the rule. A house rule is simply the way the world works. Rules are not about what you want or what your twins want; the rules are just the way it is. When my parents babysit our kids, they appreciate the idea of house rules, as grandparents tend to not like to be the bad guy. They can avoid taking any blame in their grandchildren's eyes by saying, "We don't bang on the window—that's a house rule!"

Twin Tip

Your twins may test you when family and friends come for a visit, or when you go to a party, to see if your reaction will be the same. Don't slack on the rules just because you are socializing. Toddlers are very smart and if you let your guard down on a house rule just once or twice, they will remember it like an elephant and challenge you on it repeatedly.

Time-outs

Once your children are around 2 years of age, they are starting to sense what is right or wrong. You and your spouse should discuss privately what should be considered behavior that will not be tolerated (eg, hitting or biting). Both parents and caregivers need to be on the same page when it comes to proper discipline. If one of the twins hits the other, for example, declare a time-out immediately, without delay. You need to connect the offense with the punishment for your child. The offending twin should go to a boring part of the room with no toys (we used a plain corner) or sit at the bottom of the staircase, alone, for 1 minute for each year of age. If your twin tries to escape time-out, silently march her right back. The whole idea of time-out is to remove all fun and attention.

Twin Tip

Disciplining toddlers can be very frustrating. Remind yourself that this is a difficult stage and you will get past it! Often your twins may refuse to stay in their designated time-out location. Your toddler twins may really fight you on going to time-out, but if you are consistent with your rules, you will see improvement over time. Hang in there!

Avoid the urge to yell, however mad you may truly be. Attention is attention, even if it is unpleasant and negative. Twins, as compared to single-born kids, especially crave their parent's attention, and they may actually enjoy being yelled at (on a certain level, as odd as that sounds) because they've got their parent's complete attention all to themselves. So remember, time-outs are effective only if they are used properly, meaning removing all fun and attention. When the time-out is up (an egg timer is handy to count the time), calmly get down to your child's eye level and explain why she got the time-out. Hug and move on with the day.

If a highly desirable new toy or object is causing repeated fighting, you have 2 options. Option 1: get an egg timer and give each child a 4-minute turn with the item, and then alternate turns for each twin (adjust the timing as necessary). If the fighting is really bad, use option 2: give the toy itself a time-out. Your twins need to learn that if they can't share and play nicely with something, *no one* gets to play with it. Hide it well and try again the next day if the twins are better behaved. With consistency, your kids will learn how to play nicely, for the most part. Our kids were so used to this routine that over the years we've had quite a few birthdays and Christmases where presents were opened and one of the kids ran for the egg timer to ensure fair turns.

Twin Tip

What do you do when *both* twins have violated house rules? What do you do when both twins are hitting each other in a fight over a new truck toy? Try not to ask, "Who started it?" If you ask who started it, it will teach your toddlers how to start blaming each other. And does it really matter who started it when they are now both hitting? They *both* need a time-out away from each other. Plan out 2 areas ahead of time for just this occasion. The last thing you need at this point is a fight over who gets which time-out location. How can you keep 2 kids in 2 different time-out spots? Is there a hallway in your home where you can create a confined area with a temporary pressure-mounted gate? Brainstorm to see if you can create 2 safe zones for time-out sessions.

Essentially, your toddler twins are like scientists in a real-life laboratory. They perform behavioral experiments by acting differently in certain situations. They observe your reaction to their behavior and any resulting consequences, and then they register the information in their data files. If you consistently give positive attention for good behavior and remove all fun and attention for bad behavior, your twins' data files will help them make the right decisions down the line. You will have to live through a frustrating couple of years of continued research so they can verify their findings, but if you and your partner provide a consistent framework of discipline, your scientists will emerge from toddlerhood with better manners for it.

I must warn you about self-fulfilling prophecies. If you expect a certain kind of behavior from your twins, you are likely to get it. I have often heard parents say, "Oh well, boys will be boys," for example, letting their sons get away with more than they should. Along those same lines, there seems to be a preconceived idea of twins as being mischievous (sayings such as "double trouble" come to mind). But you need to be aware of what your mind-set is. If you simply throw up your hands and say, "Oh well, they're twins, I guess they're supposed to give me a hard time," you may end up slacking on their daily discipline. Make sure you expect the best behavior out of both of them, as if they were each single-born children. If you are inconsistent, you'll end up with twins who are hard to handle. If you have high expectations for your twins and are consistent with them, you will be rewarded.

Encouraging Language Development

Toddlers improve their language skills by directly talking with the people in their world, as well as by observing other people speak with one another. The most beneficial thing you can do as a parent to get your twins talking is to simply speak with each of them—a lot! Narrate your lives together. "Here comes the shampoo. Let's scrub your head! Rinse with water. The water is warm and wet!" Surround your children with words to help them learn how to use the words.

Many people believe in a secret twin language that only your pair of twins understands. *Idioglossia* or *cryptophasia* are both terms used to describe "twin talk," or a secret twin language shared only between the pair. Personally, I feel that there isn't a secret language so much as one twin will say a word the wrong way, his twin will understand what he meant to say, and the two of them will continue to reuse the wrong pronunciation of the word. For example, "milk" is spoken "moak," and soon enough both twins are calling it "moak." If this happens, be supportive of your twins' attempts to talk, and repeat the correct word. "You would like miiilk? OK, I'll pour you more miiilk." Place emphasis on the correct pronunciation. Avoid saying negative things to the effect of, "No, that's not how you say it," inadvertently shaming your toddlers from attempting to say new words. Just keep repeating the correct words until your twins catch on.

Twin Tip

In the early talking years, some parents find mispronounced words or brand-new, made-up words to be incredibly sweet and adorable. These early words are cute; make sure you record the invented words in each twin's respective baby book and laugh about it at night with your partner when the twins are sleeping. But in the presence of your twins, repeat the *correct, real* word back with exaggerated enunciation to help them learn. Don't perpetuate repetition of incorrect words, even if they're really funny.

On the whole, twins' language development can take a bit longer compared with that of their single-born peers, simply because they are usually sharing the same caregivers. You can't have a one-on-one conversation with each twin at the same time. Just do your best and the twins will catch up. Usually by 4 or 5 years of age, twins are talking as clearly as their peers. If you have specific concerns about one or both twins, check with your pediatrician. Don't be surprised if just one of your kids needs a language boost with some speech therapy.

 Twin Tales

Sue, mom to school-aged twins, advises, "Take notice of any developmental delays to ensure proper treatment; my son had delayed speech due to hearing issues."

Toilet Training: Is It Possible?

Imagine, if you dare, a new world in which you're not changing diapers all day long…. In this magical new land, you don't have to stock up on diapers every time you leave the house! Do you dare to dream?

Believe it or not, it will happen. Your twins will indeed wear underwear one day, and they'll keep their underwear clean and dry! When will this happen? The timing of toilet training is up to your kids, ultimately, with Mom and Dad's encouragement and involvement. Toileting success may not happen as early as it did for your neighbor's kid, and it may not happen by the time your niece was wearing underwear, but don't worry—it will happen. The age of a child when toilet trained has no bearing on that child's future intelligence or status in the world. Early toilet-trained kids don't all attend Harvard; they were trained early because they had exceptional personal interest in the potty, had highly motivated and available parents willing and able to intensely train them, or a mix of the two.

And that's the key, isn't it? We're not just talking about training 1 child, but 2. You can do it! Toilet training doesn't happen overnight. Let's back up a bit and discuss the ages and stages that are involved.

📖 Twin Tales

Sheri, mom to twins in preschool, shares, "I wish I would have known a little more about potty training during the toddler stage. That was the hardest part of parenting by far! They're in preschool now and things have calmed down a little."

When and Where Do We Start?

Start talking about the toileting process with your twins when they are around 18 months of age—nothing intense, just the definition of terms (eg, *pee, poop, potty, flush*) and introduction of the topic. When one of your twins poops in his diaper, use it as an opportunity to talk about potty training. If you see him straining to poop, say, "It looks like you're pooping in your diaper! Good job!" This way he'll learn the word for what it is he is doing.

Twin Tip

Always be positive and upbeat about the toileting process. Toileting is a normal and natural phenomenon—everyone poops, after all, just as Taro Gomi's well-known children's book is titled. Resist the urge to wrinkle your nose at even the stinkiest of diapers. It is important for your twins to know that pooping is healthy and normal.

Even if you are self-conscious, I recommend an open-door policy when it comes to using the bathroom in the privacy of your own home. When you need to visit the bathroom yourself, let your twins see what happens. How will they learn if they've never seen anyone else do it? Older siblings (if they don't mind) are also useful in this regard. So much can be learned by mimicking others. Anyway, when you have toddler twins in your house, you're being followed around all day as it is, so let them learn what that big mysterious toilet is there for.

You can step toilet training up a bit when your twins are around 24 months of age. Certainly, if your twins are very eager to learn, showing the signs of readiness, and perhaps trying to be more like their older sibling, you can intensify the process sooner. Just be prepared to back off a bit if one or both of your twins are showing signs of resistance. Any power struggles will only lengthen the overall process and will really test your stamina. But around 24 months, most kids are showing signs of true readiness, including walking well to a potty, positioning themselves on the potty properly without losing balance, speaking well enough to use the proper terms, and having stronger bladder and bowel control (so as to hold it to run to the potty in time). Are your twins' diapers still dry after 2 or 3 hours? That's a good sign of toilet-training readiness.

Helpful Gear

Invest in 2 potty chairs or in 1 potty chair and a ring to place on the adult toilet seat. These could also be borrowed to save some money; ask your family and friends if they can give you their old ones. A good slip-proof step stool will help too. I had hoped that my twin boys would be eager to sit on a ring on the real toilet, as their big brother did, reducing cleanup work for me. Unfortunately, they were afraid to sit so high up; they preferred to be lower to the ground. So we had 2 identical potties (to avoid bickering over who got which seat) and kept them handy wherever we were spending time. In the daytime we were mostly downstairs, so we placed the 2 potties in our main hallway (great for decorating, let me tell you), as we didn't have enough room in the bathroom for both potties. Always having a potty nearby is not so glamorous, but this is a short-lived stage, and it does help your toddlers remember them and find them easily if they get the urge to pee. We'd bring the 2 potties with us upstairs in the evening so they were close at hand when giving baths and getting ready for bed.

Twin Tip

Stock up on children's books about using the potty by buying them or borrowing them from others or the local library. Reading plenty of these potty books will help ingrain the idea in your twins' heads and promote the whole idea. I liked to refer to it as potty "brainwashing."

Schedule Potty Time Into Your Day

Start scheduling potty time once a day—a chunk of time each day when the twins sit on their potties to practice, regardless of any result. Choose a quiet time that works for your schedule so that everyone is relaxed. Make potty time fun. Read books together, sing songs, and heap on the positive attention. If you like and are able, you can give each twin her own potty time so that she gets your full attention. The kids can initially sit on the potty chair with their clothes still on so that they get used to the idea, but soon they can take their diapers off. You're aiming for 5 or 10 minutes of pleasant practice time together. If your twins want to keep sitting longer, great, and if they run off after a couple of minutes, that's OK too. We're not looking for actual results right now; the idea of potty time is to learn that sitting on the potty is a regular part of the day and something we do every day.

Don't force the potty time or engage in a power struggle over it. If one or both twins defiantly do not want to sit on their potty chair, back off and try again another day or experiment with another time such as before the afternoon nap. You'll eventually work your way up to holding potty time 2 times a day.

Is one twin clearly more interested in the potty than the other? Many parents of twins prefer to train their kids one at a time. This seems to work well particularly for boy-girl twins, as girls seem to be interested in toilet training earlier than boys, on average.

Depending on your comfort level and the degree of success you're seeing at potty time, you can make a big production of selecting some big-kid underwear at the store. Now you can start having underwear time each day, starting with a couple of hours' worth and increasing from there. In our house, we had our underwear time every afternoon starting from post afternoon nap to bath time before bed. Every hour of underwear time, check in with each twin to ask if he needs to use the potty, "to keep your underwear clean and dry."

Motivational Tools

Success sticker charts, or potty charts, work really well for toilet training and help kids feel special. You can buy 2 big, blank poster boards at the store. Have each twin choose a distinct color, and hang the posters in a central location of your home where everyone can see them clearly.

Make a big production of writing each twin's name at the top of each poster, and draw a row of small squares at the top. Start small and make this first row only 3 squares long. Each square will get filled with a sticker (1 sticker for peeing on the potty; 2 stickers for pooping on the potty—small reward sticker collections are easily found at discount stores) and when the row of squares is filled with stickers, the child can choose a small prize. The first row should be short so that your child can have an early taste of success, and the following rows can have progressively more squares to raise the bar.

Twin Tip

Our sons' potty charts were taped to the side of our kitchen island. Displayed potty charts are not going to be the next great idea in the world of kitchen design, but potty training is a temporary situation, and our boys could watch their progress unfold at eye level in a central location in our home, encouraging them toward more success.

Some families use candy rewards during the toilet training process; however, as a pediatrician, I warn against this. Food rewards, even if given with good intentions, can unfortunately send an unhealthy message to your kids by fostering an attitude about treats that can contribute to weight problems in the future. The potty charts may require a bit more effort than just handing out candy, but the beauty of the potty chart is that your kids can visualize all their success and see how far they've come. The charts can be a real confidence builder. See what works for your family.

Accidents will happen. Expect them and be prepared for them so you are not caught off guard. Keep extra-absorbent cloths handy to help clean up accidents; burp cloths from the infancy days are great for this purpose. Have extra wet wipes handy. When accidents happen, do your best to keep your cool; remain calm and have your child "help" you clean up the accident in an age-appropriate way by giving her an extra cloth to wipe the floor. Teach your twins to put their dirty pants in a bin in the laundry area *themselves,* and where to get clean pants *themselves.* You want each child to understand how much easier and simpler it is to simply pee and poop in the potty. We kept a shelf nearby stocked with burp cloths, extra underwear, and extra pants just to make cleaning up after the inevitable accidents easier to handle.

Twin Tip

Expect setbacks, and don't be discouraged by them. Illness, changes in the daily schedule, travel, a new baby—all can cause a temporary regression in toilet training. If your toddler twins have issues withholding painful poops and progressive constipation, consult with your pediatrician. Continue to be upbeat and positive, and your twins will recover. When you're really worried, just remember, they won't be attending high school in diapers. I promise!

Toilet training is truly complete when each child makes it to the potty in time with *no* reminders from a parent or caregiver. When you're seeing that your kids are doing well, try to back off on the reminders, so that they can learn to remind themselves.

 ## Twin Tales

There are plumbing secrets every parent of twins should know. Toilet training twins is quite a task, and parents will take any help they can get. When I was training my identical twin boys, I purchased some wipes from the store. The box was clearly labeled "flushable" wipes. Anything that simplified the process of helping 2 little ones learn the language of the toilet seemed like a good idea to me.

Not coincidentally, 2 months into the toilet training process some unwelcome events occurred in our home. During the washing machine's spin cycle, water began gurgling in a shower drain. The gurgling quickly turned into overflowing in the direction water is not meant to go. Long story short: those flushable wipes had collected and clogged up the main sewer line exiting the house.

As the plumber worked on the expensive repairs, he recommended not flushing anything other than toilet paper and #1/#2 (to phrase it politely)—not even Kleenex. When I asked specifically about flushable wipes, he said there is no such thing, even if the box is labeled as such. If used, they should be thrown in the trash. A friend experienced a similar situation; her plumber joked that flushable wipes kept him in business! We compared notes and figured it was time to spread the word to others with young children, especially those who are toilet training twins. Here's hoping this story keeps your pipes clear and spares you unnecessary plumbing repairs.

Safety Issues

Continually reevaluate the childproofing in your home. Watch out for choking hazards that may have found their way into your twins' play areas. Your twins may be older now, but they may still decide to explore a small, unknown item by putting it in their mouths.

As your twins grow bigger, their style of play changes. They are faster and stronger than when they were 13-month-olds. Two or more children chasing each other can get into more accidents than just one child playing alone. Are there hazards in your home that you didn't even realize were a problem? If a part of your home comes to your attention as unsafe, correct it before someone gets injured. When our twin boys were toddlers, they both fell on separate occasions, hitting the very same wall corner in a high-traffic hallway. Ryan tripped into it, turning his forehead into one big bruised egg, and several months later Andrew ran into it playing in an exciting game of hide-and-seek, splitting his upper lip. The day after Andrew received his stitches, I purchased long foam cushions, which were made to childproof coffee tables, and taped them onto the wall corners in our high-traffic hallway. The padded-corner look may not appear in home decorating magazines anytime soon, but we rested a little easier knowing that lightning wouldn't strike at that spot a third time.

Twin Tip

Playing outside in the yard can be very stressful for parents of toddler twins. The minute you go outside, one runs in one direction and the other runs in the opposite direction. Brainstorm different ways to enjoy the outdoors safely with your twins. Our backyard deck had openings to the beckoning yard, yet I wanted the option to have family meals outdoors. Our solution was to install child safety gates to block off the deck openings. The gates weren't aesthetically pleasing, but they were worth it to enjoy family dinners outside without worrying about 2 toddlers trying to escape. We ended up eating outdoors quite often with the luxury of the gates because cleanup of crumbs and spills was much easier.

Now that your twins are walking toddlers, you'll be spending more time outdoors. Teach your twins basic outdoor rules such as staying with a parent and not running into the street. A fenced-in yard is wonderful for containing your active toddler twins; if a fence is not an option, monitor your twins' locations diligently. Don't get a false sense of security when other adults are present. Always make sure that both toddlers are being monitored when spending time outside.

Twin Tip

When you whip up a quick meal or tasty snack, are you bombarded by your 2-year-old twins begging, "I help you?" A while back I posted an item on my blog about kitchen safety and was asked by a reader if I had more tricks to share about incorporating a crowd of little kids in the kitchen. My advice? Take advantage of your kids' helpful instincts! By simply cooking together, your children can learn healthy eating habits, life skills, family traditions, and much more all at the same time—a true "high yield" activity. Looking at recipes and measuring ingredients boosts early reading and math skills in a very fun, hands-on way with edible results. Do you have picky eaters? Kids who play a role in the cooking process are more likely to try new foods.

Both toddlers in the kitchen brings up safety issues. As with all ages and stages, no magical childproofing gadget or gizmo can replace direct supervision. Parents need to keep a vigilant watch over toddlers when cooking. Mom and Dad can teach kitchen safety skills in an age-appropriate way. I usually kept my instructions clear and simple and defined certain tasks as "a grown-up job" (slicing onions, peeling pears) or "a kid job" (measuring or adding sugar, sprinkling cheese). As your children grow and develop, they'll be able to add on to their repertoire of cooking tasks. From the outset, establish clear boundaries with hot stoves, sharp knives, and other dangerous aspects of the kitchen. Over time with consistent parental guidance, your kids will learn the basics of staying safe while cooking and you'll be able to shift more attention toward the dish at hand. Some lessons will be accidental but memorable nonetheless. A couple years ago I gave myself a minor cut (requiring only a bandage) when slicing vegetables. One of my twins witnessed the event and for the next couple years, if I happened to pick up any tool that had a remotely sharp edge to it (scissors, knives, even a stapler), he would remind me, "Be careful with that, Mom!" In addition to kitchen safety, teach good hygiene by reminding your kids to wash their hands with soap and water before handling food and to sneeze in their cough pocket (crook of their elbow), not into the salad bowl.

What is the safest way to help your toddlers or preschoolers work at a standard counter height? Typical step stools are usually not high enough, but pushing dining room chairs into the cooking area can be both cumbersome and dangerous; wiggly little feet in socks standing on a chair can easily slip and fall. Since our twins have older and younger siblings very close in age, we invested in a sturdy and stable stepstool made specifically for 2 children to use at once. It had a rail around all 4 sides, was nearly impossible to tip over, allowed step height to be adjusted as our kids grew, and could even double as a puppet theater if curtains were added. I used to store ours in a closet, lugging it out each day, and then realized life would be easier if we simply kept it out and available in the corner of the kitchen. It was a bit of an eyesore, but we've consciously prioritized our children's development over aesthetic appearances. (Search for "The Learning Tower" on the internet to see some examples. Many vendors now carry it at different price points, so shop carefully if you choose to make this investment.) When you have twins, it is worth the cost of a couple meals out in a restaurant (and is healthier) to have the ability to safely cook with your children at home over the years.

Family Relationships: A New Baby?

Whether you plan it or not, another baby (or 2) may show up in the family, and it could be sooner than you think. Another baby in the house can be a challenge when your twins are mere toddlers themselves! Our twins were 28 months of age when our fourth child was born—quite an adventure. I remember the hardest aspect of those initial months was trying to nurse our baby. The boys figured that when Mommy sat down to nurse the baby, they had the next 15 minutes to explore and wreak havoc—or so they thought. I had to get really creative to crack down on the madness so that I could continue to nurse our baby girl. Have interesting activities for your toddler twins hidden away and pull them out at critical times when you're busy with the baby. You can use special crayons, a new DVD, or a special rotating toy basket that is only brought out during baby's feeding time, to be quickly stored away again when nursing is complete so it doesn't lose its appeal.

Although those early months were difficult, our twin boys were encouraged to mature with their baby sister's birth; her presence in our family has helped them "grow up." Our twins are no longer the babies of the family; they are proud to show their sister how big kids do things. So if you find yourself pregnant again when your twins are still young, there are a lot of positives that will result from the new family dynamic.

Keeping a Twin-Friendly Budget: Save Time and Money

When your twins are in the younger age groups, borrow as many clothes for them from family and friends as you can, and shop your local Parents of Multiples club resales for gently used clothing. Let everyone know that you gladly accept hand-me-down clothes. Don't worry if some items have small stains; save those pieces for home play days or as a change of pants during toilet training. Toddlers grow so fast that the borrowed items will soon be outgrown, and you'll be so glad you saved the money.

Shoes are an exception to the hand-me-down wardrobe. Every kid's feet are different (even identical twins) and every kid's walking pattern is slightly different, so brand-new shoes are preferable for molding to the feet and being shaped by walking patterns. Personally, I have made it a point to ask family and friends for their kids' old clothes, and the money that I saved by not buying new pants and shirts was diverted into buying new shoes. We have found some trusty, comfortable, reliable sneaker brands that are our standby day-to-day shoes; add a slightly dressier shoe and you're pretty much set for any occasion. When at home, barefoot is best, but proper footwear is needed to venture outside.

Twin Tip

Try to buy your twins distinctive pairs of shoes; that way, each pair clearly belongs to a specific twin, and there is no squabbling over whose shoes are whose when rushing out the door. Using color themes for each child can extend to other items as well, such as drinking cups, to quickly identify whose cup is whose.

Your kids' shoes fit properly if there's a finger's breadth distance from the tip of the toes to the tip of the insole. When the kids' feet grow, we use our favorite Internet shoe store that has free shipping and free return shipping. We can confidently order the same brand and style of shoe, selecting a half size up, maybe getting new colors to be interesting. Because we know the shoe brand well I am confident that the new shoe will fit. I spend mere minutes ordering online, and a couple of days later the new shoes arrive on the doorstep. I find Internet shopping much easier on our lifestyle than schlepping toddler twins to various shoe stores, looking for something you like, and hoping that the store will have the size you need in stock.

Internet shopping can be a real lifesaver. Many companies offer free shipping if you pay over a certain amount or will mail out special promotions for free shipping for a limited time. Be on the lookout for these offers. Try entering your favorite store's name with "coupon code" into your Internet search engine to track down online shopping deals. You are too busy with 2 or more kids to be out shopping at brick-and-mortar stores.

Twin Tip

Figure out which Internet shopping sites have good deals on shipping. Save time, effort, and gas money, and spend an afternoon having fun instead of shopping. Take a neighborhood walk or hold a block-stacking competition! If you can streamline the mundane, routine, and yet necessary tasks such as shoe shopping for ever-growing feet, you can create more free time to enjoy your family.

Having Fun

All children love to listen to music and dance. Music is such a great tension reliever for kids *and* parents, and it's a great alternative to flipping on the television. Dance parties are an enjoyable way for toddler twins to let off energy and steam. Make sure you clear the floor of toys beforehand, as the dancing may get pretty wild! Excellent new kids' music that is family friendly *and* fun for adults to listen to is more popular these days than ever. I highly recommend 'They Might Be Giants' albums specifically for kids, such as *Here Come the ABC's*.

Twin Tip

Want to really have some fun with your toddler twins? Teach them "freeze dance," the classic game where everyone must freeze like a statue when the music is paused. I guarantee a good time!

It doesn't even have to be kids' music per se; early Beatles albums are pretty kid friendly, for example. Make sure the music you listen to is fun for you *all*. Your twins will notice when you really like a certain song and will enjoy hearing you sing along, even if you are tone deaf. Keep a stash of CDs in your car, or stock up the iPod for use with Bluetooth to listen to good music while running errands and driving on longer car trips.

A word about the cleanliness of your home: don't worry about a messy house. Within reason, just let it go and play with your kids. Just make sure the floor isn't so cluttered that everyone's tripping everywhere! Your kids will not remember how clean the house was; they'll only remember the times that Mom played fort with them using couch cushions or when Dad played garbage truck with them by compacting them with throw pillows. Soon enough the kids will grow older and you can clean the house as much as you want. Reserve power clutter-busting sessions for the evenings when the kids are in bed, so that the floor actually stays clear for a while, and you and your spouse can feel like normal people again, if just for a couple of hours.

 Twin Tales

Danielle, mom to school-aged twins, advises, "Enjoy the fact that your children have a built-in playmate."

CHAPTER 7

The Preschool Years (3- and 4-Year-Olds)

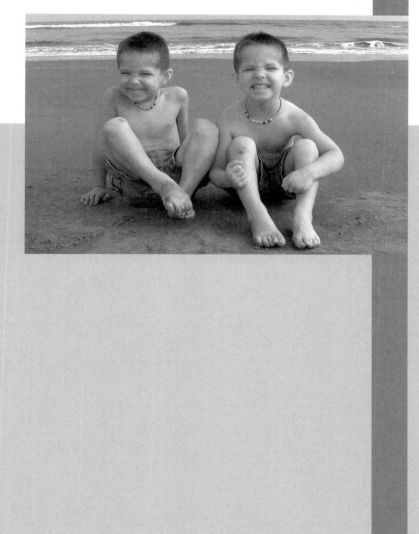

"Mommy, can you come to my restaurant?" "Daddy, would you read this book to me?" All of a sudden, your twin babies have grown into 2 wonderful people who can speak clearly and play cooperatively with one another as well as others. The preschool years with twins are truly magical, as 3- and 4-year-olds burst with imagination. Not so long ago, your home was filled with constant feedings and frequent diaper changes. Now your home is a place where the couch is a train and a cardboard box is an airplane that you can fly to the grocery store to buy a loaf of bread.

 Twin Tales

Back in those hazy days when our twins were teeny, I never imagined that one day I'd hear this at our breakfast table:

Andrew: Knock-Knock.
Ryan: Who's there?
Andrew: Rain.
Ryan: Rain who?
Andrew: Reindeer!
Both: Ha, ha, ha, ha! (in that crazy way that only twins sharing a joke can replicate)

Shared twin laughter is among the most beautiful things one can hear.

Relish these years and revel in playing like a child with your twins. Your preschool-aged children want nothing more than a parent sitting on the floor with them, following along in a make-believe scenario that they are creating as you go along. Be a customer in one child's restaurant and order a banana split with extra ketchup on top. Help your other child play garbage truck by collecting assorted toys and dumping them at a pretend garbage dump. Playtime serves a greater purpose than just fun; it is through imaginative play that 3- and 4-year-olds make sense of the world around them.

The possibilities of imaginative scenarios are limitless with 2 kids at the same creative age. You have 2 inventive minds bouncing ideas off each other. And conveniently, you have multiple actors to play out different roles—store cashier and shopper, pilot and copilot, or waiter and customer, for example.

Your twins are most likely wonderful playmates much of the time. However, do not expect your twins to play wonderfully with one another all the time, every day. Could you imagine being with the same person *all the time*? Two individuals with 2 minds of their own will have differing opinions from time to time. Disagreements between your twins are inevitable.

Is there a way to prevent inter-twin arguments from happening? Not in entirety, but there *is* a way to reduce the number of disagreements in your home. Giving each child his own personal space is one way to prolong the peace in your home. If you respect the individual opinions and personal space of your children, each will feel more self-assured, secure, and content. In this way, you can prevent some arguments from even starting.

Parents of preschool-aged twins notice that life is much easier than it was a couple of years earlier because twins can be such great playmates. However, keep in mind that your twins won't want to play together all the time, despite the convenience of such an arrangement for you as a parent. Each child needs her own distinct relationships with other siblings, relatives, and friends—all part of healthy and normal child development. These relationships help each child build her sense of identity and self-esteem. You'll notice different patterns emerging as, for example, one twin buddies up with an older sibling frequently one month, while the next month, the other twin takes great interest in a neighborhood friend. As a parent of twins, encourage these budding outside relationships. Your children will always have a unique and special twin bond, but early experiences with others will help socialize each twin as she embarks on her school years. Such socialization is great for adjusting to a classroom setting. Much of the focus of the early school years is simply getting along with others and listening to instructions. Your twins will be well prepared for school simply by socializing with the world around them.

Twin Tip

For the first couple of years, you synchronized your infant twins' schedules to make life more manageable. Now, at the preschool stage of the game, parenting twins is less about daily survival and more about nurturing who each child is as an individual. Celebrate these wondrous preschool years with your twins.

Sleep Issues

On average, 3- and 4-year-olds should be sleeping a total of 12 hours in a 24-hour period. Your twins may have given up their naps or, if bedtime is later or they've woken up early, they may take a quick 1- to 2-hour early afternoon nap. Expect a few months' time of an in-between phase. Some days your twins may need the nap, and other days quiet time will suffice. As discussed previously in the toddler chapter, encourage an hour of quiet time in the early afternoon (see page 111 for more information on quiet time). A restful break from the day's activities will help your twins be energized for the remainder of the day. Be flexible and creative with naps. One twin may like to keep napping, while his twin doesn't need to. Allow one twin to nap in the shared bedroom while you read quietly with the other twin in your bedroom, for example.

Twin Tip

After the third birthday, you may notice that your twins nap well, yet resist bedtime. Experiment with your family's schedule to improve bedtime cooperation. You may decide to transition your 3-year-olds' naps into quiet time to ensure that they fall asleep easily at a consistent bedtime. However, if one or both parents work outside the home, you may need to continue afternoon naps until your twins are 5 years of age to prevent them from being overtired at later bedtimes.

If your twins share a bedroom, one twin may wake the other twin too early in the morning. Encourage both twins to stay in bed if the sun hasn't come up yet. "When it's dark out, we sleep, and when it's light out, we can play." Teach your twins what to do in different situations; they're old enough now to understand what you expect of them. For example, teach them that if one wakes up and it's light outside but the other is still sleeping, the twin who is awake should quietly tiptoe out of the room so as not to disturb the other. You'll likely have several mornings where one twin is bright eyed and bushy tailed, while her twin is still yawning with heavy eyelids. If you don't all have to leave the house that morning, encourage the sleepy twin to go back to bed, making a teaching point for the awake twin so they can learn for the next time.

A great way to help ensure a good night's sleep is to make sure your twins get plenty of activity and exercise during the daytime. Your preschoolers are naturally filled with energy! Getting lots of motion in during the day will help the twins be more restful at night. Playgrounds help kids exercise their large muscle groups by climbing and balancing. Neighborhood and nature walks, with short bursts of running sprinkled throughout, get kids' legs moving. Get your twins practicing on tricycles, and advance to 12-inch bikes with training wheels once they're a bit taller. Don't forget the bike helmets! Make learning new physical activities fun. Simply running around the yard can provide great physical activity; you can play catch or monkey in the middle.

Twin Tip

Keep your twins active each day to promote better quality nighttime sleep. Aim for at least 30 minutes a day of cumulative physical activity. The exercise still counts if it is done in smaller bursts scattered throughout the day.

In wintertime or during bad weather, you'll need to get creative to find ways to get your twins' bodies moving and hearts pumping. Clear out your play area for a safe game of catch with a softball, or play hide-and-seek. Our family cleared the space in our unfinished basement, cushioned wall corners and sharp edges, and kept the boys' bikes there all winter. Many afternoons we'd head downstairs so the boys could strap on their bike helmets and have a ball riding their bikes around while it was freezing cold outside. See what fun ideas you can come up with to squeeze in daily physical activity to help your twins sleep more solidly at night.

Socialization: The Twins' Role Within the Family

Your 3-year-old twins are eager to learn about the world around them. When kids have a strong sense of their role within a family, self-esteem gets a boost and they more easily navigate through their lives, at all ages. How can a 3-year-old feel like part of a family? Enlist their help around the house. Taking care of the home is not just a parent's job; it is *every* family member's responsibility, and you can exercise the philosophy starting at a young age.

Preschool-aged kids *love* to help with housework. Give your twins dust cloths to clean off tabletops while you vacuum. Sorting laundry? Make a pile of the twins' underwear and have one child put the clean underwear back in the proper drawer (teach your kids where everything goes). The other child can pair socks together to put in the sock drawer. Coaching your kids to perform simple housework tasks may seem like more work initially, but the rewards are worth the effort. Your twins will learn quickly, and soon you will see that they *really* are helping. Besides, daily mundane house chores are more fun when tackled as a team.

Twin Tip

Discount stores have nice-looking nonbreakable dinnerware (Melamine as one example, usually intended for outdoor entertaining). Have a set on hand, and your twins can help set the table each night without fear of broken dishes. See page 178 for an age-appropriate chore chart.

When your twins help with household chores, the job doesn't have to be performed perfectly. Applaud each child's *effort,* not the outcome. Chores help each twin feel like a contributing member of the family, which will go a long way to boosting his self-esteem. The bonus for you? A 3-year-old who is accustomed to helping around the house will grow into an older child who helps around the house. Expect each child to help at a young age so that it becomes a natural part of everyone's routine. Eight-year-olds won't magically start tidying up their bedrooms on their own without having had some prior experience.

The most important job your twins can help with is keeping the toy clutter under control. Multiple young children in one single home can quickly result in a crowded floor of random toys. Coach them to put away toys when they are finished playing with them. Big baskets and totes can simplify the process (eg, cars in one basket, trains in another, and stuffed animals in a third).

Twin Tip

Borrow an organization strategy from preschool teachers: take digital pictures of each toy group and print them. Tape the pictures to storage bins so that nonreaders can check the picture to see what goes where.

We're not looking for perfect organization from 3-year-olds. We're simply sending the message that when you're done playing with something, you should pick up after yourself. Make cleanup fun; set an egg timer for

3 minutes and have a speed cleanup race to see how much can be put away before the timer goes off. Once everyone gets in the habit of helping clean up, it becomes part of the daily routine.

Twin Tip

Organization in your twins' closet can streamline your morning routine. Choosing one's own clothes to wear each day will help your twins feel like they have some control over their daily lives. Organize your twins' clothing into groups of play clothes or nicer clothes. Depending on the day's activities, you can instruct your twins to dress themselves in play clothes, for example, if you are all headed to a neighborhood playground. Your children get a sense of ownership by having a choice, and they are still dressed appropriately for the occasion.

Your twins will learn to interact with the outside world by getting lots of practice at home interacting with family members. Age-appropriate board or card games are a great way to teach social skills while getting in some good family bonding time. Your twins will learn to take turns and have fun whether they win or lose. They may have a hard time sitting still for longer stretches. If one runs off after only one turn, that's OK. Just continue the game with the other child as long as the players remaining are still having fun. If the first twin decides to come back, simply have him pick up where he left off. Full disclosure: when playing board games with my kids at this age, I rarely fully followed the included instructions, and that is OK. If no one wants to play anymore, no sweat. Pack up the game and try again another day. Expecting 3-year-olds to sit perfectly still through an entire board game is unrealistic. Over time and with practice, you will see that your young twins will be able to sit for longer stretches, they will be more cooperative during the game, and the games will be more meaningful for them (ie, there is more to it than just moving a red game piece around in a random circle). If one child wants to play a game with an older sibling, great! Encourage your twins to split up when they feel like it.

Preparing for Preschool

The idea of your children spending a couple of hours in a classroom setting away from their parents, siblings, and possibly each other can be quite a change for everyone involved. If your twins have spent time in a child care setting, the transition may not be as dramatic as for those who have been cared for at home or in a smaller group setting. Our generation may or may not have attended preschool back when we were young. Today, however, education experts agree that the experience of a preschool program can help kids learn more effectively when kindergarten comes along. We're talking about a fun, relaxed preschool atmosphere, not any sort of rigorous academic curriculum. In preschool, 3-year-olds usually participate 2 or 3 half days a week, while 4-year-olds can participate 3 or 4 half days a week.

Preschool registration happens at different times depending on where you live. In general for most areas, looking at preschool options a year before you plan on enrolling your twins is a good idea. Busy urban settings can be more competitive, and infants on preschool waiting lists are not uncommon in larger cities. Check with your local park district for good options and talk with your neighbors who have older kids to see if they liked their private preschool. If your children were born prematurely or needed early intervention therapy services (eg, speech) prior to 3 years of age, they may qualify for preschool through your local school district; contact your local public school district to get specifics on requirements for qualification.

In the months leading up to preschool, you'll want to provide your twins with some practice for the experience. Look around your community for options. Public libraries usually offer a story hour or craft sessions for each young age group. These story hours are a great way for your twins to practice sitting quietly in a group while listening to a story. The fact that these programs are usually free is a bonus. Your twins will learn some social etiquette by being in a room of 3-year-olds. Multiples may be accustomed to close physical contact with each another, but they'll need to learn they can't be quite so cozy with others around them.

Twin Tales

Once upon a time, I took our twin boys, recently turned 3 years of age, to a library story hour. After about 5 minutes, both boys started wandering around the room instead of sitting quietly to listen. I gathered them together in the back of the room and told them, just one time, "Let's try to sit and listen. If you can't sit and listen, we'll have to leave so we don't disturb the other kids." That day, the boys just weren't interested. I wanted them to appreciate these sorts of experiences and have positive associations with them, not to remember their mom nagging them for 30 minutes. So I simply gathered the boys up and we left. No sense in forcing the issue—this is supposed to be *fun* for the kids. Just try again another day. Keep exposing your twins to the idea of library story hour and similar experiences, and they'll learn to appreciate them.

Another way to get your twins ready for preschool is to visit your area's public and school playgrounds after school hours. Get to know a variety of parks around your home to keep the trips interesting. Your kids will have fun on different types of equipment and feel quite comfortable at their preschool playground when the time comes. Your twins will also gain a little experience meeting and playing with other kids at the playground.

Look into your local park district youth offerings and recreational youth sports. Always ask if they offer a twins discount! Soccer is a great gender-neutral choice that boy-girl twins would enjoy. Park districts often offer a 3-year-old "class," specifically for a parent to drop the child off so that the child gets used to the idea of being on his own for a bit. To ease the transition, if your twins are in the same class, they can provide some comfort for each other when their parent leaves. At these types of classes, my twin boys were so excited to see new toys to play with that they didn't mind at all that Mom was leaving for a while. I had tears myself, though, the first couple of times and didn't know if I felt better or worse that the boys weren't crying at these good-byes. With a little practice getting out there with your twins, you'll all be ready to make the leap to 2 mornings a week of preschool quite smoothly.

Twin Tip

When your twins attend preschool, they will bring home mountains of adorable craft projects and paintings. The artwork and drawings of 2 students can quickly accumulate and overwhelm a home. How can you preserve the highlights of your kids' projects while minimizing clutter? Take digital photos of each child *individually* holding his or her artistic creation(s). You'll have documentation of the art and what your child looked like when she created the art, without taking up physical space on a shelf. Your twins will beam with pride when showing off their creation. After taking a digital picture, you can even hang the artwork in an art gallery on your twins' bedroom wall by using blue painter's tape. The tape can be rearranged multiple times without damaging painted walls or woodwork. An art gallery of preschool projects is a great way to boost your twins' self-esteem and encourage future projects. If the projects get crumpled or thrown out, no worries, because you've saved the projects with your digital camera.

Many parents of twins wonder if they should keep them in the same classroom for preschool or separate them into different classrooms. If your preschool is a small program, you may have no choice because all the

3-year-olds may be together in a single class. If there are 2 separate class-rooms, you'll have to decide for your family on the best strategy. Remember that this decision is not final; every year you can reassess your family's situation to determine what classroom placement will work best for your twins for that specific, new school year.

Twin Tales

Sue, mom to third-grade twins, advises, "It is okay to separate twins into 2 classrooms; they will still feel connected. Also, don't worry if they are progressing at different stages."

For our family's situation, our decision for class placement was pretty straightforward. We felt that our identical twin sons looked so similar that the teachers and other students would be confused all year long as to who each twin was. We didn't want our sons to hear the question, "Which one are you?" all year long. I wanted to de-emphasize the boys' "twinness" and give the boys a chance to show others who they are as a person, as an individual. I also felt that 2 mornings a week of being in 2 separate classrooms wouldn't be that big of a deal, considering the boys are together the other 5 days a week, 24 hours a day. In addition, I felt that after some practice with separate preschool classrooms, the transition into separate classrooms in the higher grades should be a little easier.

Twin Tip

If your twins are in 2 separate classrooms in school, prepare in advance for special school days such as Meet the Teacher Day. Arrange for both parents to attend or have Grandma or another trusted adult help on the special day. Let the teachers know your situation in advance and that you plan on spending time in both classrooms to see both kids and both environments. If only one parent can attend, explain the situation to the teachers so they can fill you in on important information that you may have missed while moving between the 2 classes.

The issue of twin placement in classrooms is currently a big issue, as many families feel that their kids would do better in school if their twins were in the same classroom. These families argue that they, not the school, should make the final decision of class placement. New legislation has been popping up in various states giving families the final say in whether twins are placed together or separately. Each family must assess its own situation and decide what will work best for their particular situation. Some families find that keeping twins together in the early years helps smooth the way for eventual separation in the higher grades.

Twin Tales

Michelle, mom to identical boys in third-grade, recalls, "I recommend flexibility and using your best judgment. I had so much pressure to separate my boys, so I did, but they were not ready and melted down. We kept them together until third grade, at which time we felt they were ready to separate. They are now doing great! Each boy has different likes and needs, and I accommodate them as 2 individual people."

Parents can observe the classroom dynamic, meet classmates, get to know the teacher better, make their child feel special, and help out the school all in the matter of a couple of hours by volunteering in their children's classroom(s). Preschools usually love parents' hands-on involvement in the classroom, and kids get a real ego-boost to show off their class and parent to each other. My kids' school experiences were somewhat of a mystery to me until I spent some time assisting in the classroom. After you spend a little time with the class, you'll be able to ask each child specific questions about friends or workstations because you've seen the class in action firsthand. Even if you work outside the home, I recommend arranging for a morning off from work to spend an hour or so with the class. If your twins are in 2 separate classrooms, be sure to post your volunteer dates prominently on the family calendar, and talk about the timing with the kids to prevent any jealousy or concerns about fairness.

One-on-one Time: Still Very Important

Continue to carve out as much one-on-one time as you can with each of your twins during their preschool years. Recognizing and stealing moments for special time throughout a regular day is a good strategy. Read with one twin while the other is playing with airplanes, for example. Continue to take just one child alone on outings with you when another parent or adult can help out.

We've taken one-on-one time to a new level in our family with special airplane trips with Mom. We have extended family scattered around the country and have found airfare for 2 family members much more affordable than for the whole family of 6. We can reduce traveling costs, visit faraway family, and squeeze in special time with each child, all at once. We rotate these trips through the birth order to be fair to all 4 of our kids. These special trips are such a treat for our kids, and I always come away from each experience with a new appreciation for who each of my children are as individuals.

Two Distinct Individuals, Now More Than Ever

Whenever I meet someone who happened to grow up as a twin, I always ask if there was anything he would have preferred his parents to have done differently. Most of the time the response I hear is some variation on a similar theme: I wish our parents didn't…"give us the same thing for our birthday," "dress us in identical outfits," "expect us to share everything."

While some people assume all twins are the same, others take it to the other extreme. Many people ask me if my twin sons are opposites: Is one social while the other is a recluse? Is one more talkative and the other quiet? Or, my favorite, "Which is the good one?" These questions imply that each twin's character traits are defined as the opposite of those of his twin brother. Of course this is not the case; they are individuals, and each child is complete on his own.

 Twin Tales

Amber, mom to fifth-grade twin girls, advises, "Don't compare your children. They are individuals and will socialize and learn at their own pace."

Any individual can be similar to another in some respects and different in other ways. Everybody, whether born as a twin or not, desires to be treated as an individual. Parents of all twins, identical or same-sex twins more so, need to think about this on a daily basis. You're a busy parent and it may be quicker or more efficient at times to treat your twins as a unit, but I encourage you to treat your twins as siblings who happen to have been born on the same day.

A great way to encourage individuality is to read their bedtime stories to them separately at night. When our twin boys were babies and toddlers, we were operating in survival mode, so we usually read to them simultaneously. As the years progressed and our twins were easier to care for, we saw that it would benefit both boys to have their bedtime stories read to them one-on-one. Reading to each twin separately boosts early reading skills and creates a calmer atmosphere in which to quiet down and settle in with a good book. The time and work to read to your twins individually is well worth the effort. The twins don't distract each other and they get a lot more out of the experience. Try to alternate which twin reads with which parent each night. Be realistic, though, and on late nights or if one parent is handling bedtime solo, gather everyone to snuggle up for the bedtime stories.

Twin Tip

My identical twins didn't quite realize that they were different from other kids until their preschool years. All of a sudden they realized that not everyone else has an identical-looking brother the same age! Whenever someone would ask one of my twins, "Which one are you?" he would look at them with bemused disbelief. If your twins are the same sex, dress them in different clothing to help friends and classmates know who is who. If your twins look a great deal alike, *talk* about it with them. They are so used to life with a twin that they may not realize that others can't tell them apart. You can even role-play social situations; teach your twins to introduce themselves clearly, and teach each child how to politely correct someone who has guessed his identity incorrectly.

Multiples know how to share well, having shared their parents with each other since they were newborns, but expecting them to share *all* their things *all* the time is unrealistic. You'll want to have a system to give each child her own personal space. Even if your twins share a bedroom, you can provide each one with a distinctly colored box, or even their own shelving unit (safely strapped to the wall to prevent falls, of course), that they can keep their special things in—a rock collection, a favor from a friend's party, whatever they decide is important to them.

Twin Tales

Bonnie, an adult identical twin, states, "While I appreciate everything my parents did for me while I was growing up, there are several things that I would do differently if I had twins or I would suggest to those that have twins. Growing up, my mom dressed my sister and me the same until about seventh grade. Looking back, I kind of wish she would have let us dress in our own style. We were in the same class in school until we were in high school. Unfortunately, we went to a small school so there wasn't a choice, but this led us to have the same friends again until high school."

Remind each twin to respect their siblings' personal space—older and younger siblings' space as well, as twins can outnumber an older brother and confiscate a special toy by sheer manpower alone. Give each twin her own distinct-looking piggy bank to collect loose coins. Institute a house rule that you can only check your own piggy bank's contents.

In your living and play areas, create separate play stations so that there are interesting things to do at different places in the home. One twin can play Lincoln Logs in one area, while the other goes in another room to listen to a kids' CD player. Don't expect your twins to play with the same items all the time. Give each child some space and breathing room and your days will be more harmonious.

On birthdays and holidays, give each child distinctive presents. At 3 and 4 years of age, each child has particular interests. Pick up on these differences and use them as inspiration for giving separate gifts. Adult twins groan when they remember all the times they received 2 of the same item, maybe in different colors. When our twins were 3 years of age, we noticed that sharks fascinated Ryan and Andrew was interested in fire trucks, so on their birthday we ran with these themes. The shark-themed books and toys lived on as Ryan's, and Andrew's new fire truck was Andrew's. Emphasize to gift-giving family members to look for distinctive gifts for your twins; they'll likely appreciate a little coaching.

If your twins are identical or of the same sex, it is inevitable that friends and family will occasionally be stumped—who is who?

Every week at my identical twin sons' preschool, a friend or teacher would mistake each boy for his twin brother. Such confusion becomes a part of life, a routine, and each twin gets plenty of practice reminding people who they are.

There is one special day each year, however, that twins should not have to repeatedly remind others of who they are—their birthday. When my twins turned 5 we threw a big party inviting friends and classmates from both boys' classrooms. I wanted to minimize any confusion over each twin's identity. I found a great online store that lets you customize T-shirts any way you choose. Each boy wore distinctly colored T-shirts at the birthday celebration with their name printed on the front and back, as well as "It's My Birthday!" on the front (I added that because I figured classmates' parents would not necessarily know who the birthday kid[s] were).

All toys that enter your home will eventually get shared extensively; after all, playing with all the cumulative toys, rather than just your own portion, is more fun. But initially, on gift-giving occasions, give each child at least a day or so with his new toy before he is expected to share with others. After the first couple of days or a period that seems appropriate, the new items can become part of the public domain, fair game for all.

If your twins are squabbling over who gets to play with a new item, use the egg timer trick. Give each child a timed turn with the toy, and rotate turns. The egg timer helps reassure your twins that the turns will be fair.

Twin Tales

Danielle, mom to school-aged twin boys, advises, "Accept that they will develop different interests. Accept that they have different needs—one child requires more sleep, one child eats more, etcetera."

Another way to emphasize each twin's individuality is to assign a signature color to each child. At the preschool age kids usually have preferred colors; use these colors for clothes, coats, toothbrushes, and backpacks to clearly indicate who the owner is and streamline the process of getting ready each day. The more distinct the twins' personal items are, the less confusion as to whose coat is whose will occur. Ah, family harmony.

Expanding Social Circles: Party Invitations

For several years our boys were in 2 separate classes in school, and usually a classmate would invite just the boy who was in the same class to his birthday party—this is a *good* thing. Attending a friend's party without one's twin is a great learning opportunity.

Starting as early as the preschool years, social experiences independent of one's twin will help each child gain confidence as an individual. My twins are identical, and often in social situations where both boys are present, a lot of time is spent answering the question, "Which one are you?" I have observed that when one boy has a chance to play with friends on his own, more time is spent in meaningful interaction rather than clarifying his identity.

If one of your twins tends to be shy without the nearby presence of her twin, the experience can be especially beneficial to her emotional maturity. Preschool parties are usually just a couple of hours, anyway—a brief and fun way to practice being on one's own.

I have heard of instances when only one twin is invited to a party and the parents ask if they can bring along the other twin as well. I recommend against this practice. Yes, it requires more effort to arrange for trustworthy child care for your other kid(s), but it is well worth the effort for your invited child to have the party experience solo.

Are you concerned that your other twin will get jealous? Kids are resilient, and the experiences will even out over time. Matter-of-factly explain, "Today it is John's turn to go to a party. Soon it will be Joseph's turn." Kids follow their parents' emotional cues; if you are calm and matter-of-fact about the situation, your children will be as well. Plus, a little planning will provide the non-partying twin with special time as well (such as a trip to a playground)—a win-win situation for everybody.

Consistency and Discipline

By the time your twins are 3 and 4 years of age, they should have a clear understanding of what the house rules are and a sense of what is appropriate behavior. Hopefully you've been able to lay down a consistent framework of rules in the twins' toddler years on which you can continue to build. High expectations of your twins' behavior from an early age have a lot of benefits. Instead of having to undo a year's worth of poor behavior, you are providing positive reinforcement for appropriate behavior.

While more mature than toddlers, 3- and 4-year-olds are still growing and learning and will continue to test limits and rules. The testing of limits is age-appropriate behavior and not a deliberate attempt on your twins' part to drive you insane! Your kids will test you in different situations to see if the rules still hold water. Your twins are also meeting new friends at school and recreation programs who behave in different ways, and they will wonder if they can try out some of those new behaviors at home with you. As parents, you need to hold strong and stick to the house rules.

If your child disobeys a rule, don't just give endless warnings with no consequences; give a *time-out*. Remember that a proper time-out takes place in a boring location for 1 minute for each year of the child's age (ie, 3 or 4 minutes for preschoolers). (For more on discipline, read the toddler chapter, specifically the discipline section on page 119.) When time is up, tell your child in 1 or 2 sentences what she did wrong, have her apologize to the appropriate person if the situation calls for it, and move on with your day. Don't dwell on the misbehavior or give it undue attention; you don't want to reward poor behavior with extra attention.

Twin Tip

Your twins are smart. As an example, let's say one of your twins throws a bouncy ball in the kitchen. You warn your child, "No balls in the kitchen. Take that out of here or Dad will take the ball." If the other twin heard this conversation and proceeds to throw her own ball in the kitchen, you should follow up with taking the ball away, even if it was the second twin who misbehaved. Why? You do not need to give each of your twins separate warnings about the same issue when they are both present for the original warning. Let your twins know, "When I say something to one of you, I am saying it to both of you." If you use this consistent pattern to deal with twins' misbehavior, you'll save a lot of time and energy down the line by preventing your kids from experimenting to find different parental responses.

Balancing the Family Dynamic

You may notice a new phenomenon in your home now that your twins are preschool aged—teaming up against other siblings or friends. By this age they have a tight bond with each other and consider each other teammates of sorts. Be aware that your twins may, perhaps unwittingly, gang up on others. Nip this sort of behavior in the bud. Explain to your twins that you expect them to be kind to and share with *all* of their siblings, not just their twin.

Preschool-aged twins may preferentially share things with each other, yet instantly become territorial if their older brother or younger sister shows interest—the tight twin bond illustrating itself once again. Monitor these situations to make sure the single-born siblings aren't getting railroaded or just passively allowing certain situations to keep the peace. This is a form of bullying and it shouldn't be tolerated.

Don't forget, as discussed in the Kind But Effective Discipline section in the toddler chapter on page 119, you should never ask, "Who started it?" A fight takes 2 kids and if you ask who started it, your twins will learn to manipulate your reactions. You want them to learn how to settle their differences on their own, without an ever-present parent mediator, not how to pin the blame on the other guy.

Expectations on Outings

As your twins grow older, you're probably going on more family outings to area museums, zoos, and the like. New situations run more smoothly if you remind your twins what you expect of their behavior *beforehand*. When you get to the zoo, before everyone unbuckles to get out of the car, take a moment to talk with the kids about what you expect. Remind them, "The zoo can be a busy place and there are lots of cool things to see, but everyone has to *stay together as a group*. Don't just run off if you see the giraffe! Tell Dad you want to see the giraffes and we'll all go together." Exercise good crowd control by reminding your twins beforehand, when everything is calm, before any such moment occurs. Your kids will be reminded to use their self-control and you won't lose them in a crowd of strangers. Give your kids lots of practice and they'll learn with repeated outings.

Anticipatory talks before new situations can help the kids remember how to behave. These talks are a kind and gentle way to lay out expectations that you can draw upon if someone behaves poorly. If you're all going to have to wait in line at the post office, remind your twins beforehand that you expect them to stand quietly with you and not run around loudly. If you are going to a friend's house for lunch, remind everyone of proper behavior before you get out of the car.

When my 4 kids were quite young, I took them to museums and zoos by myself numerous times. I suppose I wasn't truly by myself—I had my 4 kids with me! We've had some great adventures, the kids learned a lot, and the trips boosted my confidence as a parent. I always received comments from other parents, though, who were apparently shocked that my kids weren't running away from me. I've heard, "I don't know how you do it alone; I couldn't because my kid's a runner," many times.

Twin Tip

How can you keep your kids together as a group during an outing? Again, before getting out of the car, remind everyone of the rule of staying as a group. Then, during the outing, if one of your kids does run off she should temporarily lose the privilege of walking independently "like a big kid." She should hold your hand or hold onto the stroller (if you're using one for a younger sibling) for the next 10 minutes, and if she is well behaved, she can earn back the privilege of walking with the group.

If one or more of the kids are not getting the message and are repeatedly running off, you'll have to cut the outing short, explaining to your kid(s) that because they can't follow the rules, they cannot stay and have fun. Cutting a zoo trip short if someone's misbehaving is unpleasant, but letting your kids know that behaving properly and staying with the group is more important.

When Twins Collide

Twins are extremely close, yet when they fight, look out! Twins' fights can be more extreme and emotional than fights between other siblings precisely because they are so close; feelings are hurt more deeply when a stronger connection exists.

How can you reduce the amount of infighting between your multiples? Look for frequent trouble spots and figure out solutions. In our family, car seat location was quite a hot topic. After a particularly bad week filled with fights over who got to sit in which car seat, I had to lay down the law. We would alternate between 2 car seats on a monthly basis. Andrew would sit in the preferred seat during September, for example, and Ryan would sit in that seat during October, and so on. Everyone knew what to expect, and our kids knew their parents wouldn't waffle, so they didn't bother trying to change the system. The bonus of this system is that your kids learn the months of the year. Perhaps your twins both desire the same chair at the dinner table. If your twins are having repeated arguments over the same issue, strategize to see if a new system can promote peace.

Interactions With Other Siblings

Be aware of the dynamic between your twins and their other siblings, whether older or younger. Patrick, 12-year-old brother to 10-year-old twin girls, does note that "sometimes they gang up on you." My singleton children would agree with this statement. It is somewhat inevitable with the team-like nature of the twin bond, but it is something for parents to be aware of. It is also a reason to promote one-on-one time, and make sure you experiment with different groupings of your kids. For example, bring only one twin and your oldest singleton with you on a Saturday to run errands, leaving the other twin home with your partner.

Twin Tip

An environment rich with words will help boost your children's language development. Even the busiest of parents can use everyday time with their kids to narrate out loud what is happening in their daily lives. You may feel a bit like a news reporter, but even mundane tasks such as preparing the morning breakfast can be a speech-boosting session. Turn off the TV, turn your cellphone to vibrate and put it away, and focus on your kids. Simply being *present* and communicative with your children will go a long way toward boosting their future speech and cognitive skills. For further advice on boosting your kids' language development, visit the American Academy of Pediatrics official Web site for parents, HealthyChildren.org.

Advanced Toilet Training and Independence

Do not despair if your twins are not fully toilet trained by their third birthday. Continue to be as patient and supportive as you can be, which is easier said than done. Toileting accidents can be extremely frustrating, more so for us parents of multiples and more so if your kids have been training for a while. After the third birthday, toilet training can take on a new dimension. A 3-year-old can be more stubborn than a 2-year-old and is more likely to dig in his heels if there is a battle of the wills.

Power struggles can be more frequent and severe than in the past. As a parent, you need to relax as best you can, as frustrating as the situation may be. If you get more emotional and upset with your twins, they may resist toileting even more, in a vicious cycle, as a result. At the preschool age, a child truly has a mind of her own and ultimately, she has to decide for herself to toilet on her own.

> ## Twin Tip
>
> Sometimes one twin may backtrack and start having toileting accidents and as a result get more attention during cleanup, as well as lectures. Be careful of paying one twin too much attention for accidents; his twin may start to also have accidents in a subconscious attempt to get some more attention.

If you have a difficult week filled with accidents, you may have to back off for a while. Make sure your twins help clean up their accidents, and have them get their own fresh clothes from the drawer to help them realize how much easier it is to pee and poop into the toilet, not in one's underwear.

Use success sticker charts in the case of toileting regression. You can make the charts as specific as you like. If only one twin is having poop accidents, for example, create just one poop chart for her to help her get back on track.

True toilet training is complete when your twins do not need reminders to use the toilet. When you notice that they've been doing well with parental reminders, back off a bit and see if they remind themselves. The sooner your kids learn to remind themselves to use the toilet, the more independent they will be. If you require further assistance with toilet training, or your twins are having problems such as constipation, consult with your pediatrician.

A friend with triplets had a challenge when her kids were 3½. While 2 of her kids were happily and successfully using the potty, her remaining daughter, despite prior successes, refused the potty in a classic display of 3-year-old power. Toilet training is a whole different ballgame once a child is older than 3 years.

Three-year-old kids are smart, have a better sense of how the world works, and continue to realize that their actions have an effect on their caregivers and environment. Twenty-four month-old kids are no strangers to the concept of power struggles, but it is quite different to deal with a 3½-year-old's efforts to assert her independence and control over her own body. As always, every child is different, and you know your kids best. If you have specific concerns about your child, or are worried about underlying problems, consult with your pediatrician.

A special note for parents of twins (or triplets): all too often, toilet training advice found in books and parenting magazines can be geared toward situations where a caregiver and child are one-on-one in some sort of magical bubble with no interference from the real world, family and work schedules, or even siblings. Most of us live in homes full of little people and action. For any family, but especially when training twins or triplets, there are many factors at play that can have a big effect on the progress of training.

Twin Tip

Parents of twins, cut yourself some slack. And remember that the age at which toilet training is achieved has no bearing on a child's intelligence or future success. There also seems to be many different definitions among parents of what it means to be toilet trained, so don't get stressed if you share notes with your neighbors. True toilet success is not caregiver driven; it is achieved when a child pees and poops on the potty *without* reminders from Mom or Dad.

Ultimately, a 3-year-old is in control of her own body, and she needs to be the one making the decision to toilet properly; she cannot be forced (the phrase "you can lead a horse to water…" comes to mind). There is no quick, overnight fix; toilet training is a process. But parents of 3-year-olds should remove the use of disposable pull-ups during daytime hours. Many mistakenly think of pull-ups as "training pants." But let's be honest: they are simply a disposable absorbent diaper in pull-up form. And too often they prolong the course of a child's learning to use the toilet because they are an out; the child doesn't need to run to the toilet when he feels the natural sensations to pee or poop, and he can simply do the deed in the convenience of the pull-up he is already wearing. That being said, a pull-up for overnight sleep, until nighttime dryness is consistent, is perfectly fine.

The ultimate goal is for your child to wear clean, dry underwear. To reach that goal, your child needs practice wearing actual cotton underwear during increasing stretches of time over the course of a day. He will learn what happens if he does not make it to the potty in time. Yes, this means accidents for 2 or more kids. But mistakes are a part of life and are part of the learning process. Your child should also be sitting on the toilet or potty seat at regular times each day, regardless of result (eg, first thing in the morning, after lunch).

Parents of twins can preserve some sanity by having systems in place to simplify cleaning up the inevitable accidents. Three-year-olds are developmentally ready to become active participants in self-care, so they can (and should) help when accidents occur. When a child is an active helper with accidents, she'll see that peeing and pooping in the toilet is much simpler (and more rewarding with positive reinforcement) than all the cleanup. Whenever a child has an accident, caregivers should keep their poker face on (more on this later) and direct the child straight to the potty. "Oops, you need to pee. Let's go to the potty." Even if nothing else will come out, you need to help your child make the connection that the sensation of needing to pee or poop is associated with sitting on the toilet. After your child has been sitting on the toilet for a bit, help remove the wet or soiled clothing, and have your child take the wet clothing to the laundry area herself. To minimize stress over laundry, we used to keep a bucket in our utility sink in the laundry area to streamline the eventual laundering. Place a kid-friendly step stool in front to help your 3-year-old reach the bucket. Then your child should be the one to get fresh underwear and clothes and put them on.

Now, onto the floor. When toilet training all 4 of our kids, we kept a huge stack of absorbable cloths (repurposed old burp cloths from the baby days) handy in a cabinet in a central location of our home. The adult caregiver will perform the bulk of the "real" cleaning of the floor (eg, wet-dry vacuum), but the child should go get a couple cloths from the stack, come "help" clean the mess (meaning an honest, 3-year-old effort), and bring the dirty cloths to the laundry bucket to be dealt with later.

Twin Tip

When you deal with the inevitable toileting accidents, you may feel angry and frustrated, but do your best to keep your cool. Even negative attention is attention, and when you have children who share a caregiver most of the time, the desire for attention can complicate matters.

Throughout the toilet training process (and always), make sure each of your kids is getting plenty of one-on-one time on a weekly basis, helping them feel valued and loved, as well as lessening any desire for them to act out in undesirable ways. Also, be mindful in your language. Many of us instinctively say, "Don't you want to pee on the potty like a big kid?" However, coaxing your child with this phrase is not always helpful. To a 3-year-old, the idea of being a big kid with all the added expectations and responsibilities may not sound so desirable. Your 3-year-old may think that life as a baby, with the cuddling and oodles of caregiver attention, sounds like a pretty good arrangement, thank you very much.

An additional note about pull-ups, specifically during naptime, day care, or preschool hours: talk with your day care providers to make sure everyone is on the same page. Preschools often ask for pull-ups during school hours; however, this can complicate matters. Some kids save up their daily poop for that 2-hour stretch when they know they're going to wear pull-ups. Similarly, many kids older than 3 years who wear pull-ups for naps may poop specifically at nap time. Depending on your child's age and progress, talk with your child's caregivers at school and work together toward a plan. A 2-week winter break without travel plans would be an example of a good time to focus on wearing normal underwear for increasing stretches of time without any interruptions from a school schedule. Ultimately, map out a timeline for "raising the bar" for your child to rise to the occasion and make good progress.

Emotional and Social Support for Parents

Your day-to-day routine with your twins is much easier than in the past, but it's still a lot of work. Parents of young children need to seek out ways to relieve the stress and laugh about the current craziness of their lives. A positive mental attitude will go a long way in helping you survive the chaos of each day. Spilled milk? Kids not listening the fifth time you've told them something? The next time you feel yourself losing your temper, try to see the humor in the situation.

Is there splashed bathwater all over the bathroom floor? Have your crew grab towels with you and mop it up, telling them, "Well, this is one way to get the floor clean!" There are a lot of mishaps that can occur each day; life will be more fun if you can laugh about it and move on.

Twin Tip

Some days you may feel like you're telling your preschoolers the same things 100 times! Use humor so that you don't lose your cool. Your twins learn how to handle tense situations by watching you. When one of my then-4-year-old twins was not listening to me one evening, I wondered aloud, "Can we buy Andrew some new ears at the Ear Store? I think his are broken—he's not listening to his mom!" Andrew knew I was being goofy (not sarcastic; there's a big difference) and amidst the giggling, he understood that I was trying to get his attention. I had made my point in a fun way, not in a nagging, unpleasant way. And once I got him laughing, lo and behold, he was a lot more receptive to what I was saying.

Parenthood can be a tough road, but having comrades with you helps. Now that your twins are participating in more activities and attending preschool, you have a lot more opportunities to meet other parents of similar-aged kids. Reach out to meet new acquaintances. It is very therapeutic to share war stories and see that some of the struggles in your home are happening in other homes as well. You're not alone. Parents share many of the same issues, whether or not they have twins. You can laugh about the struggles and move on, remembering that each phase will pass quickly. If you're a naturally shy person, practice making small talk with other parents at a public park. Even if small talk doesn't lead to a lifelong friendship, it boosts your mood and takes you out of your own little world.

📖 Twin Tales

Enjoy the fact that you have the interesting family dynamic of multiples. Sheri, mom to preschool twins, shares, "My son Evan is always perplexed when he sees only one baby with a mommy and always asks where the other baby is." How wonderful to grow up as a twin, and what an interesting perspective!

When out around town running errands, our family saw that the comments from strangers about our twins did not slow down. If anything, having a fourth child close in age increased the amount of comments we received. Far and away the most common comment is, "You've sure got your hands full!" Sometimes this line is delivered in a pitying tone with some head shaking, as if to say, "Wow, poor you!" Don't let these comments get under your skin. I am so used to hearing this phrase by now that I am ready with my reply: "They're very good kids, and we're so lucky."

Twin Tip

As your twins grow older, keep trying your best to attend your local Parents of Multiples club meetings, even if you only attend once in a while. You may feel that you've outgrown these meetings because you've moved past the newborn stage, but if you can give another new parent of multiples some baby advice that you've lived and learned, you can see how far you've come on your parenting journey now that your twins are older. That can be quite a confidence builder, which can keep your spirits up.

View the interactions with interested strangers from your children's point of view. What should my twin sons think when we go out in public and people seem to feel sorry for their mom because of *them*? I never want my twins to feel that they are a burden on me. Even though I am talking to the stranger and not my kids, I want to send the message to my twins *everyday* that they are loved, wanted, and wonderful.

Twin Tip

I find that interactions with inquisitive, curious strangers can be a helpful way to boost my twins' self-esteem by complimenting them to others. An overheard compliment can be a lot more effective than simply telling your kids directly, "You are good kids and I love you."

Budgeting and Practical Matters

Parenthood can be expensive, even with just one child. Twins need many of the same things at the same time and therefore can seem much more costly. When you're providing toys and experiences for your twins, remember that cost does not determine quality. Preschool-aged children can have a grand time with an empty cardboard box; it can be whatever you imagine it to be and can change on a whim. The box can be a spaceship, train, house, or whatever your twins are in the mood for. The less a toy does, the more the kids think.

"Grocery store" and "restaurant" were 2 of our all-time favorite games to play at these ages. Save empty food containers such as butter tubs and cake mix boxes, clean them out, and use them as your groceries. You don't even need a toy play kitchen; you can create one out of an empty box by drawing a range on top with markers and decorating it however you please.

Twin Tip

Don't blow the bank buying toys for your twins. Think outside the box for interesting playthings. I found tailor's measuring tape at a craft store for a dollar, and my kids spent an afternoon measuring everything around the house. In fact, the first time I heard my son Ryan count to 50 was when he measured my bathroom countertop with the measuring tape. Some of the best toys don't have to be toys at all.

The public library can be a parent of multiples' best friend for sticking with a budget. Make a point to visit the library as much as you can to treat your twins. Let each child pick out his own book or more to give him a sense of ownership over the book. Having plenty of books available in your home will encourage your twins to become lifelong readers.

Twin Tip

Another bonus to museum and zoo memberships is that it is easier to plan spontaneous outings. Busy parents of twins don't have lots of extra time to research and explore countless options for a day trip. With a museum or zoo membership, you can take your family out without having to think or plan too hard. Once you've made a museum trip a couple of times, you'll really get to know the lay of the land. Bring your lunch along and you've got quite an affordable family day.

Budgeting for a family vacation is difficult when your family has 4 or more people. Airfare can be quite steep, especially because airlines charge kids older than 2 years the same fares as adults. You can take more vacation in your local area by considering family memberships to your area zoos and museums. Memberships are quite cost-effective for larger families and often pay for themselves in fewer than 2 visits a year. When you use a family membership, you don't feel pressured to see all the exhibits in one day. If one of the kids is cranky, you can leave early. We like having local memberships so that when the weather is nice, we can go to the zoo, and during hot or snowy seasons, we can go to the indoor aquarium.

Twin Tip

When you take your preschooler twins on outings, keep a stash of sandwich-sized plastic bags with your supplies. Distribute a healthy snack such as clementine sections or apple slices during the outing by handing out individual bags to each child—a more cost-effective method than purchasing convenience-sized packages (which usually contain processed, unhealthy options) at the store.

Another way to have some affordable family bonding time is with family movie picnics. Spread out some blankets in your family room, pop some popcorn, and put in an age-appropriate DVD. Let the cuddling and bonding commence! These picnics cost hardly anything and can be so much fun for all of you.

Rainy Days: Painting for a Crowd

"Mom, can we paint?" Even 1-year-olds can scribble and paint; it is a great way to boost hand and finger (fine motor) skills, feel the sensation of paint underneath fingertips, and just have some fun. Even older babies like to practice "painting" with pureed food on their high chair tray. As toddlers grow into preschoolers and beyond, the artwork matures into more significant forms and meaning, and painting, whether with fingers or brushes, is a great way to spend some time on a rainy or snowy day.

As a busy parent with 2 or more kids, though, you may sigh an inward groan as you visualize 20 minutes of prep time, 2 minutes of painting, more paint on the children than the paper, and, inevitably, the post-painting cleanup. Our 4 kids loved painting when preschoolers, so we needed a system to make it easier on everyone.

An old mattress pad easily covers the kitchen table quickly and soaks up paint spills. Old pillowcases cover the chair backs for when kids get squirmy and lean over to check the progress of their siblings' project. Old adult-sized T-shirts provide great art smock coverage, fastened in the back of the neck with a clip. The supplies can be stashed in one of those plastic zippered storage bags that new mattress pads come in at the store. Everything is stored together, easy to pull out and set up quickly.

When your Picassos and Monets are finished, simply pile up all the messy smocks and pillowcases in the center of the mattress pad, pull up the corners, and make a tidy little bundle. All the messy stuff is safely contained within, and you can put the bundle in the laundry area and wash it when you have the time. Any washable paint–laden brushes can soak in the sink and be dealt with later.

The choices in washable paints and markers these days are dizzying, and kids don't even need fresh paper; painting on old cardboard boxes or paper rescued from the recycling pile is just as fun. See what streamlining systems you can develop for your family so that cleanup after a fun time is a breeze.

Enjoying the Here and Now

Savor playtime with your preschooler twins. Enjoy the fruits of your labor over the last 4 years. You've put in so much effort and energy into your kids, and now you can stand back and enjoy these wonderful people that you have nurtured and guided. Don't be in a rush for the next stage of life. Play an extra game of Uno or Candy Land with your twins and enjoy this magical stage of their lives.

CHAPTER 8

The School Years: As Your Twins Grow

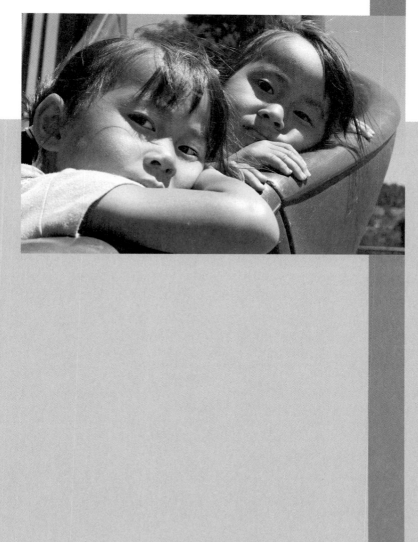

Our twin sons have always looked up to their big brother, and as preschoolers, they loved to accompany him to his bus stop on school mornings. One morning was garbage and recycling pick-up day. After the big kids' bus zoomed away to school, we returned to our home with 2 large, now empty bins sitting at the end of the driveway. Without hesitation, Ryan and Andrew each grabbed one of the wheeled containers and began to roll the behemoths back into our garage. The bins towered well over their heads, and I called out, "That's OK, guys, I can get those!"

They quickly replied, "Mom, we're strong; we can do it!" Andrew and Ryan returned each bin to its usual place in the garage, and I praised and thanked each boy, thinking, "Wow, this is the life!" After years of tending to my *twins'* every need, the boys were now turning the tables and pitching in with our *family's* needs. As twins grow older, they can play a larger role in helping the household run smoothly. There is more to be done in your home because of the number of kids, yes, but these kids can and should learn to contribute to and help out with all the numerous household tasks.

Raising twins through their early years is quite an endeavor. Parents of twins learn so much through the process, but we learn just as much about ourselves as we learn about our children. Did you know that you have an unlimited capacity for patience and love? You fed 2 babies around-the-clock, changed endless diapers, resolved conflicts between warring toddler twins, and so much more.

Your twin parenting skills will continue to adapt through the years as your children grow in their school years. In the early days, parents of multiples keep a synchronized schedule of feeding and constant care. Now as your twins grow older, your job as a parent shifts to managing the psychological aspects of raising 2 loving yet independent people.

What do the school years hold in store for your family? The school years offer new challenges and choices to be made regarding academics, classroom placement, extracurricular activities, and sports. Each of your children has strengths, weaknesses, and personality quirks that will affect how you parent during their school years. Over time, each child will evolve, requiring frequent reassessment to see what strategies are working and what needs to be tweaked.

Among other fun adventures to come your way, your twins will one day be eligible for learners' permits for a *driver's license*. Many parents of older twins have joked with me, "It gets easier all the time, but just wait until they're driving!" We parents of multiples will navigate drivers' education and other hurdles the same way we've adjusted to our other milestones—one day at a time.

Now that your twins have grown past the hectic early years, the school years have their own set of challenges and issues. In this chapter we will discuss school classroom placement, identity issues, managing household chaos during these busy years, bedroom and shared space issues, family dynamics, and travel and having fun, as well as hear from multiples themselves from all age groups about the experience of growing up as a twin (or more!).

Built-in Life Lessons

Your twins learn built-in, significant life lessons growing up with siblings so close in age. They learn *patience,* as their parents have more than one child for whom to care. They learn how to *share.* They have been sharing their mom and dad from the beginning, and as they grow, their sharing skills get lots of practice each day, as they almost always have other playmates nearby. Twins learn *empathy.* Being so close to their siblings, they develop an understanding of other people's points of view. Many experts believe that school-aged twins can be more socially savvy than their single-born peers because they have continual practice negotiating and interacting with others.

The twin bond is beautiful and will always be special for your children and family. However, as your twins grow, continue to give your kids plenty of opportunities to be individuals and pursue their own interests. They will have different strengths, and these strengths should be celebrated. Twins will almost always have a strong relationship, but each twin will go on to make his own friends, participate in different sports and activities, and have different life experiences.

Classroom Placement

The issue of classroom placement was initially raised in the "The Preschool Years: 3- and 4-Year-Olds" chapter (for more information, see page 139). It is important for parents of twins to remember that the decision of classroom placement for their children is not a one-time only decision. Every year your children are growing and maturing, and they may have different, distinctive needs as time goes on. I strongly recommend that parents reevaluate their family dynamic each spring to determine the best path for the upcoming academic year.

 Twin Tales

Danielle, mom to third-grade twin boys, shares, "Our twins are in different classes at school. This has always been a great balance for our family—time apart at school and time together at home. It has helped them to not compete with each other on tests and grades."

Kim, a first-grade teacher who has taught several sets of multiples, is also mom to quadruplets in kindergarten. She has special insight both personally and professionally into the issue of classroom placement for twins. She advises that it is important to identify if your twins lean, or rely, on each other too much. Every set of twins is different, and if yours are independently minded, being placed in the same classroom may not be that big of a deal.

It should be noted that same-sex twins, regardless of whether they are identical or fraternal, may have more issues to consider regarding classroom placement compared with boy-girl fraternal twins. Boy-girl twins, by virtue of the ease with which others can tell them apart, do not have nearly the same amount of identity and independence issues that are wrapped up into the classroom placement decision. For more on this, refer to the Straight From the Source: What Do Twins Themselves Have to Say? section later in this chapter on page 188.

 Twin Tales

Sue, mom to third-grade twins, advises, "Be your child's advocate. Be wary of teachers who may view the children as a 'package deal' where one child's progress is compared against the other's. They are individuals and should be treated as such."

In 2005, Minnesota was the first state to legislate that families should have the right to decide how their multiples are placed in the classroom, and since then Illinois, Texas, Georgia, and other states have followed suit. Check to see if your children's school has policy regarding classroom placement, and discuss your concerns with the appropriate administrative members from your district. Many districts do not have a formal written policy; in these cases, advocate on your kids' behalf. Each child's personality, needs, and learning style, as well as the twin relationship as a whole, will all play a role in your decision.

Of course twins have a special relationship, but as parents we need to be mindful of the give-and-take between the siblings. If one twin tends to become shy without the comfort of his co-twin, parents should be aware and make efforts to give him increasing amounts of practice interacting with others on his own. Over the summer, as well as during the school year, twins can participate independently in different activities or sports, which will ease the transition and help each individual be able to function to his full social and academic capacity.

 Twin Tales

Leigh, mom of 4, including fraternal twin girls, shares, "When our girls started school, we made the decision to keep them together. For the most part it went very well. It was easier for me to know that they had the same homework and classwork on the same days. It helped keep me organized. They didn't seem to have many problems with having their own identity while still being in the same class. We made the decision to split them in fourth grade because they would move to a more departmentalized class schedule…. They each have their own strengths, and fortunately, we have not witnessed much sibling rivalry. They seem to be aware of what their own strengths are and seem truly happy when the other one does well. I hope this continues as they get older."

Competition

A bit of friendly competition between twins, or siblings of any age, can be a good thing, pushing each child to their full capacity. Olympian Michael Phelps had 2 older sisters who swam, which had an effect on him in his formative years, and NFL quarterback Tom Brady had 3 older, athletic sisters who similarly encouraged him. Everything in moderation, though. As parents, we should ensure that competition between our kids, multiples or not, remains of the healthy variety. And for twins, the tendency to compare is ramped up a bit; siblings cannot get closer in age than multiples. Over-exuberant competition can result from twins sharing the same birthday and being in the same grade in school.

One way parents can help avoid excessive competition amongst their kids is to avoid labeling their kids. As individuals, it is a fact of life that your children will differ in their academic, musical, physical, and artistic talents. Be mindful of how you encourage your children: if a child is labeled as smart or sporty, she may experience limited confidence in other areas. Siblings, especially twins, may also subconsciously underachieve in certain areas so as to differentiate themselves from their family members. Praise your child's *effort,* not the *outcome,* whether it is a report card or a basket-ball game. Examples include "You worked really hard on creating a beautiful poster for your class project; I like the details you included," as opposed to "You are so smart." Telling your child, "I am proud of you; you swam really hard and beat your best time," as opposed to "You came in second!" places the emphasis on effort, over which a child has more control, instead of how they placed.

Twin Tip

Amber, mom to fifth-grade identical twin girls, advises, "Let them explore academic, extracurricular, and athletic options independently, as well as find their likes and dislikes away from their sibling(s)."

From preschool through third grade, our twin boys were always in different classes. This worked really well for our family and helped each boy establish himself as an individual within their grade in our school district. The boys could focus on their early education without constantly remind-ing teachers and young classmates who was who. Recently my son recalled, "Back in kindergarten a lot of kids didn't even realize I was a twin!" which he seemed to have frankly enjoyed, a nice change of pace for him. There was one day when all the classes were lining up after recess, and Andrew's class was instructed to line up before Ryan's. The teachers shared with me that quite a few 5- and 6-year-olds were calling Ryan, telling him he had better line up, thinking he was an Andrew not paying attention!

The fact that the boys lived together; shared a bedroom, family, and home; and so much more meant plenty of together time. So for us, a few hours apart during school came with an added benefit of appreciating each other more during after-school hours. As a mom, I felt the boys got along much better with the occasional separation.

For fourth grade, for a variety of reasons, we chose to have Ryan and Andrew in the same homeroom for the first time (our district rotates all fourth graders between 2 classrooms for the day's subjects). The boys had spent the prior 6 academic years separated and for the most part did quite well with being in the same class for the first time. The novelty of it definitely was a plus. The annual geography bee did give us a taste of competition, however. Each year our school gives all the students in a grade the same geography examination. Each homeroom winner advances to the grade-level finals, held before all the students in the grade, and each grade-level winner goes on to compete in the school finals. While Ryan performed extremely well on the qualifying test, Andrew was the class winner, earning the public spot of competing in front of the grade (and parents of the grade-level finalists), clearly an honor for Andrew. This made for some interesting conversations about winning and losing gracefully, and we were mindful of how we spoke with our sons, choosing our words of praise carefully. A point we emphasized with Ryan was that it was Andrew's special time during that particular week; there would be other times when we would celebrate Ryan's achievements, and we would all (including Andrew) cheer for Ryan at those times.

A great strategy for a healthy family dynamic is to focus on *fairness over the long haul*. There will be some days, weeks, and even months when one child has special achievements or needs. Other occasions, the siblings will need more from us parents. In the long haul, it will even out; each child will have his or her own day in the sun.

Twin Tales

Lisa, mom to 9-year-old twin boys, shares, "I am so glad we chose separate classes for my twins. It gave them the chance to flourish and make their own friends, instead of being Jack-and-Max, the single unit of twins."

Balance: Pursue Individuality, Yet Avoid Activity Overload

While we know as parents we should nurture each child's interests and allow them to pursue individual interests, including extracurricular activities, we do live in the real world, with financial and time constraints. Especially for families with parents who work outside the home, simply getting multiples and siblings off to where they need to be can be overwhelming, let alone affording the lesson fees, team costs, and so on. Use common sense and realize it is OK for some activities to be shared. Try not to compare your family situation with that of your neighbors' family, who have 2 children spaced 5 years apart. Those of us with multiples have different challenges;

look at the big picture and prioritize those activities that are most enjoyed, weaning where needed.

Our 4 kids were born within a 4-year span, so there has been a fair amount of overlap with their extracurricular activities. As a family, we have prioritized school as #1, and everything else follows. I try to follow a personal rule of school followed by religious education, an instrument, and a sport to avoid an overwhelming schedule, but we maintain flexibility and do our best to honor each child's truest interests. In this day and age, many school-aged kids are burdened with excessive extracurricular activities, so try not to feel guilty if your kids are not signed up for as much as their classmates; know that unscheduled free time is just as important for their development.

Boosting Literacy

Learning to read is a process, and it starts when your babies gnaw on their first board books. Add time and encouragement, and your kids will grow into confident readers who get absorbed in the plot of a chapter book. Surrounding your children with words (of both the spoken and written varieties) is key toward boosting literacy skills and nurturing a lifetime love of reading.

Each of your twins will develop reading skills at her own unique pace. Do not be surprised when one seems to take off with reading more quickly than the other. Make a dedicated effort to read to each of your twins one-on-one as often as possible, so as to work at each child's pace and comfort level, without his siblings interrupting the experience.

Twin Tip

The days get busy, and as our twins learned to read, despite reading every night at bedtime and during daytime opportunities, I always looked for more ways to incorporate words and reading into our weekly routine. I found a wonderful chalkboard at our local craft store for about $2. It was simple, only measured about 7 by 8 inches, and was easy to stick up in a corner of the kitchen with double- sided, removable picture hanging strips. The strips stayed together with Velcro, so I could take the chalkboard up and down every day. We started out writing kindergarten sight words on the board, but later we wrote the dinner menu on it—the special of the day, as it were. The kids got a kick out of writing the menu themselves, making the board a fun way to reinforce writing skills as well—quite the mileage out of $2.

Managing Household Chaos

A friend with school-aged triplets plus an older singleton posted in January on Facebook: "It's been a successful winter break from school. Our oldest is now trained to load the laundry, measure detergent and fabric softener. The triplets are trained to move laundry from washer to dryer and start the dryer. They all have to cooperate to lug a basket of laundry up the stairs. What should the next life skill be?" We are raising future adults, after all; for the kids' own sakes, plus the practicality of having help around the home, parents are to be applauded for encouraging teamwork and age-appropriate chores for all family members.

Age-Appropriate Chores for Kids

Kids who perform basic household tasks help the home run more smoothly, and the earlier the idea is introduced, the more it becomes the norm for a family. As kids grow, their responsibilities gradually increase with their skills. Early initiation of chores paves the way for preteens and teens to perform further household tasks. Contributing to the home boosts self-esteem, relieves boredom, and instills good life skills that will be infinitely useful once a child grows into an independently living adult. In the earlier stages, resist the urge to help your younger child with a particular task. Yes, of course the task is handled 3 times as fast by a parent; however, time and experience will help your child master the task, and kids need to start with baby steps. Applaud the effort, don't strive for perfection, and keep the big picture and goals in mind.

Toddlers (Ages 2–3)

- Pick up toys/place into toy bins
  (tip: attach photos of what goes into which toy bin to help with sorting [eg, train bin, block bin]).
- Set table at mealtime with nonbreakable plates, simple flatware.
- Dust surfaces/sweep floors
  (recommendation: provide commercially available fiber cloths that "trap" dust and dirt—a game for kids).
- Fetch supplies for care of younger siblings (diapers, wipes, new clothes) or during meal preparation (vegetables, other simple ingredients).
- Place dirty clothes in laundry hamper.
- Help move clothes from washer to dryer.
- Make/neaten bed.
- Perform simple cleaning after craft/art projects.

Preschool/Kindergarten (Ages 4–5)

Earlier tasks, plus

- Put dirty dishes in dishwasher.
- Set table/clear table at mealtime
  (suggestion: nonbreakable plates).
- Wipe up spills
  (kids should know where rags and paper towels are kept).
- Straighten bedroom space.
- Sort clean silverware.
- Prepare a simple healthy snack.
- Dry, put away dishes.
- Use handheld vacuum to help clean messes.
- Wipe out bathroom sinks, clean bathroom counter surface
  (suggestion: use household disinfecting wipes).
- Water indoor plants.
- Feed pets.
- Fold dishtowels, washcloths.
- Match clean socks.
- Clean up after art/craft projects, put away supplies.

Early Elementary (Ages 6–8)

Earlier tasks, plus

- Collect trash through house
  (tip: reuse plastic bags from stores as trashcan liners for bathroom; kids can pull out filled bags and replace with fresh bags).
- Fold towels of all sizes.
- Vacuum, dust/mop floors.
- Empty dishwasher, put away clean dishes.
- Outdoors: pull weeds, rake leaves, pick up sticks before lawn mowing, sweep porch.
- Peel vegetables.
- Prepare a simple salad (wash vegetables, find ingredients, perform simple cutting).
- Replace toilet paper roll.
- Prepare a simple breakfast with some supervision (eg, cereal, toast).
- Wipe bathroom sinks, counters, toilet
  (convenience household wipes are good for this purpose).
- Retrieve mail/newspaper.
- Wipe down microwave.
- Write needed items on a centrally located grocery list.

Elementary (Ages 9–11)

Earlier tasks, plus

- Take garbage/recycling to curb.
- Clean toilets, clean bathrooms.
- Vacuum.
- Sweep out garage.
- Help load washer/dryer.
- Hang/fold clean clothes.
- Put groceries away.
- Water indoor/outdoor plants, garden.
- Walk pets.
- Wipe off table.
- Prepare simple meals (eg, sandwiches).
- Help prep school lunches the night before school days.

Middle School and Older (Ages 12+)

Always consider your child's abilities and developmental level when introducing new household tasks. Not all 12-year-olds have the same level of maturity and respect for safety. I include these tasks so you can plan for your child's future chores. As always, practice safety first with good instruction beforehand; make sure your child demonstrates a good handle on the tasks, good decision-making, and an understanding of how to handle situations that do not go as planned.

Earlier tasks, plus

- Clean bathroom tub/shower.
- Make full meals and plan for future meals.
- Bake cake, cookies, bread.
- Contribute to grocery shopping list.
- Clean refrigerator, freezer.
- Mow lawn.
- Supervise younger children's chores.
- Change lightbulbs
  (with proper instruction beforehand).
- Wash/vacuum car.
- Wash windows.
- Supervise younger siblings.

Families with twins have a lot of people that need to get out the door on time each morning. I'm always looking for ways to help my kids take more personal responsibility. When our twins were in the first grade, they were working on reading analog clocks and I wanted to help them apply that sense of time to their everyday lives. The twin goal of *time proficiency* and the practical matter of *timeliness* inspired me to post a reminder by the clock in our entryway. The project took me about 5 minutes from start to finish. I used a "how to tell the time" children's book that had a pretend clock with moveable hands within it. I moved the hands to the appropriate positions and made 2 separate copies to illustrate the times we had needed to head out to the bus stop and when the bus would actually arrive.

If your home is anything like ours, you might find yourself repeating similar messages each day to a crowd of kids. Use your imagination to tackle some of the more common themes while boosting your kids' independence at the same time.

Twin Tip

In a home filled with growing twins, you have a lot of little people eating a lot of food and a lot of little people who, over time, are fine-tuning their reading and writing skills. This tip is a simple way to boost literacy and at the same time make sure your fridge and pantry stay well stocked.

Keep pads of paper and pencils or washable crayons in a central location of your home. Whenever any member of the family (grown-up or child) notices that you're running out of milk, bread, or even toilet paper, encourage him or her to write it on the shopping list. Younger kids can even draw a picture of the item or get spelling help from a grown-up or older sibling. Practicing writing items on a shopping list is fun for kids in elementary school, and they don't realize they're gaining valuable literacy practice at the same time.

If kids are encouraged to add to the shopping list on a regular basis, it will become a habit. You'll be instilling good responsibility, teaching each child to contribute to the household. Just don't be surprised if you walk by the list one day and see that a child has scrawled "chocolate" or another such kid-endorsed "necessity" on your shopping list.

Teaching Your School-aged Twins
Vital Safety Information

Technology marches forward, and phone numbers are all programmed into smartphones these days; yet when helping your school-aged twins learn life skills, learning important phone numbers is high on the list. Consider maintaining a list of important phone numbers as a word processing document on your computer, and post a printed version in a central location of your home, such as on the refrigerator. Customize your list to include any numbers you deem important; it is yours, so go ahead and include your favorite takeout restaurant's number below the emergency numbers. We keep key information on ours such as

- Mom and Dad's cell and work numbers
- Grandparents' and neighbors' phone numbers
- Pediatrician office number
- School numbers and absentee hotline numbers (very handy, as my 4 kids attend 3 different schools)
- Poison control number
- Local pharmacy numbers, including that of the nearest 24-hour pharmacy

A posted hard-copy list is always available and easy to reference, and it never needs recharging. If parents head out for work, date night, or a rushed, unexpected emergency, the hard-copy list is ready for your children's caregiver with all pertinent information—no need to worry about preparing the information every time you leave the house. Just as carrying an umbrella seems to ward off the rain, being prepared for unexpected scenarios seems to give peace of mind. If the master document is kept on your computer, you can easily make corrections and updates as needed. Print out extra copies for nearby relatives or neighbors, and they'll have your contact information ready. A bonus: as our kids grow older we coach them, in an age-appropriate way, how to handle emergencies and other various situations. Even our youngest knows where the master contact list is, and if need be, she can use the house line to call her dad's cell phone, or Grammy, in a jiffy. While most cell phones have phone numbers saved, your child probably won't have access to your device in an emergency.

Multiple Kids, Multiple Shoelaces

Kids master many milestones in their early years—drinking from a sippy cup, toilet training, tying shoelaces, reading independently. For families with twins or more, these milestones can sometimes be overwhelming as you are teaching 2 or more children at the same age (and usually developmental level) the same new skill. The logistics of coaching 2 kids at once, as well as dealing with inter-twin dynamics (eg, hurt feelings when one twin catches on sooner than the other), might lead a parent to buy Velcro sneakers for life. However, once your twins achieve each milestone, their increased independence is well worth the effort. Our strategy to teach our twins to tie shoelaces was similar to what we've done for other milestones—a mix of group time and one-on-one time. Working in our favor was the fact that our twins look up to their older brother; we borrowed his terminology for tying shoes (the bunny runs around a tree, jumps into the hole, and gets locked inside with a knot). If your twins do not have older siblings, ask a beloved older cousin, family friend, or neighbor for help; a kid-to-kid demo can sometimes be more effective than merely watching a grown-up perform the task. Exciting new shoes and books about lacing shoes (with actual laces) help too. Plenty of YouTube videos give visual, play-by-play tutorials as well. Make it fun, and know when to take a break. As your twins encounter new milestones on their developmental journey, hang in there, be patient, treat each twin as an individual, and soon they will master the new skill du jour (of the day).

Bedroom Spaces

If you have the ability and space to give each of your twins their own bedroom, wonderful! You can skip ahead to the next section. For those who need your kids to share, read on. That being said, some families do get creative. Jill, mom to 6, including sixth-grade twin boys, shared that recently, one boy moved out of their lifelong joint room into a tiny non-room so he could have his own space.

Because of space constraints in our home, our twin boys need to share a bedroom; yet each boy has divergent tastes, has varying degrees of cleanliness and orderliness, and is growing and changing every day. If your twins need to share a bedroom like ours do, here are some issues to consider.

- Each child deserves protected, special space for his treasured objects and to express his distinctive personality.
- Each child needs some degree of privacy.
- Kids' interests change quite rapidly; choo-choo train decor may quickly be outdated with new fascinations.
- The belongings of 2 kids takes up twice the space, and the clutter can easily become a mess.

If you opt for loft or bunk beds, make sure your kids are developmentally ready for them (the American Academy of Pediatrics has safety tips at www.healthychildren.org). Clean, simple bookshelves are a great showcase for more than a reading collection. Select 2 narrow bookshelves to conserve space, and designate one to each child to display her own treasured objects, special crafts and creations, souvenirs from a trip, or whatever she is into that month. Furniture shopping in brick-and-mortar stores is time-consuming (and almost always an adventure with kids in tow); instead, browse the Internet for affordable strategies to contain the clutter and carve out unique areas for each child.

Brainstorm together with your kids for decor that will be appropriate for longer than one year's duration. I found affordable laminated world and US maps online that not only look nice on a wall but come in handy when your kids want to know where Peru and Transylvania are.

Family Dynamics and Behavior

Have you noticed your kids' behavior can take a turn for the worse during particularly hectic weeks? Often this phenomenon is not just a poorly timed coincidence. Think of "feeding the meter" as a discipline strategy; effective discipline strategies are a must for busy families with twins. Even at our busiest, we parents need to feed our kids' "meters" on a routine basis to encourage good behavior. Clearly life is more pleasant with well-behaved children, but if you're a parent of multiples, good discipline techniques are a requirement to keep your household running smoothly. Think of discipline as an overall framework where good behavior is rewarded and inappropriate behavior has consequences (for more on discipline, see pages 119 and 155 in the toddler and preschooler chapters). We've all heard of a time-out for poor behavior, but even more important is "time-in"—positive, pleasant, one-on-one time with a parent. Time-in boosts your child's self-esteem and strengthens your emotional connection. Having a good relationship is wonderful in and of itself, but in addition, it is the setting under which you can most effectively guide your kids' behavior. Positive quality time with a parent on a regular basis helps your child know that he does not need to act out in order to get your attention.

So how can you feed your kids' meters? Even if both parents work outside the home, it is possible to squeeze in meaningful one-on-one time each week. As you prep dinner, let one of your kids help with simple, age-appropriate tasks as you talk to each other, leaving the TV off. On weekends, take just one child with you to the grocery store, ignoring your cell phone or other distractions. Sit with your kids and simply color and doodle with them, sharing peeks at one another's artwork. Over time you can fairly distribute time-in amongst all your kids, strengthening bonds and improving overall behavior.

Travel and Having Fun

These days, a family is considered large with more than 2 kids, so those of us parenting multiples as well as singletons automatically fall into this group. Day to day, I don't consider our family of 6 particularly big because it is our personal version of normal; however, I can't help but notice the costs adding up when we buy tickets for an event or airfare.

Budget-Friendly Outings for Twins

We often take advantage of early bird rates for a summer family membership at a nearby community pool. The school year can be hectic, so we look forward to a loosely scheduled summer vacation. The pool is a nice option for those pleasant lazy days when nothing in particular is on the calendar. Signing up, there is a bit of initial sticker shock (especially because many base rates are for a family of 4), but when you calculate the cost of admission for 6 family members for 2 or more visits, the numbers work out similarly; any subsequent visits over a year's time are free. Memberships are available for your area's museums, zoos, aquariums, and more. Do the math, and you might find it'll save your family some money too.

Another benefit of the up-front investment of a membership is that you won't feel stressed to spend the entire day at the museum or zoo. This membership is particularly handy when you have younger kids in your group. Too much action packed into one day can be over-stimulating, and a crew with young kids will need to head home for naptime at some point. Many museums have reciprocal partnerships with other cities' attractions, so you can even take advantage of discounts if you're hitting the road this summer. Having a couple memberships on hand means not having to think too hard for activity ideas; pack up a homemade lunch for your crew, and you've got an affordable, low-stress, fun, and educational activity for the day.

Traveling With Older Twins

With each passing year you'll notice that outings and travel are easier and easier. This is your life; don't be afraid to head out on adventure, whether by car or airplane. A positive mental outlook definitely helps; treat the travel portion as part of the excitement, not just as a means to get to the destination. For longer car trips, prep containers ahead of time with sliced fruit and veggies, ready to go, only requiring to be passed around. Food prepped at home is healthier and more budget-friendly than hitting fast food restaurants while en route. Have each child pack her own backpack with books and age-appropriate activities. Visit the library or bookstore in advance so you can pull out new books on the trip. Buy special markers designed to draw only on paper, not the car. Try to stop every 2 to 3 hours for kids to let off steam, or as I call it, get out their heebie-jeebies. Giving kids an opportunity to run around and stretch their legs will earn better behavior in the car. The American Academy of Pediatrics recommends limiting children's access to TV and computers, but on a lengthy trip it's OK to pull out the DVDs for designated amounts of time, as long as there is an educational component. Be mindful of overly long stretches of screen time, as your kids will become zombie-like, and a lot of kids can get motion sickness if they don't regain their sense of balance and horizon by simply looking out the window from time to time. Our family uses a timer on road trips, with designated chunks of time for conversation, car games, snacks, and limited screen time.

For air travel, it may be worth the investment to purchase each of your multiples a small, wheeled bag in which to carry a beloved teddy and activities onto the flight. Families with twins need more stuff; put your kids to work by having them help carry the load in an age-appropriate way. Your younger travelers will enjoy feeling like a jet-setter, pulling their own wheeled mini-suitcase! When possible, choose direct flights to reduce traveling mayhem and disruptions.

Straight From the Source:
What Do Twins Themselves Have to Say?

Life with school-aged twins can be just plain funny. When my boys were in kindergarten, we played the board game Candy Land. When one of them landed on the same space as his twin, he exclaimed, "Look, we're *double* twins!" When they were in first grade, someone asked Ryan, "What does it feel like being a twin?" He shrugged and responded, "Pretty normal." When my boys were around that same age, I tried to explain to them what it was like when I was pregnant with them. Two babies squeezed into one belly (for several months, no less) is quite a concept. The boys began telling jokes about how they spent that time together, and through endless giggles they agreed, "We were playing checkers!"

Twin Tales

Here are some other goofy or frustrating questions my identical twin sons have heard.
- Do you ever mistake yourself for your brother?
- Do you ever think you're Andrew? (directed to Ryan)
- Which one is which?
- I know people ask you this all the time, but who are you? (Ryan and Andrew note that both adults and kids have asked them this.)

My twin boys have shared that it is frustrating when family and friends know clearly who their older brother is and who their younger sister is, yet lump them (Andrew and Ryan) together as a nameless unit and don't even try to remember who is who, despite different clothes, eyeglass frames, haircuts, etc. As a parent, be your child's advocate, be mindful of these situations, and if needed, provide a gentle reminder to the family member or friend, if you are comfortable doing so.

Regardless, your twins will find the joy and fun, despite the frustration at times, of sharing a birthday with a sibling. What do twins have to say about their experiences?

Jill, who grew up with a fraternal twin brother, is now a mom to sixth-grade fraternal twin boys herself. Her experiences growing up as part of a boy-girl twin team give her special insights into parenting her twin boys. She shares, "Their main sport is basketball, and they have always made the same team. However, this past fall they both played a different sport that the other would not be playing. They *loved* having it as their own. One boy said, 'Sometimes I wish I had my own grade and all my own friends. It gets old when people confuse me with my brother.' They really do like each other, however, and do have similar interests. It was totally different for me growing up because I had a twin of a different gender than myself. I always thought it was a really neat thing, being a twin. I never felt like I needed my own identity or felt any competition."

Dani grew up with an identical twin sister and is now mom to 3 girls, including twins. She shares, "My parents would say, 'Dani's the social one; Kara's more academic,' probably to make Kara feel better about not having a lot of friends. But I thought she was smarter until high school, when I was scared to be in the advanced physics class with all of her friends. Guess who ranked #1 in the class and went on to an advanced degree in physics and math? But I wonder what would have happened if I hadn't taken that ranked class to prove that I was really as smart."

Dani also has some funny stories. "My first-grade teacher suggested we switch classes to fool Kara's teacher. The teacher didn't guess; it was only when I took my shoes off and the teacher told me to put them back on that another student told her 'That's Dani, not Kara.' After that, we switched one day every year and the students always could tell but the teachers didn't. Another time we went to my grandparents wearing customized shirts with our names on them, only switched. When we told them that we were really the other twin, they wouldn't believe us! Now that we're adults and she lives overseas, most people in my life don't even know I'm a twin. Before my wedding, though, Kara was mingling with guests in the foyer and finally had to go in back because all of my friends thought she was me."

Alexis is a junior in high school, as is her fraternal twin brother. She shares, "We appreciate how our parents look at us as individual people and not as a 'unit.' We were encouraged to seek out our own interests (hobbies, sports, music, etcetera) and are not compared in our accomplishments. This may have been easier for our parents, as compared to some parents of twins, since we are different genders."

Madeline and Catherine are identical twin girls in fifth grade. They share, "We have a special bond with each other that is hard to describe but is stronger than our bond to our other sisters and our friends."

Brian, now a dad to twins himself, grew up with an identical twin brother. He says, "In general, it bothered me when people would ask, 'Are you the good one or the bad one?' Really, people, who asks kids that question? And no, if you punch him in the leg, I do not feel his pain!"

Shelby and Payton are 8-year-old twin girls. Shelby says, "You always have someone to stick up for you if someone is bullying you." Payton says, "The best thing about having a twin sister is you always have someone to have your back." Their mom Michelle shares, "I love that they watch out for one another without smothering each other."

Taylor and Jaden are 8-year-old twins. When asked what they wanted others to know about being a twin, Taylor said, "It is hard to share the same birthday." Jaden wanted classmates and family members to know, "We are not identical."

Emily and Jack are 9-year-old twins. Jack shares, "It's hard when one twin is doing better than the other in school or sports. But it is good to have a built-in friend because if you are bored you can ask them to do something." Emily shares, "Twins can be different, especially boys and girls. It's OK to do different things—sports, interests. I wish my friends knew that twin brothers aren't annoying. Sometimes it's not fun to have to play boy games, but I do it because I know my brother doesn't like to be alone."

Emily and Maddie, 10-year-old fraternal twin girls, share, "Sometimes it is hard to be a twin because you have to share everything and people get you confused. It is fun because you always have a person to play with and talk to, and you always have someone to support you and stick up for you." Their mom, Leigh, mom to 4 kids total, says, "The most frustrating thing as a parent is that others don't realize that even though they were born together, they are not the same. Our twins are like night and day, and it is hard to see people expecting them to have the same disposition and personality. I am thankful for the unique personalities they each have."

Magda, 75 years young, has a fraternal twin sister. She shares, "I was born and raised in Germany [1939] until my freshman year in high school [1952]. We lived through the war, so some of the twin 'specialness' may have been lost early on, as times were rough. Once the war was over and school was regularly back in session, there was only one classroom per grade, so we were never split up into different classrooms. We were always the leaders of the class in such things as school processionals and parades, which were common because it was a Catholic school. Everyone knew who we were. We were always dressed alike, and at that young age we looked very much alike, despite being fraternal. Upon our immigration to America, we were split up in high school classes and it was then that I realized how much I really liked and valued that. It was the first time in my life that I could actually achieve something on my own without direct comparison to my sister. I was able to just be myself. I think it is important for twins to nourish their own identities. I was not particularly bothered that we always dressed alike when younger; that was more a function of the war and everyone being poor."

Lois, 90 years young, grew up with her identical twin sister. She also comments on the generational differences for multiples, between her youth and these days, now that multiples are more commonplace. "My mother always dressed us alike. We were 'special,' as there were not many twins in our hometown—really, anywhere. We always loved the attention that we got from the public, from complete strangers who would always comment that we were twins. We recognized our own strengths and weaknesses. We were our own best friends; we had each other and were the 2 youngest of 5 girls. We did the typical swap dates, who happened to be our future husbands. They didn't even know they were with the wrong twin. We only told them when they put their arms around us. We all laughed because they had no idea. Another time, I was asked out on a date but the young man actually wanted to ask my twin. He just didn't know who he was asking out. We were always in the same classes; everyone got confused without us actually doing anything. We loved going to Twinsville, Ohio, and seeing hundreds upon hundreds of twins!"

CHAPTER 9

Support, Emotional Health, and Time-savers for Families With Multiples

My childhood friend Lisa is a parent to boy-girl toddler twins as well as 3 older siblings, and it has been a joy to follow along with her growing family's adventures. With her family, as with the families in my pediatric practice who have twins and triplets, I marvel at how each of our parenting journeys are uniquely ours. Well-meaning friends and family will offer you advice, which is wonderful; however, you will often hear a variation of the phrase "been there, done that." Nope! No one has walked in your shoes, no one has had your specific family structure, and no one has parented your unique children before you.

When her twins were first born, Lisa received advice on how to best raise her babies by anyone and everyone. Sometimes the advice was solicited, and sometimes, not. Trust us; taking a walk in public with a hugely pregnant belly is the best way to attract the attention and comments from random strangers passing by. When I visited Lisa in the hospital, her nurse came in to check vitals and told her, "You know you *have* to feed the babies 30 minutes apart, right?" Lisa, aware that I am a big fan of feeding infant twins simultaneously, smiled and said, "OK, thanks!"

Here's the deal: although others may have parented themselves, although others may have raised twins or triplets, their experience is not your experience. Listen to the advice and well wishes of others, but know you will find your own path. Some twins are born first to a family. Some triplets are born third, fourth, and fifth to a family with 2 older kids. Some of us have local family members able and willing to help; others do not. Each family's needs will be different, and each situation and circumstance will affect how you handle infant feeding schedules, bedtime routines, naps, and more. Your neighbor's method for soothing her infant's colic may not work for your infant. Some babies love swings; others, not so much. You only know until you try it out. This is a great reason to borrow others' infant equipment; when our twins were babies, we borrowed a swing—thank goodness, because none of our 4 kids were a fan of it, and no money was wasted.

Listen to other's advice, and feel free to tinker and experiment to see if their strategies will work for you. But ultimately, each child, and each family, has individual needs. When offered advice from others, smile gratefully and store it in your mental notebook; use it if it sounds like it's worth a try. Have faith in your abilities, and remember that you know your children better than anyone on this planet. Once you've ensured your children's health and safety, sometimes a certain degree of flexibility, with a dash of trial and error, is needed before determining how to best tackle the current parenting stage or challenge.

New parents of multiples need all the support, tips, and encouragement possible, and while no single book is one size fits all, families need support and troubleshooting ideas to handle the myriad issues involved with raising multiples. Just as every child is unique, and what works for one child may not work for another, all families are distinct. Each family will create their own rulebook, and no 2 will look the same. This support chapter aims to *empower* parents of multiples like you to gather information and advice, use common sense, speak with your pediatrician, and see what works best for *your* family.

The Teamwork of Raising Multiples

When you have 2 or more newborns to care for, both parents need to roll up their sleeves and get to work. Some fathers may not have planned on being a hands-on type of dad; yet when twins are born, more manpower is needed. By necessity, fathers become proficient in feeding, burping, and changing diapers for their babies. Such tasks are not mundane; feeding and diaper changes are ideal times for parent-child communication and bonding. Hands-on fathers not only have more fun but also provide a boost to their children's development by providing a different kind of interaction from that experience with Mom. As an example, Mom may be gentle and nurturing, while Dad is goofy and blows more raspberries on the babies' bellies. The combination of 2 different styles leads to a more well-rounded experience for your children.

Parenting Tip

To use a basketball analogy, parents of singleton babies play 2-on-1 defense; parents of twins play man-to-man defense; and parents of twins and more play zone defense, my personal favorite. The teamwork of parenting twins benefits both the kids and the partnership.

Seek Support

Reach out to extended family and friends during your pregnancy to establish "help lines" to assist with the challenges lying ahead. If possible, designate one close family member or friend to act as a contact person who organizes help with tasks that must continue despite possible bed rest and the birth of multiples (eg, preparing meals, house cleaning, babysitting). Online resources are available to coordinate a meal chain for a family blessed with multiples. MealTrain.com, CareCalendar.org, and TakeThemAMeal.com are some examples of Web sites dedicated to organizing assistance with meals and ensuring that multiple meals aren't delivered on a single day.

Parenting Support

Amber, mom to 4 kids, including fifth-grade identical twin girls, recommends, "Have a support system in place to help you; you will need it. If someone offers help, take it! Multiples are overwhelming, and it's OK to have those feelings that maybe this is not going well. I was already a mother, so I thought, 'How hard can it be?' Well, a lot harder than I thought. The best advice I would tell my 32-year-old self is don't be so hard on yourself; you really are doing the very best you can. Those babies are doing just fine."

If finances allow, a sitter, "mother's helper," nanny, or designated night nurse can help ease the chaos of the early weeks with multiples. Our family was fortunate to have the help of a local middle school student who was eager for more experience with kids. Her help progressed to full-fledged babysitting and she came over often as a mother's helper to play with our older children when our fourth child was born. A great bond was formed, and as the years progressed she has been a significant person in my children's lives, currently a college student and our summer sitter when home on break from college.

Parenting Tip

Meal planning, both by prepping and freezing meals ahead of time, can help immensely once your babies are born.

Child Care Aware is a useful resource for families looking for quality child care close to home. For more information on nannies, au pairs, and home day cares, please refer to the early infancy chapter, specifically the Returning to Work section on page 75.

Parenting Tales

Jon, dad to infant twins, says, "Though by no means a simple or haphazard personal expense, hiring a night nurse for a majority of the nights in a week to take over feeding, changing, etcetera, has been an invaluable decision, worth every penny. We tag teamed the night feedings and care with our first singleton and managed to come out fine, albeit a bit exhausted, on the other side. With the twins, if we didn't have a night nurse and instead were doing everything ourselves [and in partnership], neither of us can conceive just how unproductive the rest of our lives would have been."

Families expecting multiples should reach out for local support through their communities and places of worship. More specific to families with twins, triplets, and more, multiples organizations (on the local level as well as state and national levels) support families both through in-person meetings and camaraderie, as well as with online social networking groups.

Multiples of America

Multiples of America, formerly known as the National Organization of Mothers of Twins Clubs, serves to support families raising multiples, to advocate for education and research in the field, and to foster friendship and community. Their Web site, www.nomotc.org, has a search function to help you find a Parents of Multiples club in your area, either by zip code or city.

The Parents of Multiples club that I was assigned to during my twin pregnancy held monthly meetings on a night of the week that my husband regularly worked late hours, making it difficult for me to make it to meetings. Fortunately, living in the populated Chicago suburbs, I was able to investigate alternative local options, which included a smaller, cozier club that met a different night of the week and was a better fit for me, personality-wise. Don't be afraid to investigate different options to better fit your needs.

Parents of Multiples clubs usually hold monthly meetings to gather for camaraderie and support. Often each monthly meeting has a guest speaker or topic related to raising multiples or parenting in general. Clubs often hold separate, more casual gatherings to get the kids together or to arrange for a mothers- or fathers-only outing. Seasonal clothing resales are often held twice a year and are a fabulous way of not only finding excellent deals on baby clothes, equipment, and toys but also passing them along when your babies have outgrown certain items.

Parenting 4-month-old twins does not leave one with much free time. Add in other kids, work, maintaining a household, and finding time to eat, sleep, and exercise properly, and not much time remains to maintain friendships, let alone seek new ones. Yet maintaining those social lifelines, as well as making new connections with other parents of infant multiples, can be rejuvenating.

Parenting Support

When our twins were younger, the last thing I thought I had time for was attending my local Parents of Multiples club's monthly meetings; yet somehow when able to swing it, I was so grateful I did. There is something instantly comforting about sitting in a room full of people who *get it*. Sharing tricks, tips, and ideas, and just plain venting about the twin parenting experience, can be downright soothing for your soul.

Social networking allows families with multiples to connect online with local and regional multiples groups as well. There are several public groups (watch for the globe icon, which indicates anyone can read the posts, photos, and comments), but many groups have a private forum to post questions and suggestions, making it even easier to stay connected, even if unable to leave the house for a meeting. If you belong to public groups, be mindful that your posts and photos may be viewable to anyone; keep your kids' privacy in mind when social networking on the Internet.

Parenting Tip

Michelle, mom to third-grade twin boys, shares, "The single most important advice for me when pregnant with my twins was to get into a support group or some kind of monthly activity that gives you time away from the kids. When you get a chance to step away, even when there is so much to do, it gives your mind a rest and you feel refreshed coming back to it."

Emotional Support

A study published in the April 2009 issue of *Pediatrics* was "Multiple Births Are a Risk Factor for Postpartum Maternal Depressive Symptoms." This article strikes a personal chord for me, stating, "Undergoing a high-risk pregnancy and delivering multiple births are stressful life events, and the unique demands of parenting multiple infants can result in high levels of parental stress, fatigue, and social isolation." Looking back at my twins' early months, housebound by the needs of twin babies plus a 1-year-old, I would agree with this statement.

The study results, while not surprising, are of vital importance. With this study, families and health care professionals can anticipate and understand the relationship between multiple births and stress. Knowing that the odds of depression are greater, families can enter the world of multiples with their eyes open, ready to be proactive with some prevention strategies.

In the hectic early months with twins or triplets, prioritize what is most important, and streamline elsewhere—you can't do it all. Is each of your kids safe, fed, and loved? If yes, then declare the day a success; the other stuff can slide for now.

Every parent is different. Some parents' outlook may improve with day-to-day logistical help or talking with loved ones, but others may need counseling and further assistance to get on the right track. If you are feeling overwhelmed, you are not alone. Be a squeaky wheel, and reach out for support.

Be *specific* in how you ask for support. Instead of vaguely hinting, ask your partner *directly* for what you need. For example, "Please change the babies' diapers." Necessary tasks that may seem apparent to you may not be clear to others; don't expect your partner to read your mind.

Good communication between Mom and Dad is key, as is utilizing your wider support circle. Friends lend an ear so you can vent, and relatives with older kids remind you that your kids' current stage will soon pass. The parents in your local Parents of Multiples club truly understand what you're going through. Also look to your place of worship and to your pediatrician, who wants to know how *you* are faring. Your babies' growth and development are intricately related to your family dynamic.

II

Parenting Tip

Darwin, dad to school-aged twins, recalls some good advice when they were expecting twins: "Exercise patience." As the parent working outside the home each day, he knew that he would come home to a house in which things had to be taken care of, and he would need to help out. The babies did not always stay on routine, so patience was needed.

IIIIIIIIIIIIIIIIIIIIIIIIIIIIIIIIIIIIIIIIIIIIIIIIIIIIIIIIIIIIIIIIIIIIIIIIIIIIIIIIIIIIIIIIIIIIIIIIIIIIIIIIIIIIIIIIIIII

Mental Health: Keep the Big Picture in Mind

Georges Seurat's *A Sunday Afternoon on the Island of La Grande Jatte* is one of the better-known works of art in the Art Institute of Chicago collection. It was featured in the movie *Ferris Bueller's Day Off* and was the inspiration for Stephen Sondheim's *Sunday in the Park with George*. It uses the technique of pointillism; up close to the canvas you can see individual dots of color, but from a distance the bigger picture, an overall scene of people enjoying a park, unfolds.

I am mentioning painting techniques to illustrate a mental health point: when faced with parenting challenges, we often find ourselves standing too close to the canvas, unable to see the bigger picture. Every child is different, and our initial strategies to help our kids navigate developmental milestones may be hitting a brick wall. If we remember to step back and observe the scene as a whole, we can refresh our perspective. By reestablishing our priorities and goals and rebooting our parenting energies, we'll be able to see the forest for the trees.

How do we reboot? Parents need to take personal breaks to maintain sanity and nurture who we are as people. Moms and dads should ensure that they have an outlet, an activity or hobby unrelated to parenthood or their careers that nourishes the inner spirit and rejuvenates them for engaging and caring for children. This will be challenging during your multiples' early weeks of life, but especially after your babies are 6 or so months of age, it is something to think about. Look at a typical week's schedule and see where your personal protected time can be squeezed in. Even the busiest of us can use creativity to unearth 30 minutes, 3 times a week for this purpose. Enlist the help of your partner, family, friends, or sitters to make it happen. Also consider waking up earlier than the family, or when your babies are older and have more consistent schedules, utilize the magical time between their bedtime and your bedtime.

Meeting our own needs helps us properly care for others. My husband and I work together to cover for one another, protecting each other's time on a weekly basis. Whether you exercise; are an avid photographer, scrap-booker, or gardener; or love to experiment in the kitchen with new recipes, make an effort to set aside time each week to pursue your passions. Your family will be rewarded with a refreshed parent who has the big picture in mind.

On the most challenging days? At the end of the day, ask yourself, "Is everyone safe and fed properly?" Then declare the day a success!

Keeping Your Cool

It is quite a challenge to keep a cool head when your children misbehave. Handling 2 or more young kids at the same age can test the patience of a saint. It is crucial for parents to stay calm in the heat of a discipline moment for many reasons, a significant reason being that kids learn how to handle stressful situations by observing how their parents handle such situations.

One tip to preserve your emotional health as a parent, especially when your twins are toddlers and your patience is being tested day in, day out, is to take a refresher course on the developmental milestones and charac-teristics of your kids' age groups. Families can find some comfort knowing that it is *age appropriate* for older babies, toddlers, and even preschoolers to test limits. Unfortunately, toddlers' temper tantrums are also age appropri-ate. They result when your 2-year-old realizes she has her own ideas about the world and is, in fact, a separate person from her parents and her twin. (For more on toddler discipline, please see toddler chapter on page 119.) Throughout your twins' early years, they are continually trying to figure out what their boundaries are; it is a function of how children operate and is *not* a conscious, deliberate attempt to drive you insane. As frustrating as the tough days can be, it is our job as parents to consistently and rationally illus-trate appropriate boundaries to our kids. For an excellent resource on your children's progressing developmental stages, refer to the American Academy of Pediatrics *Caring for Your Baby and Young Child: Birth to Age 5.*

How can you model reasoned, rational behavior to your kids when you have reached your capacity for patience? Counting to 10 and "going to your happy place" may not be enough to keep you, a parent of multiples, calm. Some goofy yet effective ideas to stay cool include imagining an audience in the room with you (or security cameras, or the camera crew from a reality

TV show) watching you as you handle a tough situation. Alternatively, you can pretend your toddlers are from another country and you're teaching them the ways of your land. Silly ideas, but sometimes fresh new tricks are just what parents need to remain calm and handle a situation objectively, properly, and without anger.

While we raise our twin sons, I keep adding to an ongoing, lengthening list of the benefits of parenting more than one child at the same age.

- *Self-reliance. Kids learn self-reliance early on when they outnumber the parent(s).* Believe it or not, being outnumbered can be a good thing. The very logistics that pose such a challenge in the first year of life encourage your children to become more independent as they grow and develop over time. We've all heard of "helicopter parents" who can be overly involved in their kids' lives and activities. Parenting twins or more decreases the chances that you'll be micromanaging each aspect of your kids' experiences. I have a personal tendency to swoop in and help too much; however, with 4 kids born within 4 years of age, I can only help each child as much as humanly able. My now school-aged kids are pros at packing their backpacks for school, helping put away laundry, setting the dinner table, and more, not necessarily because of my parenting skills but because of the logistics and needs of our larger-than-average family.

- *The oft-cited multiples catchphrase "You can't scare me; I have twins!"* Once you've parented multiples for any stretch of time, you realize you are capable of more than you may have expected. You quickly learn the ropes and can handle a multitude of situations, which is empowering. This sense of empowerment can carry over to other areas of your life such as handling your career and your personal relationships. If you've raised multiples through the exciting first year, you can handle anything.

- *Resilience. Multiples coach their parents on how to roll with things and adapt.* Time flies quickly when parenting multiples; we tackle current issues and then move on to a new set of circumstances. Even during a difficult stage, rest assured. Time will pass, the stage will pass, and you'll be onto the next milestone.

Healthy Family Dynamics

Do you sometimes worry that your twins get too much attention, leaving their younger sibling on the sidelines? Or are you like a friend of mine who worries that her toddler twin boys are neglected because of their older sister's busy schedule of school and activities?

When 2 or more children are involved, well-intentioned parents do their best to maintain a fair family dynamic by providing equal amounts of love and attention to each of their kids. These efforts can be fraught with guilt, however, as it is *impossible* to provide exactly equal amounts of interaction with 3, 4, or more children. Life is just so variable—how *could* your attention be spread equally? One week, Kid #1 is sick; another week, Kid #2 has a school play; then the following month, Kid #3's best friend moves out of state. I often find myself fretting if I have not had enough special time with one of my 4 kids, even if there are very good reasons that some kids needed more of me during a given week.

Having twins or triplets in a family can intensify the issue of relationships. By their very nature, multiples are a rare, special occurrence, and they are fascinating as well as time-consuming. I have friends who happened to grow up as a single-born sibling of twins. They warned me, when I was pregnant with my twins, to not forget my oldest son. These warnings intensify my feelings of guilt during those hectic weeks when some of my kids get more attention than the others.

I think the best strategy for a healthy family dynamic (and fret-free parents) is to focus on *fairness over the long haul*. There will be some days, weeks, and even months where one of your kids will need you more than your other(s). And that is *OK*. In the long haul, it will all even out, and each child will have his or her own special moments with Mom and Dad.

Always remember that each of your twins is an individual. It is fun to celebrate the special status of twins, but keep a healthy family dynamic by treating each child, twins or not, as if they were a single-born child.

Time-saving Strategies

Time is a tricky thing. We have 24 hours each day to spend as best we can. Families with multiples need to utilize time-saving strategies whenever possible. Manipulate your daily schedule to budget your time effectively. Creative thinking can streamline your home's daily tasks and make your life easier.

Take dinner prep, for example: when your twins are newborns, the dinner hour is the "bewitching" hour. Babies tend to become more anxious and unsettled during the late afternoon and early evening hours, and colicky episodes usually peak right at dinnertime. What superhero could cook and serve a meal while also caring for 2 fussy babies? Even as your twins grow into toddlers and preschoolers, they may be bouncing off the walls come late afternoon. During the school years, your twins are getting off the bus in the afternoon and have homework and various extracurricular activities scheduled. Frozen pizza 7 nights a week isn't the healthiest option, but the forces of the universe seem aligned in a mission to thwart homemade dinners forevermore.

The solution? Make a "do-ahead" dinner at a time convenient for you and your schedule, and then assemble or reheat it right at mealtime. Personally, I am a morning person and my kids, when little ones, were usually more agreeable and cooperative in the morning hours. If able, I would assemble lasagna, to be baked off later, or roast chicken parts so they would only require a microwave reheating. A slow cooker is a valuable kitchen device to use this strategy, with countless online recipes. Come 5:00 pm, most of the prep is complete, and even if it is a hectic afternoon, you can quickly toss together a decent meal for your hungry family. Mornings aren't the only alternative. Families with busy work schedules may find that weekends are a good time to assemble a few nights' meals in advance. See what works for you and your situation.

Parenting Tip

If you need to make a trip to the grocery store and don't have time to make a list, take a picture (or several) of the inside of your refrigerator with your smartphone to see what things you have or don't have and the amount that is left.

The point is that you can "twist time" to make it work for you. Dinner can be made in the morning. Laundry can be done when the kids are in bed. Prime time TV shows can be recorded or watched later on the Internet. Hectic mornings can be alleviated by placing backpacks in the car the night before. Identify your trouble spots and experiment with new strategies, and you'll find yourself a more relaxed, hence more effective, parent.

Strategies for Special Occasions

Holidays and birthdays are terrific occasions to get together with family and friends. However, when you have young babies, your day-to-day life can be hectic enough. The thought of hosting a get-together can be daunting. Consider the possibility of making your life easier by hosting at your home, as opposed to traveling a distance to visit a family member's home for the holiday. Think about it: your twins' cribs are there, as well as all your baby supplies, milk, and even a changing table. Having your loved ones come to your home means that you don't have to pack and travel to get to another destination.

Most importantly, your children will be happier and healthier if they consistently use a routine nap and nighttime sleep schedule, even on holidays and special occasions. It is inevitable that from time to time, life will get in the way of a perfect schedule for your kids, but if you can entertain at your home on a holiday, it will be easier to respect your normal routine.

An easy way to host a gathering is to plan for side dishes and desserts that can be made a couple days ahead of time. Then, on the day of the event, all you need to do is focus on a main dish and reheat the rest as needed. This plan not only frees up your event day but also spreads out the cleanup of prep dishes over a few days' time. Better yet, delegate the sides, beverages, and extras to your guests to bring as potluck items.

It is not cheating to get a little help from the grocery store, either. Take hummus as an appetizer example; open up a store-bought tub and scoop into your own dishware to make it your own, if that makes you feel better. It will taste great, and the hostess is happy and relaxed, not overworked and exhausted from adding more prep bowls to the dirty dishes.

Family get-togethers are about loved ones gathering, not about how clean the house is or what food was served. Keep this as your focus and you'll be a calm hostess, ready to enjoy her own holiday.

Parenting Support

Michelle, mom to 8-year-old twin girls and a 13-year-old singleton, states, "My girls make me laugh every day. They have taught me so many things like to appreciate the little things in life. A spotless house isn't as important as the tea party they are having. Even though days are sometimes hard and seem like they are never going to end, when a little hand takes your hand and asks to go snuggle and read stories in the 'big bed,' everything else can wait for a moment. Cherish those moments. Important lesson learned. Whether outside on a sunny day or dancing in the rain, imagination is a wonderful thing. I find it's important to be silly with them."

Modified Expectations

I once read a holiday survival article in our local newspaper. It had good advice, yet I believe that the year-end season is not a hardship to endure; rather, it is a gift. Parenting twins or more keeps you busy *every* month of the year. During this month, as with any month, prioritize what is truly important and enjoy the spirit of the season without overwhelming yourself or your children. Despite various family, social, and religious events, *you* are in control of your schedule for the most part.

Embrace your most treasured traditions, such as an afternoon spent decorating cookies with your kids or taking the family to see glorious outdoor light displays. Make time for these experiences by saying no to items lower on your priority list. You can't do it all. Realistic expectations for the holidays, especially when your twins are young, can help maintain some serenity. Traditions from years past can be reevaluated as well. Hosting family or friends at your home may be simpler than packing and traveling with a crew of young children.

The concept of saying no may be difficult for many of us, but we often need a reminder that we have permission to do so. We owe it to ourselves and to our children. Your infant twins cannot speak up for themselves, so you need to be their proactive advocate. If you avoid over-scheduling, you'll prevent meltdowns, illnesses, and behavioral setbacks. I am not endorsing the life of a hermit who declines all outside invitations; rather, I am suggesting *balance* in how you spend your precious family time.

Ultimately, keep in mind that your twins' early years are fleeting. Accommodating the needs of young twins is a temporary situation that will be just a blip on the radar screen over the course of your lives. Streamline your days during the holiday month of December to enjoy each member of your family, your traditions, and the true peaceful spirit of the season.

Finding Lessons in the Mishaps

During a particularly hectic week for our family, I decided to take it easy and pop a frozen pizza in the oven for dinner. The timer rang and the pizza somehow broke into two pieces upon removal, resulting in big glops of cheese, sauce, and bell peppers falling onto the oven floor and racks—so much for a painless dinner. Was I happy about the now-smoking oven?

Definitely not! However, my usual audience of 4 little kids was watching to see how I would handle this unexpected suppertime dilemma. I decided to laugh about it and call the kids over to watch (from a safe viewing distance) as I attempted to extricate some of the burning cheese blobs. At the time, the kids were 7, 5, 5, and 3, so of course they found this entire scenario hilarious. We then rallied together to open as many windows as possible, laughing at the mess Mom made, hoping the smoke alarms didn't start blaring.

How do children learn to deal with mistakes, disappointment, and difficult situations? During early childhood, Mom, Dad, and other important caregivers model attitudes and coping strategies, whether they are aware of it or not. Keeping this in mind, I consciously chose to take the lighthearted path and joke about the smoking oven. Despite our best efforts, parents are human and our kids will see us lose our cool from time to time. Do not fret if that occasionally happens; emotions are a part of life. If you've found yourself yelling or otherwise exhibiting less-than-model behavior, it is OK to simply talk to your kids about it (eg, explaining that you shouldn't have used those particular words). Use daily life events and mishaps as illustrative scenarios to help your young children learn to navigate their emotions and maintain their self-esteem, even when things go wrong. You're raising future adults, who need to know how to move forward from the inconvenient bumps in the road.

Where's the Answer Key?

Do you ever wish there were right and wrong answers to your parenting dilemmas, a nice, clear-cut, straightforward way to go? It sure would make life easier! As your children grow and your family's dynamics evolve, parenting quandaries arise that have no obvious correct answer.

When our then 5-year-old twins were ready for new bikes, we had a dilemma of modest proportions. We had a perfectly good hand-me-down bike, courtesy of our older (singleton) son. So who would get the hand-me-down bike, and who would get a new bike?

Parenting Tip

Lisa Henderson, mom to 5, including boy-girl twins, shares, "Every family is different. Every situation is different. I have several friends who are moms of twins and while we commiserate and exchange information, something that worked for one family may not necessarily work for the other. Whether you are a first time parent or have been around the block, whether you are expecting multiples or are having a single baby and have picked up this book to see how your life could be more complicated, don't try to do everything. Figure out what's important to you and the health and well-being of your family, and discard the rest."

Our solution: I tossed a coin to determine who got the new bike, and we figured in a couple more years when the boys need bigger bikes again, we'd alternate between the twins as to who got the hand-me-down and who got the new. My son who lost the coin toss was pretty bummed, and I started to feel pangs of guilt as I reassured him. Nothing that I said, though, made him as happy as when he simply hopped on and rode his bigger and faster bike, beaming with pride at how much he had grown! A bonus was that he had instant gratification; his hand-me-down was ready to go, waiting in the garage for him. His twin who won the coin toss had to wait for his new bike to be assembled from the box.

There may not be an exact answer key for your parenting dilemmas, but remember that regardless of the paths you choose, kids are resilient. Each family and each child is unique, so follow your instincts with love and fairness, and you'll make the right decision for *your* family.

CHAPTER 10

If Your Multiples Are Born Early

*M*ost twins do well after delivery. However, multiples have a greater chance of premature delivery compared with single-born babies. This is a sensitive subject and is not meant to scare you; rather, this chapter provides an overview of issues that preterm babies might face, as well as some terms and therapies that a family may encounter in the neonatal intensive care unit (NICU), should you find yourself in this situation. If you are pregnant with multiples, do your best to keep a positive spirit and healthy outlook on your pregnancy, but do familiarize yourself with some of the following issues to prepare in case your family has a premature delivery.

According to the American College of Obstetricians and Gynecologists, *preterm birth* refers to all deliveries at fewer than 37 weeks of gestation; this classification includes *very preterm* (<32%7 weeks), *moderately preterm* (32%7 to 33%7 weeks), and *late preterm births* (34%7 to 36%7 weeks). The fractions in these gestation time periods range from %7 to %7 and indicate additional days per a 7-day week; every day in the womb counts. *Term birth* refers to deliveries that occur from 37%7 to 42%7 weeks, and *post-term birth* refers to any delivery occurring after 42%7 weeks.

Newborns born between 34 and 36 weeks of gestation (near, or late, preterm births) are the majority of all preterm births in the United States, and in 2007 the American Academy of Pediatrics recommended a change in terminology from *near term* to *late preterm* to better delineate the special health concerns of infants born at these dates.

A full-term pregnancy is 37 weeks or longer, yet twin pregnancies usually deliver, on average, around 36 weeks. The National Vital Statistics Reports (NVSR) from the Centers for Disease Control (CDC) show that 57% of twins born in 2011 arrived prior to 37 weeks of gestation. The final weeks of pregnancy are a time for growing babies' weight gain and lung maturation. For this reason, if your babies are born early, they may face low birth weight and respiratory difficulties.

The 2011 CDC NVSR statistics further illustrate that 11% of twins were born "very preterm," meaning at fewer than 32 weeks of gestation, increasing the chances of the therapies and treatments described in this chapter. Triplets were born prior to 37 weeks of gestation 93% of the time in 2011, with 36% born prior to 32 weeks. Quadruplets were born prior to 37 weeks 93% of the time, with 67% born prior to 32 weeks.

Some multiples who are born a little early may need time in the NICU to gain weight before going home. Other babies may have respiratory difficulties in addition to a need to gain weight. More significantly preterm twins may have additional issues. Each newborn will be evaluated and treated individually, and it is possible that they may have dissimilar needs at birth. Premature delivery can be scary for parents and families, but the good news is that modern medicine has made wonderful advancements toward care for preterm babies.

For more valuable information about newborn intensive care, an excellent resource is *Newborn Intensive Care: What Every Parent Needs to Know*, by Jeanette Zaichkin, RN, MN, NNP-BC, from the American Academy of Pediatrics.

The NICU: Different Levels of Care at Different Hospitals

The neonatal intensive care unit, or NICU, is a special place that most people, including parents, might not already be familiar with, unless they had family or loved ones who already required the services of a NICU. Most people's planning and pregnancy preparations do not include familiarity with the NICU; however, because multiples tend to deliver early, it is wise to be aware of what the NICU is all about.

Parenting Tales

Kim, mom to quadruplets, recalls, "When I was on bed rest in the hospital, they gave us a tour of the NICU facilities ahead of time. This was very helpful. I saw that the NICU had an open area, in which all the babies were cared for; there were no private rooms. They showed us a baby who was about the size that they expected my babies to be when born; that was a surprise. Usually when you see pictures of babies they are larger full-term babies, not the reality of what a premature baby looks like. Although even with this advance preparation, the NICU experience is totally different when it is your own children being cared for."

Talk with your obstetric team about your delivery hospital options. Be aware of the different levels of care available at different hospitals. If your pregnancy has been followed by a maternal-fetal medicine (high risk) team, you will likely have more information about the level of care available for your babies after delivery. Every hospital can handle emergencies, but many community hospitals prefer to transport pregnant women at higher risk to the region's medical center where staff is more experienced at managing complicated pregnancies and sick newborns.

In 1976, the March of Dimes categorized obstetric and newborn services at hospitals as Level I, II, or III, depending on the availability of resources and the complexity of patients served.

Here is a breakdown of each of these levels.

- **Level I:** Basic nursery services, designed to care for healthy term babies. Babies born at fewer than 35 weeks of gestation are transferred to another facility.

- **Level II:** Nursery services designed to care for babies born at more than 32 weeks of gestation who weigh more than 1,500 g (3 lb, 5 oz). This level of nursery has been further divided into Level IIA and Level IIB, with B having the capacity to care for babies who need mechanical ventilation (respirator) or continuous positive airway pressure (CPAP), a form of support for babies with breathing problems, for a day or less.

- **Level III:** A subspecialty service that offers comprehensive care for all newborns. Often located in a regional medical center, this type of facility is equipped to provide neonatal intensive care. Level IIIA cares for infants born at more than 28 weeks of gestation who weigh more than 1,000 g (about 2 lb, 3 oz), while Level IIIB cares for infants born at fewer than 28 weeks of gestation who weigh less than 1,000 g. The Level IIIC NICU provides the highest category of care for the most complex issues, including those who need extracorporeal membrane oxygenation, or ECMO, which is cardiac or lung bypass, and surgical repair of complex birth defects.

Early in your pregnancy, talk with your obstetrician about how your pregnancy is progressing and what will be the best facility with the proper resources for your babies.

Parenting Tales

Kristine, mom to first-grade triplets, shares, "All the staff and nurses in the NICU were awesome. The only scary part was seeing my babies with all the wires, breathing tubes, etcetera. But the nurses were so great at explaining everything, so that gave me comfort."

Nutrition

If you are physically able, you can start pumping breast milk soon after delivery. Breast milk is the perfect nutrition for small or preterm babies. Pumping your milk on a regular basis will help boost your milk supply. If your babies cannot yet tolerate feeding by mouth or a nasogastric (NG) tube, which goes from the nose to the stomach, the milk can be frozen and fed at a later date. A high-quality, hospital-grade breast pump can help you double pump breast milk quickly and easily. Recruit your nurses and the hospital lactation consultants for assistance and advice. Your neonatologist (newborn pediatric specialist) may recommend boosting the calorie content of your breast milk with human milk fortifier (HMF, a powder that increases the caloric and nutritional value to the milk, adding iron, for example).

Breast milk is ideal, but there are also formulas specially made for babies born before 36 weeks. Several options have more calories per ounce than standard formulas to maximize your infant's nutritional and energy requirements, a key step toward growth and proper catch-up weight gain. In addition, supplemental iron will help boost preterm babies' blood supply.

The suck and swallow reflexes are developed with gestational time, and your preterm baby may not be able to suck. Babies who cannot yet suck and swallow from a bottle may benefit from nasogastric tube feedings, during which breast milk or formula is fed via a small tube that enters through the nose and leads to the stomach. Tube feeding helps the stomach and intestines stay healthy and accustomed to digesting milk until the baby develops her own suck reflex to feed.

Parenting Tales

Kim is mom to first-grade quadruplets born at 29½ weeks and recalls her family's NICU experience: "The hard part was the ups and downs. You would have what seemed like a good day with progress made only to get a call at one in the morning with a problem that one baby was experiencing. To describe the NICU, you go through a journey where you take one step forward and 2 steps back. Then 2 steps forward, 2 back, and so on until you are moving forward without regressing. It seems like an eternity to get there, but you do. Developing a strong relationship with the NICU nurses is hard and emotional but also critical."

Respiratory Difficulties

During the final weeks in the womb, the lungs form a substance called *surfactant*, which helps the lungs develop elasticity, like a balloon, to open up and take air after delivery. Babies born early may lack this substance and may develop respiratory distress syndrome (RDS) as a result. Corticosteroids such as betamethasone are usually given to a mother in preterm labor before 34 weeks to help prevent RDS. If a baby has signs of severe RDS, surfactant treatment is given to the baby soon after delivery and in the first couple of days of life, and the baby will require the help of a breathing tube and ventilator. Babies with less severe RDS may require a nasal tube with oxygen. Preterm babies who require supplemental oxygen for longer periods may go on to develop chronic lung disease, or CLD.

Chronic lung disease is not the same thing as chronic obstructive pulmonary disease, or COPD, which affects adults. For babies born early, chronic lung disease, also known as bronchopulmonary dysplasia, or BPD, refers to persistent inflammation, injury, and scarring of lung tissue that occurs as a result of underdevelopment of the preterm lung, as well as the treatments needed to support the immature lungs. Each baby is an individual and it is difficult to predict what the next couple of years upon discharge home from the NICU will require, based on what occurred during the NICU stay. In other words, even kids who require intubation and ventilation for any amount of time may do better than expected. In general though, a longer ventilator time period indicates that preventive medications will likely be needed upon discharge home from the NICU. The length of time can be quite variable, and it depends on the child and his progress. Some infants require daily preventive medications (possibly including inhaled medications with a nebulizer machine) for the next couple of years, while others may only require medications during the winter months of cold and flu season. And still others may do quite well on their own without specific prescriptions. Infants with respiratory concerns should be followed closely by their general pediatrician as well as a pediatric pulmonologist for at least a year after going home from the NICU.

Preterm babies commonly have apnea of prematurity, which means they have episodes when they forget to breathe, requiring stimulation to continue breathing. Stimulant medication can help control apnea of prematurity, which usually resolves by the time the baby is at 40 weeks of post-conceptional age.

Parenting Support

Reach out to other families who have had NICU experiences with their children. Sue, mom to third-grade twins, shares, "I had just found out I was pregnant when a close friend delivered 28-week twin boys. I honestly had never seen a breast pump before, let alone a premature baby or a NICU. I was very fortunate to have my friend as a resource during my pregnancy and the immediate weeks following my twins' birth. My twins were born at 32 weeks, with a 4-week stay in the NICU. Her advice to me during that time was invaluable."

Jaundice

Jaundice is a yellowing of newborns' skin and eyes. It happens when a chemical called bilirubin builds up in the baby's blood. Bilirubin is a by-product of old red blood cells and is removed by the liver. Most newborns, even if healthy and full-term, have some degree of increased bilirubin because the immature red blood cells of a newborn break down more quickly. In addition, the liver is immature and not fully handling the extra bilirubin.

A simple laboratory test measures the amount of bilirubin in the blood to evaluate the degree of jaundice. Pediatricians are concerned about jaundice because high levels of bilirubin, if left untreated, can cause deafness or brain damage. Light phototherapy can reduce the bilirubin levels if needed. A baby receiving phototherapy looks like a baby visiting a tanning salon; skin exposure helps the treatment be more effective, and the baby will even wear mini-sunglasses to protect his eyes.

Parenting Support

Amy, mom to preschool-aged twin boys who were born at 24 weeks, shares, "The only way to keep moving every day is to think *when*, not *if*. When will your baby be off the ventilator? When can you hold him? When can you bring her home?"

Other Concerns

- Low-birth-weight or preterm babies who need help maintaining their body temperature are placed in radiant warmer beds or Isolettes (incubators).

- Infections are a concern for preterm babies with an immature immune system.

- Babies born extremely early will require eye examinations to screen for retinal problems, as well as head ultrasounds to evaluate for any bleeding from fragile blood vessels.

- Some babies have patent ductus arteriosus (PDA), in which a normal fetal connection within the major heart vessels does not close after delivery the way it should. A PDA can be treated with medication; if the medication fails to close the connection, surgery may be required.

Bonding in the NICU

Give your babies names as soon as possible. Naming your babies will help your family and hospital staff bond with the babies. Get to know the NICU staff; they are knowledgeable and will become part of your extended family. Bring in family photos and special mementos for each of your babies' bedsides.

Initially, it may not be safe for parents to hold a preterm baby. When the babies are medically stabilized, you will be able to hold them and participate in direct skin-to-skin contact with them, which is great for moms *and* dads and is as beneficial for parents as it is for the babies. Parent-child bonding thrives on the sense of touch.

Parenting Tales

Kristine, mom to first-grade triplets, shares, "One regret I have is not going to the NICU often. As long as you are a patient in the hospital, you can go any time you want, as long as the NICU team is not doing their rounds. One of the nurses called me once at 2:00 am to see if I wanted to come see Rocco. I was thinking to myself, I wish I had known, and I would have been there every night. At the time, they had 3 nurseries— NICU, intermediate, and the regular nursery. Everyone was in the NICU and Isabella and Ava left after a day, but Rocco stayed for 3. I did have a lot of nurseries to visit, but I could have had extra visits with Rocco in the wee hours."

As your babies grow over time, you will be able to become more involved in their day-to-day care. You'll learn when your babies' care times are, and you can help take temperatures, change diapers, reposition the babies, and even give baths. Continue pumping breast milk and nurse your babies one at a time if you are able.

Going Home: When Is the Right Time?

It is possible that one of your babies may be able to come home before the other. Babies who are ready to go home from the hospital should be able to regulate their body temperature, take all their feedings by mouth, be gaining weight in a steady pattern, and have a home plan for any ongoing medical issues.

Your babies may need breathing and heart rate monitoring at home. Hospital staff will train you to learn how to use any necessary equipment. If one baby is able to come home before the other, use the opportunity to get into a routine before the other babies comes home. When all babies are home, coordinate feedings and nap times to occur at the same times each day.

Parenting Support

Expect to feel anxious upon your multiples' homecoming. Kim, mom to quadruplets born at 29½ weeks, shares, "I was so used to reading monitors in the NICU to know how my babies were doing that when I got home and there was no monitor, I was so scared that there would be a breathing problem and I wouldn't know. When my first baby came home, I think I woke her up 4 times throughout the night to make sure she was still breathing."

If your babies were born before 35 weeks of gestation, needed oxygen at birth, or are still on oxygen, ask your pediatrician about monthly injections to prevent respiratory syncytial virus (RSV). In older kids or adults, RSV presents itself similarly to a bad cold. Babies born prematurely or who have chronic lung disease can develop a serious lung infection if they catch RSV. In addition, ask your NICU staff and your pediatrician about developmental clinic follow-ups to monitor your babies' developmental growth after being discharged from the hospital.

From the NICU and Beyond

Your multiples may have quite different medical needs whether born very preterm, moderately preterm, or late preterm. Good communication continues to be important as you work with your team of physicians and therapists. Your general pediatrician should serve as your children's medical home, helping coordinate specialists and necessary developmental, speech, and other therapies. Continue to write down concerns and questions as they occur to you during the course of a busy week so that you can ask the appropriate people at a scheduled office visit or during an additional phone call. Looking forward, believe in yourself and your abilities as a parent to advocate for your children.

CHAPTER 11

Triplets, Quadruplets, and More

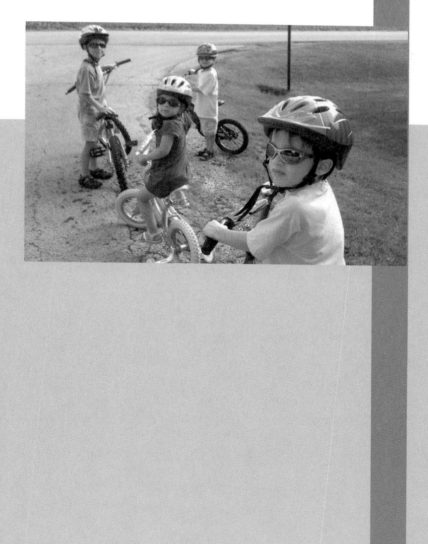

Our twin boys are 18 months younger than our oldest son, so when our family goes out and about, strangers and passerby often ask us if our sons are triplets. Even though we had 4 kids within 4 years, our kids were born on 3 different birthdays, which was a much different scenario than if we had triplets plus one, or quadruplets. I have so much respect and admiration for families with triplets and more, as well as the unique challenges they face in the early years. All families with multiples can benefit from the lessons families with triplets or more have learned to streamline care for their infants and keep their family organized.

To prepare this special section, I spoke with many wonderful families with triplets or quadruplets. Each of these families has beautiful multiples, and in many cases, single-born children as well, yet all of them have different structures and family schedules. Some moms work full-time, some stay at home to care for their children, and others are back at school to further their education. Despite dissimilar family structures, these families' successes have some consistent themes, such as organization and teamwork.

Pregnancy Preparation

Just as with twins, parents of triplets or more need to be prepared for a premature delivery. Please refer to the triplets and more statistics on premature delivery in the "Multiples: Facts, Lore, and More" chapter on page 229. Mothers carrying triplets or more should expect to go on some form of bed rest around the 20-week point of the pregnancy. Bed rest may be at home initially with modified activities and then advance to fully hospitalized bed rest. Mothers of triplets need to eat considerably more calories on a daily basis to help their babies grow. Some moms find protein shakes are a healthy and convenient way to obtain extra calories.

Even during the pregnancy stages, parents of multiples can join local Parents of Multiples clubs, as well as Internet support groups (for more on this, please refer to the "Support, Emotional Health, and Time-savers for Families With Multiples" chapter on page 193). Reaching out to other families with triplets can provide practical survival tips, as well as reduce feelings of isolation. Internet support groups and social networking pages specifically deal with various stages of triplets' lives, from pregnancy through the teenage years.

While you are pregnant with your multiples, begin to research various options to recruit volunteers to assist your family during the challenging early months. Ask family, friends, neighbors, and your place of worship for support. It would be helpful to designate a point person (a close family member or friend) to coordinate such tasks as a meal train plan to which others can contribute. You and your partner will be immediately busy with the pregnancy and delivery of your babies, so assigning this task to a third party may prove useful and stress reducing.

Synchronized Schedules

Most triplet families stay sane their first exciting year by coordinating their babies' feeding and nap schedules. Families that start out feeding babies on a more casual as-needed basis quickly find themselves overwhelmed and adjust to streamline the process.

Often when babies are sent home from the neonatal intensive care unit (NICU), they have a consistent feeding schedule, such as every 3 hours. Many triplet families take advantage of the existing NICU schedule and keep their babies on the same pattern upon their homecoming, tweaking the 3 babies' schedules to work together more efficiently. (For more on the NICU experience, please refer to the "If Your Multiples are Born Early" chapter on page 211.)

In the early weeks and months, many families obtain outside help with frequent feedings. With a second adult's assistance, infant triplets can feed at the same time; 1 adult can feed 2 babies simultaneously while a second adult feeds the third. Alternatively, when a parent handles the 3 babies solo, 2 babies are fed simultaneously followed by the third. Nursing moms can nurse 2 of the babies together and then feed the third baby a bottle of pumped breast milk.

Parenting Tales

Take advice from Kim, mom to kindergarten-aged quadruplets, and a first-grade teacher herself. She incorporated her professional know-how for keeping her classroom organized into how she managed the first year with quadruplets. "We had stations for all the major tasks—a food station to prepare the milk and bottles, a diaper station, a bath station, and so on."

Surviving the Early Months

Different families have different strategies for handling the challenging weeks when they first bring their triplets home. Volunteers can help immensely in the daytime and nighttime. Ask your helpers to perform specific duties. They can feed the babies, do laundry, cook or bring along a meal, clean the house, or just hold the babies.

Many families arrange to have help with the first month of overnight feedings. One family that I spoke with had help from relatives. The grandmother arrived at the home each evening to handle overnight feeds for the first month the triplets were home; she would leave in the morning to refresh and return again the following evening.

Some families have the babies sleep in the same room initially and split the babies up later as needed, usually into boy or girl bedrooms for multi-sex triplets.

‖‖

Parenting Tip

Stash important supplies (diapers, burp cloths, and the like) in convenient places on each level of the home to minimize time spent running around retrieving necessary items.

‖‖

Friends can help families organize meal programs. One family's church arranged a schedule to deliver meals to the house 3 times a week in the early months. Families find it beneficial to give helpers and volunteers very specific instructions of what needs to be done to minimize confusion (eg, how much to feed the baby, how often to pause for burping breaks, how long to hold the babies upright after feeding). Don't be shy with how you ask for assistance and what assistance you ask for; this is not the time to be proud and try to do too much yourself. Be specific in what you ask of your helpers and how these tasks should be accomplished. Make sure all volunteers are healthy and virus-free.

Organizing the Multiples Way

Organizing bottles, nipples, and formula streamlines the feeding process. Many families buy supplies in bulk and store them in a designated location, to quickly assess what supplies are needed before embarking on another shopping trip.

Dry-erase boards are very useful for families with multiples. Many use a dry-erase calendar to keep track of volunteers in the early months at home. Other families use large dry-erase bulletin boards to keep track of the triplets' feeds, wet and dirty diapers, moods, and medications. As your triplets grow older, the bulletin boards can transition to keep track of school calendars, assignments, and extracurricular schedules.

|||||||||||||||||||||||||||||||||||||||||||||||||||||||||||||||||||||||||||||||||||||||||||||||||||||||||||

Parenting Tip

One family with triplets and 3 older single-born children created a buddy system in case of emergencies such as a house fire. Each older sibling was instructed to take her assigned baby and exit the house quickly if need be.

|||||||||||||||||||||||||||||||||||||||||||||||||||||||||||||||||||||||||||||||||||||||||||||||||||||||||||

A mother of older triplets keeps her smartphone on all the time. She programs in her children's appointments, school functions, and activities, as well as has the phone beep 24 hours ahead of time as reminders to keep her on schedule.

Color-coding helps families with multiples keep track of each child's items. Give each child a signature color starting in infancy to help identify personal items, as well as identify who each child is in pictures.

Toilet Training Triplets and More

Families with multiples often find toilet training 3 or more kids at once to be overwhelming for everyone involved. One family began potty training their triplets, at the same time, but as the mom describes it, "It was a circus!" They abandoned that idea and began training each child separately, starting with the child who showed the most signs of readiness, with much greater success. The extra one-on-one attention each child received with separate training led to better successes on the potty. (For more on toilet training, please refer to the toddler chapter on page 126.)

Parenting Tales

Kim, mom to kindergartener quadruplets, shares, "Toilet training was one of our more difficult stages. Each child ultimately had to decide when they were ready. One of our girls trained first, which inspired 2 of her siblings. We used incentive charts to keep everyone motivated. Further along, however, our daughter who was the first to train did have a few months of regression, needing a few more months to get back on track."

Interpersonal Relationships, Individuality, and Emotions

How can spouses support each other during the early challenging months? Sleep deprivation affects everybody's mood and can have an effect on even the strongest of marriages. Many families find that a consistent, early bedtime for the children gives the parents some quality quiet time together. Other families squeeze in good spouse conversations whenever possible— even if at 3:00 am, if that is the only time that both parents are awake and together—with no disruptions.

When navigating the early years with triplets, a go-with-the-flow attitude helps. Once one stage or schedule is mastered, things change and you need to adapt. Try to anticipate and be prepared for the triplets' next developmental stage.

Be realistic in what you can accomplish in one day. Lower your daily expectations if you must! The early months can be a haze of constant feeding and care; take things one day at a time. A calm parent is a more effective parent.

Try not to stress about the need to give each of your triplets identical experiences. Strive to be fair among your children instead. One mother of triplets noticed that one of her triplets hit his milestones a bit earlier than his siblings and was a bit more self-sufficient. It is now years later, yet she still feels twinges of guilt about him; she worries that he missed out on some of the motherly attention that his siblings received for being needier. You cannot give your children identical experiences; you've just got to do your best to be fair, not equal.

Most families will notice that as their triplets grow older, each child will exhibit unique talents. One family I know had a son who excelled at baseball. They encouraged him and noticed that his self-esteem blossomed, while his siblings participated in completely different activities. It is wise not to place all the kids in one single activity; rather, encourage each child to find his special area of interest.

Triplets can be quite a team. They are socially savvy because they are almost always interacting with other children their own age. They always have each other, and they tend to be quite outgoing in new social situations.

Being raised as a triplet or more provides plenty of built-in life lessons. Triplets have learned to share and be patient from infancy, by virtue of their family logistics, and have a less self-centered view of the world because they have siblings the same age.

The importance of treating all your children as individuals, regardless of birthdays, cannot be overstated. One triplet family I know has a terrific method of ensuring quality one-on-one time with each of the children on a weekly basis. On Saturday mornings, Mom has a special outing with one child, Dad has an outing with another child, and the remaining children stay at home with a trusted babysitter. A rotating schedule is used to be fair to everyone and help the children know what to expect and when their special time is coming. Even in a large family, with a bit of planning and strategizing, families can spend quality one-on-one time with each of their children.

The Adventure of a Lifetime

Families with multiples agree that the early weeks and months are challenging, but they are more than worth it to have their beautiful family. Organization and streamlining strategies will help families with triplets or more stay sane and happy. Enjoy each of your child's stages. Soon the stage will be over and you will all be on to the next chapter!

CHAPTER 12

Multiples: Facts, Lore, and More

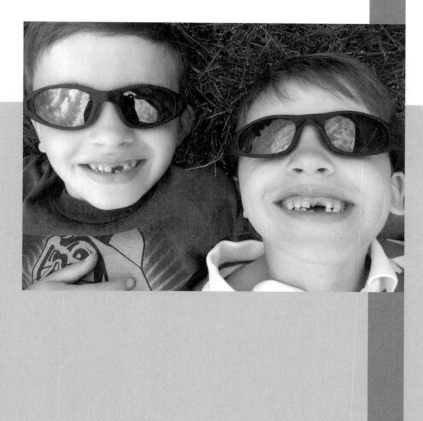

"*D*o twins run in your family?" "Are they identical or fraternal?" Parents of multiples are no stranger to such questions. Just try to make a quick grocery store trip, kids in tow, for just a couple of items without fellow shoppers stopping you to inquire about your family history. It's time to dispel some myths and separate fact from fiction. Now that you are a parent of multiples, your multiples' community is relying on *you* to help spread the truth!

Twins can either be identical or fraternal twins. *Identical* (monozygotic) twins result from a single fertilized egg that has divided into 2, giving each twin identical genetic material. *Fraternal* (dizygotic) twins result from 2 separate eggs being fertilized by 2 separate sperm, giving each twin different genetic material.

Identical twins occur at about 1% of all births around the world. Identical twinning appears to be unrelated to family history, maternal age, or ethnic, geographic, or socioeconomic patterns, and it has so far eluded explanation as to its occurrence. So even though everyone will still ask if twins run in your family, and even though there are plenty of instances when an individual who is a twin herself may conceive identical twins, statistically across the board, identical twins do not run in families.

Fraternal twins, on the other hand, can and *do* run in families. Fraternal twins have varying percentages of occurrence in different populations and places in the world. Fraternal twins are associated with a family history of twinning, advanced maternal age, and the use of fertility treatments. A family history of twins affects the maternal lineage, meaning that the tendency to produce twins is carried only by the mother, not the father. A twinning family history is a tendency of mothers to ovulate more than one egg at a time in a single monthly cycle. Despite the popular belief, twins do not skip a generation because these ovulatory events (ie, how many eggs mature in a single monthly cycle) are random each month.

Triplets, quadruplets, and more may have different variations of genetic material. All 3 babies may be genetic siblings (ie, fraternal, all developed from 3 separate, fertilized eggs), or there may be interesting combinations. A pregnancy may begin as 2 separate, fertilized eggs (meaning fraternal twins); however, one zygote may further split into 2, meaning that the triplets will be 2 identical twins plus a fraternal triplet.

The Distinction Between Identical and Fraternal Twins

Because fraternal, or dizygotic, twins are 2 separate fertilized eggs, they usually develop 2 separate amniotic sacs, placentas, and supporting structures. Identical, or monozygotic, twins may or may not share the same amniotic sac, depending on how early the single fertilized egg divides into 2.

If twins are a boy and a girl, clearly they are fraternal twins, as they do not have the same DNA. A boy has XY chromosomes and a girl has XX chromosomes. Girl-boy twins occur when one X egg is fertilized with one X sperm, and one Y sperm fertilizes the other X egg.

Sometimes health care professionals identify same-sex twins as fraternal or identical based on ultrasound findings or by examining the membranes at the time of delivery. The best way to determine if twins are identical or fraternal is by examining each child's DNA. Occasionally a family is told that their twins are fraternal based on placenta findings, when they are in fact identical. Other times, a family may see the minor differences in identical twins and declare the twins fraternal based on these differences in appearance.

There are a few commercial laboratories that, for a fee, will send families DNA collection kits to determine if the twins are identical or fraternal. The families swab the insides of each child's cheek for a DNA sample and send the kit back to the laboratory to await results.

We were initially told our sons were fraternal twins based on the fact that they had 2 separate placentas and supporting structures. However, because of natural curiosity, a concern for future medical issues, and the fact that the boys had countless physical similarities, we decided to use a commercial DNA kit to determine their zygosity once and for all. (I had initial plans to wait until the boys were at an age that they would understand and learn the news themselves with us; however, I was too impatient to wait!) The kit was easy to use and we had our results back in a quick turnaround time. Our suspicions were confirmed, and the boys are identical—very handy if one of them ever needs an extra kidney down the line!

Identical twins have the same DNA; however, they may not look exactly identical to one another because of environmental factors such as womb position and life experiences after being born. Our family jokes about one of our twin's stitches for a lacerated upper lip was that he wanted to distinguish himself from his identical twin brother. In addition to life's bumps, bruises, and differing hairstyles, a child's DNA is constantly adapting from that child's experiences. Different stretches of one's DNA can turn on or off in response to environmental surroundings; therefore, over time, a pair of identical twins' DNA becomes more and more distinctive. All twins, whether fraternal or identical, are truly 2 separate, unique individuals.

More and More Twins: The Statistics

If you feel like there are more multiples these days compared to when you were a kid, you're not mistaken. Multiples (twins, triplets, and more) are more common these days than a generation ago.

Each year the Centers for Disease Control and Prevention National Vital Statistics System publishes reports analyzing birth data along a wide variety of characteristics. The rate of twin births rose 76% from 1980 to 2011, but the pace of increase has slowed in recent years. From 1980 to 2004, increases averaged nearly 3% a year, but from 2005 to 2011, the pace of increases slowed to 0.5% each year. In 2011, the twin birth rate was 3.3% (33.2 per 1,000 total births), essentially the same as in 2009 and 2010.

The triplet and higher-order (quadruplets and more) multiple birth rate was also essentially unchanged from 2010, at 137 per 100,000 (roughly 0.14%), but it has declined 29% since 1998. The decline in more recent years is a change from the rapid increase from 1980 to 1998, more than 400%.

Statistical Trends

The National Vital Statistics Reports found that the most important trends leading to the rise in multiple births are maternal age and the use of fertility treatments. Older women, without any intervention, have a higher chance of ovulating 2 eggs during a single monthly cycle. In addition, women who undergo fertility treatments or hormone therapy to induce ovulation are more likely to ovulate multiple eggs. The recent decline in triplet and higher-order multiple birth rates has been associated with updated guidelines from the American Society for Reproductive Medicine, as well as improvements in assisted reproductive technologies such as in-vitro fertilization, or IVF. That is, there are fewer embryos transferred per IVF cycle. In 2009, 19% of all twin births and 34% of all triplet and higher-order births were estimated to have been conceived with IVF.

Where do the most twin births occur in the United States? Multiple birth occurrence ranges widely by state. Interestingly, the National Center for Health Statistics report showed that for the years 2009 to 2011, twins accounted for 2.5% of births in New Mexico, compared to 4.5% in New Jersey. Twin rates were greater than 4% in Connecticut, Massachusetts, and New Jersey for this 3-year period. State-specific triplet and higher-order multiples ranged from 0.06% in Montana to 0.2% in New Jersey; 3 states reported triplet and higher-order birth rates higher than 0.2%: Nebraska, New Jersey, and North Dakota (Births: final data for 2011. *National Vitals Statistics Report.* 2013;62[1]:1–70).

On average, most single-baby pregnancies last for 39 weeks; for twins, 35 weeks; for triplets, 32 weeks; and for quadruplets, 29 weeks. For more on pregnancy, please refer to the pregnancy chapter on page 11.

Twin Lore and Twins Around the World

Star gazers know that Gemini, Latin for "the twins," is a well-known constellation in the starry night sky. Castor and Pollux were twin brothers who were transformed into the constellation, according to Greek and Roman mythology.

The Yoruba, a tribe in Nigeria, has the highest dizygotic twinning rate in the world (4.4 % of all maternities). Some attribute the high twin rate to a diet high in yams; however, because the tribe clearly has a strong family history of fraternal twins, this plays a large role in the continued trend.

Each summer, Twinsville, Ohio, is host to the Twins Days Festival, the country's largest gathering of multiples, with several events over the course of a 3-day weekend. You can learn more about the Twins Days Festival at www.twinsdays.org.

Guinness World Records

The Guinness World Records state the most prolific mother ever achieved her status with the efficiency of giving birth to multiples on several occasions. The wife of Feodor Vassilyev (1707–1782), a peasant from Shuya, Russia, had a total of 69 children. With 27 pregnancies in all, she gave birth to 16 pairs of twins, 7 sets of triplets, and 4 sets of quadruplets. Numerous sources support this story, suggesting that while improbable and statistically unlikely, it is in fact true.

Also from the Guinness World Records, Michelle Lee Wilson gave birth to the heaviest triplets on record in July 2003. Her children weighed 8 lb, 9.4 oz; 7 lb, 5.4 oz; and 6 lb, 13.8 oz at birth, and all delivered within 2 minutes of one other. These babies were carried to 36 weeks and 5 days. They, and their incredible mother, are a testament to the fact that the human body is incredibly adaptable and resilient.

The Representation of Twins in the Media

As a child, I attended school with a pair of identical twins and naively wondered if they could read each other's minds. Later on as a middle-schooler, my friends and I devoured the *Sweet Valley High* books about the Wakefield twins, which later ran as a television series (and is buzzed to be a movie in the works.) Elizabeth was a "good girl," but Jessica often schemed and showed her wild side. I had limited exposure to twins in the real world, yet viewed plenty of dramatic representations on TV (*Super Friends*: "Wonder Twin powers activate!") and in the movies (Stanley Kubrick's *The Shining* famously using the image of twins as a sign of foreboding); as a result of all of the above, I perceived twins to be magical and mysterious.

Fast-forward a couple decades later. I am now a lucky mom of 4, including a set of identical twins. Forgive the pun, but twins live dual lives in the 2 worlds of reality and in media. Each of my twins is a complex, textured individual with a unique identity, and knowing each boy with the depth of our parent-child relationship, I understand that being a twin is only one facet of their hundreds of interesting personal quirks. Parenthood expands one's breadth of experience, and one of the many life lessons we learn when we become parents is that those we formerly considered under other exotic categories are now understood in a clearer light. Yet, as a mom of twins, I often find myself answering questions such as "Who is the outgoing one, and who is the shy one?" or "Is one sporty and the other artistic?"

In life and in the media, labels and stereotypes abound. Pop culture tends to reinforce these notions, which are not always accurate. As parents, we can recognize our own misconceptions, as well as guide our children's understanding of the variety of people in this world. We can teach our kids that people are not to be generalized or compartmentalized; each of us deserves consideration as a *person*, not as a *category*.

An important role we play as parents is helping our kids responsibly navigate and interpret what they see in the media, including helping your children understand how media impacts their view of others in the world. (CommonSenseMedia.org is a great family resource.) Watch programming with your family and discuss, in an age-appropriate way, different characters and their representations with your kids. Are all twins jokesters à la Fred and George Weasley in the Harry Potter series, or are they good and evil counterparts such as PBS Kids Ruff and Scruff Ruffman? The good-twin/bad-twin stereotype perpetuates thinking of the twins as a unit; one twin's personality is defined as how it contrasts with the other twin's personality. Most importantly, emphasize to your kids that each of us has a unique spirit that defines who we really are.

Not all media representations are negative or misleading, and with a little homework, parents can use TV or movies as an educational tool with their families. As an example, when Dora the Explorer became a big sister, she was surprised to gain not 1, but 2 new siblings (boy-girl twins). This Dora episode is a helpful way to prepare a preschooler who will soon become a big sibling to multiples. Look for positive, realistic, and age-appropriate examples of characters when watching programming with your kids. If you see a scenario that doesn't agree with your family's principles, use it as a talking point to discuss the issue. Media surrounds us, and parents can use them selectively and wisely to open family discussions about human behaviors and interaction.

Resources and Web Sites
for Families With Multiples

Breastfeeding

The New Mother's Guide to Breastfeeding
American Academy of Pediatrics
Edited by Joan Younger Meek, MD, MS, RD, FAAP, IBCLC

The Nursing Mother's Companion
Kathleen Huggins

General Parenting and Health Resources

HealthyChildren.org

HealthyChildren.org is the official parenting Web site of the American Academy of Pediatrics. If your child has a mild illness or minor injury, the KidsDoc Symptom Checker tool on the Web site can help you decide what level of care is needed and how to provide symptom relief for minor issues you can manage on your own. A KidsDoc Symptom Checker app is available for smartphones as well.

Remember that no Web site or app can replace the medical care and advice of your health care professional; always address specific questions about your child's health with your pediatrician, and in an emergency situation, call 911 immediately. For those situations in which you are unsure if you should call your doctor, the Symptom Checker is a useful tool to help you make an appropriate decision for your child.

Text4baby

Text4baby is a free mobile service designed to provide pregnant women and new parents information on maintaining healthy pregnancies and babies, provided by the National Healthy Mothers, Healthy Babies Coalition. Parents can sign up for the service by texting BABY (or BEBE for Spanish) to 511411 to receive 3 free SMS text messages each week, timed to their due date or baby's date of birth—a helpful way to get reliable advice while on the go. Check out their Web site at https://text4baby.org or their Facebook page for more information.

Meal Assistance Coordination for Bed Rest/ Multiples' Homecoming

MealTrain.com

CareCalendar.org

TakeThemAMeal.com

Media Resources

CommonSenseMedia.org
CommonSenseMedia.org is a Web site you can use to determine if a film is age appropriate for your kids and much more!

Neonatal Intensive Care Unit

Newborn Intensive Care: What Every Parent Needs to Know
Jeannette Zaichkin

Sleep

Sleep: What Every Parent Needs to Know
American Academy of Pediatrics
Edited by Rachel Moon, MD, FAAP

Solve Your Child's Sleep Problems
Richard Ferber, MD

Specific to Twins and Multiples

Emotionally Healthy Twins: A New Philosophy for Parenting Two Unique Children
Joan Friedman

Healthy Sleep Habits, Happy Twins
Marc Weissbluth, MD

Multiples of America
www.nomotc.org

Raising Twins **Facebook page**
www.facebook.com/RaisingTwins

Shelly Vaziri Flais official blog
www.pediatricianmomoftwins.blogspot.com

Twins Days Festival in Twinsburg, OH
www.twinsdays.org

Twins **magazine**
www.twinsmagazine.com

Toilet Training

Guide to Toilet Training
American Academy of Pediatrics

Mommy! I Have to Go Potty! A Parent's Guide to Toilet Training
Jan Faull, MEd, and Helen F. Neville, BS, RN

Index